LIGHT OF SOHAM

This light of Soham inside us, sheds its luster on our whole life and makes it full of happiness. Sri Gajanana Maharaj

LIGHT OF SOHAM

THE LIFE AND TEACHINGS OF SRI GAJANANA MAHARAJ OF NASHIK

COMPILED AND EDITED BY
ABBOT GEORGE BURKE
(SWAMI NIRMALANANDA GIRI)

"I think that the present work–the life of Shri Gajanana Maharaj–has come into existence for the sake of those human souls who have been reborn in the Western Countries, but were in their previous lives followers of the Nath Pantha." (An Anonymous Disciple of Sri Gajanana Maharaj regarding the biography of the Master.)

LIGHT ᴼᶠ ᵀᴴᴱ SPIRIT
PRESS
CEDAR CREST, NEW MEXICO

Published by
Light of the Spirit Press
lightofthespiritpress.com

Light of the Spirit Monastery
P. O. Box 1370
Cedar Crest, New Mexico 87008
OCOY.org

ISBN-13: 978-1-7325266-7-9
ISBN-10: 1-7325266-7-2

Library of Congress Control Number: 201994175

Bisac categories:
1. BIO018000 BIOGRAPHY & AUTOBIOGRAPHY / Religious
2. OCC010000 BODY, MIND & SPIRIT / Mindfulness & Meditation
2nd edition
03302022

CONTENTS

Sri Gajanana Maharaj (Gajanana Murlidhar Gupte)

FOREWORD

Never man spake like this man (John 7:46).

Over half a century ago I was blessed and fortunate to discover Sanatana Dharma and Yoga. Two years later I discovered India as my spiritual home. I eagerly took in everything without discrimination and in the ensuing years began sifting through all I had embraced with increasing scrutiny and discrimination.

The capstone of this process was my completely accidental discovery of the contents of this book. Reading the life and teachings of Sri Gajanana Maharaj (Gajanana Murlidhar Gupte–not the famous sadhu of Maharashtra, also called Gajanana Maharaj) was a veritable revelation to me of what a true yogi and ideal master teacher should be, shorn of so much superstition, nonsense and charlatanry regarding gurus and disciples that prevail today in India and abroad–and at that time, in my own mind. There, too, I discovered the authentic Nath Yogi tradition of Soham Yoga. (See the book *Soham Yoga: The Yoga of the Self* for a complete explanation and exposition of Soham Yoga meditation practice.)

For over fifty years I had been reading books from India, many of which I had collected myself during my various pilgrimages to India. And during those pilgrimages I had met or seen and heard many renowned yogis and gurus–and some unknown great ones in obscure and unexpected places. Every one of them left a sacred impression in my mind and heart. Yet in reading about Sri Gajanana Maharaj I encountered a holy personality that eclipsed all others for me. I still revered the others, but in Maharaj I found the following unique features that awed me and altered my perspective on what yoga, yogis and gurus should be.

1) He did not call or consider himself a guru, but called those he spiritually taught and advised his "friends." To one of those friends he said, "Paithankar, I can only say that as I do not consider myself as anybody's guru, I do not look upon anyone as my disciple. Some of my young and old friends, owing to their merit acquired in previous lives and owing to the practice of meditation, have reached the state of samadhi. But I do not consider any of them as my disciples. I simply give the mantra of Soham to my friends and ask them to practice meditation."

2) He embodied the Nath Yogi principle that the guru does not seek the disciple, but the disciple seeks the guru. Shunning all publicity and prohibiting his friends from even speaking of his existence, he ensured that he would meet those whose karma, samskaras and intense aspiration and desire for Self-realization qualified them to meet him and receive benefit from him.

3) His open, honest and pointed speaking to those met him, never flattering or enticing or manipulating them in any manner, was proof of his being worthy of their trust. Equally admirable was his complete indifference to others' opinion of him.

Since it could not help but happen that some people would come to meet him unbidden, he used his plain-speaking to rid himself of any return visitation. For the same purpose he chain-smoked and openly drank wine to disgust and repel the unwelcome ones, though his friends easily noted that there was never the smell of burning tobacco when he smoked and that when he offered the wine to someone to drink they discovered that it turned into fresh milk in their mouths!

He dressed in ordinary but stylish clothing with no marks of a sadhu or yogi at all. For most of his life he lived in the homes of various friends, and toward the end lived in a room at the back of a shabby house in an obscure area of Nashik. In that room there were photographs of saints, but no trappings of religion, and no kind of religious functions took place there. He did not speak on spiritual topics at all unless a visitor initiated talk on such subjects. And as a rule no more than two or three people could be found with him at a time.

4) He prohibited anyone of his friends from moving to be near him. Further, after a friend had gained experience and made some progress in Soham sadhana, he would sometimes tell them that they did not need to visit him any more. As one friend wrote in a publication, "There is not even the idea of any dependence on him. Rather he makes us independent and free." This was in total contrast with the manipulative, emotional idea of a guru being eternally destined for the disciple and "offering shelter for the ages" to those who "took refuge" in him rather than in their own eternal Self.

5) Perhaps the most amazing aspect of Sri Gajanana Maharaj was his having a newly-instructed friend sit before him and (often with his hand on the friend's head) taking him through astounding experiences. Such a friend would see visions of deities and far away places (even other planets) and experience all kinds of inner experiences such as divine sounds and various manifestations of the kundalini. Many would see all the chakras in turn, and he would ask some of them to read out for him the letters on the petals of the chakras. When they did so, it corresponded exactly with the descriptions and pictures found in authoritative texts on yoga. These experiences at the hand of Maharaj might happen just once or many times over some days or even weeks—according to Maharaj's direction.

All these experiences were the things considered by most yogis and gurus to be evidence of either enlightenment or the nearing approach of enlightenment—and therefore liberation (moksha). But then they would stop, and Maharaj would tell them that all such experiences were of little or no value and that from thenceforth, leaving them behind, they would be able to make real progress in sadhana, that now was the real beginning for them. This implied that all such experiences are really obstacles in the path of the yogi and may even cause him to fall into delusion and self-deception, thinking he has attained much when he has attained nothing, and worse than nothing.

This ability to give such experiences at will and thus to protect his friends from future misperceptions is truly awesome and only possible through association with a siddha of siddhas.

Those who read this book and ponder its contents thoroughly and well will surely agree with Mr. Ambadas Gopal Paithankar, who said to the matchless sadguru, "Maharaj, I see in you what I have never seen before, and I hear things explained by you in a manner never heard by me before," and the simple reply of Maharaj, "What you say is true."

In many places in this book there are references to Sri Gajanana Maharaj as living. I have retained them as I wanted to change the words of Maharaj's disciples as little as possible. I have sometimes given explanatory words and comments in brackets to elucidate matters for the Western reader. I hope the glossary at the end will be helpful in understanding unfamiliar words and expressions.

May the blessings of all the Nath Yogi masters, including Jesus Christ who as Sri Ishanath was one of their number (see Appendix One of *Soham Yoga, the Yoga of the Self,* and *The Christ of India*), be with those who read this book and follow the eternal wisdom set forth so ably by Sri Gajanana Maharaj.

Swami Nirmalananda Giri
(Abbot George Burke)

Sri Gajanana Maharaj of Nashik

CHAPTER ONE

THE LIFE AND CHARACTER OF SRI GAJANANA MAHARAJ

"He should be called a saint who has known God, and who has definitely ascertained what is eternal and what is non-eternal" (Samarth Ramdas). A perusal of the life of Sri Gajanana Maharaj will convince us that he is one of these extraordinary personages. Regarding him one of his spiritual friends (disciples) wrote: "In the first half of the twentieth century there lived in Nashik a man who had reached a high level of Yoga. This remarkable man was unmarried, and his name was Gajanana Murlidhar Gupte. His surname, Gupte, means invisible. His spiritual knowledge and everything about him was invisible to the world at large." Fortunately we do have the following information about him.

Birth and early childhood

The worldly name of Sri Sadguru Gajanana Maharaj was Gajanana Murlidhar Gupte. His father, Murlidhar Bajirao Gupte, was originally a resident of Pen in the district of Kolaba, Maharashtra. His family were the Inamdars of Pen, Vasi and some six or seven more villages. (Inamdar was a feudal title prevalent before and during the British Raj, including during the Maratha rule of Peshwa and other rulers of India. The title was bestowed upon the person who received lands as Inam–grant or a gift–rewarding the extraordinary service rendered to the ruler or the princely state.)

But owing to financial adversities, Murlidhar left Pen and went seeking some employment elsewhere. He obtained a government position at Malkapur in the district of Buldhana. He, however, found that the wages were too meagre to enable him to meet his expenses and to lead a life of comfort and ease. He therefore read law side-by-side with his work and succeeded in passing with credit the barrister's (attorney's) examination which was then taken in Marathi. He then began to practice as a barrister at Yeotmal. At that time there were only two or three other barristers there. He very soon made good progress in his profession and became well known as a successful and rising barrister.

His wife's name was Rajubai. This couple gave birth to eight children: five sons and three daughters. The fifth son was named Gajanana.

Sri Gajanana Maharaj was born at Yeotmal in 1892. In the third year of his age, he suffered a very strong attack of smallpox, owing to which his right foot became permanently crippled. He was taken to Amraoti and was examined and treated by various doctors, but all the remedies were of no avail. He remained a cripple throughout his life. This caused great sorrow to his parents.

Both of Gajanana's parents fell ill some time later and died within a month or two of each other. At the time of her death the mother of Sri Gajanana Maharaj, Rajubai, called her sister Balubai near her, and having placed Gajanana's hand in hers, said, "I shall shortly cease to be a denizen of this world. My Gajanana is a cripple, as you see. Be a mother to him. Love and cherish him deeply and bring him up in such a way that he will never even think of me. If ever you happen to meet a saint, place my Gajanana on his feet. By the blessings and grace of a saint, Gajanana's life will be happy and blessed."

This aunt of Gajanana, Balubai, was a widow from her childhood, and had immersed herself in devotion and passed her days doing good deeds. [At that time throughout India there was the practice of marriages being performed for small children, arranged by the parents. If the girl died, another marriage could be done. But widows were never allowed to remarry, so if the boy died the girl was condemned to be unmarried. This was a terrible evil that caused great suffering. Some "child widows" turned their minds to intense spiritual study and practice–and such was Balubai. *Editor's note.*] Having no other relatives, she was staying with her sister. All the members of Gajanana's family had feelings of deep affection for her. She, to the last, never slackened in her care of Gajanana and as soon as an opportunity occurred as desired by Gajanana's mother in her last moments, this aunt did not fail to take advantage of it and carry out the last wishes of her departed sister.

The death of the parents of Gajanana within a few days of each other was a very serious calamity. The responsibility of the whole family then fell upon Mr. Narayanrao, the eldest brother, and upon the aunt, Balubai. But it appeared that God himself had taken the family under his special protection and slowly light began to be seen in the grim darkness of adversity and the three sisters were married one-by-one and left for their husbands' houses. Gajanana's Sacred Thread Ceremony (Upanayanam) was celebrated at the age of nine. This event occurred in 1901.

Refuge in a saint

When Gajanana was about ten or eleven years old, his brother Rambhau wrote a letter to Akola regarding Sri Narayana Saraswati Maharaj, asking Narayanrao to go to Chikhli with the whole family to meet this great saint. Narayanrao accordingly obtained leave for two months and went to Chikhli with all the members of the family. At about a distance of six or seven miles from Chikhli, there is a village called Antri, near which there are many hills and dense thickets of trees. In this forest near the village of Jambore, there is a samadhi (tomb of a saint) and some underground rooms. The well-known yogi siddha, Sri Narayana Saraswati Maharaj, lived there. His name had spread far and wide and devotees from Punjab, Delhi and Bengal used to visit the place for the darshan of that great yogi. The whole family went to Antri from Chikhli in bullock carts.

The place of residence of Sri Narayana Saraswati was very charming. Just nearby was a big plaza, in the center of which there was a samadhi of a saint of great antiquity. On the four sides of the plaza there were apartments and some underground rooms built of bricks and mortar.

The apartments were well lighted and contained accommodation for ten or fifteen persons. In the thicket of trees near the square there was a beautiful well of good-tasting and wholesome water. People performed their sandhya adorations and their japa near it and also ate their food there. Near the samadhi there was a cot on which Sri Narayana Saraswati usually sat. Early in the morning there was arati, at noon worship and arati, and in the evening again arati after which there was bhajan (chanting of devotional songs).

The Gupte family went immediately on their arrival for the darshan of Maharaj, who assigned to them an apartment for their stay. The aunt separately went for the darshan of Maharaj, taking Gajanana with her. Gajanana immediately firmly caught hold of the feet of Maharaj. The aunt said to Maharaj, "Oh Maharaj, take pity on this crippled child. He has neither father nor mother to take care of him. How will he fare in his future life? Except the Almighty God, there is no one to support him. You are a great saint and have become one with God. You possess all the powers of the Almighty God. Kindly take this child under your protection."

She further said, "My sister who was this boy's mother, was a pure and noble woman. Just before her death she entrusted this child to me and asked me to place him on the holy feet of some saint, saying that only by the grace of a saint would his life be blessed and happy. The present occasion has been brought about only by her good wishes."

Blessings from Sri Narayana Saraswati

Maharaj was pleased at these words of the aunt. He turned towards her and said, "Mother, both of you sisters had practiced yoga in your former births and the present occasion has been brought about by the great merit acquired in those births. This Gajanana was a yogi in his former birth. After some years he will become known as a saint and will be a guiding light to aspirants on the spiritual path. From his eyes I can see that he is a yogi of the Nath Pantha and practiced Dhyana Yoga in his previous life. Do not be anxious about him at all. But mother, you are not destined to witness his spiritual mission. So now let your anxiety regarding him disappear."

Sri Narayana Saraswati, guru of Gajanana Maharaj

He further told her, "His elder brother, Narayan, will become a great poet. His poetry on spiritual subjects will be superior to anyone's." That happened exactly as he said. His brother, Narayan, who, was born at Malkapur in 1868, from his childhood showed great intellectual capacity and righteousness of conduct. This Narayanrao was the intellectual and learned poet of Maharashtra known by the name "Bee," though he disliked celebrity. A collection of his poems was published under the title *A Handful of Flowers* (*Fulanchi Onjal*).

Maharaj then asked all to go and cook their food. After taking their food, all went to sleep. It had been agreed that at 4 a. m. all were to attend the morning arati. All were awakened in due time and went to attend the arati. However, Gajanana appeared to be sleepy and he remained sitting on his bed in a state of half sleep and half wakefulness, and he was found so sitting when the others returned.

Spiritual vision

When all others had left for the arati and Gajanana was sitting on his bed, half awake and half asleep with his eyes open, he had the following vision.

There was dense darkness everywhere and Gajanana found himself walking on foot in the darkness. Occasionally he saw a star shining and again there would be darkness. Rain began to pour down, sounds of thunder were continuously heard and there were intermittent flashes of lightning. The way was full of serpents, some black, some white, some with marks like cowrie shells. Some were of the thickness of a man's wrist while others were as thick as a man's thigh. The serpents entwined themselves round Gajanana's feet and waist. The largest among them encircled Gajanana's neck and got upon his head. Gajanana was observing this and still walking on. While walking his body became that of a stout and strong man and he was going ahead pushing all the serpents aside. He was feeling a mixed sensation of fear and joy. He could not get any idea as to what distance he had travelled. Then he began to feel lightness in his body. The serpents, however, were still there. But the darkness disappeared and there was a clear light spreading on all sides. In the light Gajanana saw in front of him a beautiful samadhi adorned with various kinds of flowers giving out fragrant smells. There was a small ghee lamp lighted and camphor was burning on one side. A beautiful damsel was standing near the samadhi. She had a gold waist-band, from which a shining sword was hanging. As Gajanana was about to bow down to her, she became invisible.

Gajanana was surprised as well as delighted. He felt a curiosity to know what saint's samadhi it was, and felt a keen desire to get the darshan of that saint. Inwardly he prayed, "Oh please give me your darshan. I am an orphan, a pauper and a beggar."

Next moment the samadhi broke in twain and a grand personage of dazzling appearance came out. There was a great sound of SOHAM. Gajanana felt as if that very sound was coming out of his own body. At the sight of that grand personage–having a long beard, wearing a gerua robe, having garlands of rudraksha beads round his neck and with a crown of matted hair on his head–Gajanana's eyes were dazzled and he felt that the sound of Soham was issuing out of his own mouth just as it was coming out of the mouth of that personage. Then the form of that personage assumed a mild appearance, there was a sound of "Machhinder Adesha" [Matsyendranath's Instruction], and the whole scene vanished.

After the vision

Gajanana then became fully awake and sat up on his bed. His body and clothes had become wet, and a sweet fragrance was coming out of all his body. He was rubbing his eyes. Although the sun had arisen a long time previously, still he was feeling a great darkness before his eyes and hence he was a little bit frightened. Looking at his wet body, Gajanana as well as others thought that Gajanana in his sleep had upset with his foot the pot of water which was near his bed.

Seeing Gajanana's terrified condition, the aunt's mind became full of fear and anxiety and she took Gajanana and placed him on the feet of Maharaj, who turned towards the aunt and said, "Have you understood? He is a real yogi. You need not be anxious about him." He turned and said to Gajanana, "Your birth is now fulfilled." He then asked Gajanana to repeat the mantra which had been given to him in his dream. That mantra was reverberating in the ears and the whole body of Gajanana, and "Soham, Soham" was going on continuously in his ears and body. Gajanana, therefore, replied only "Soham." Maharaj then said, "Even at such an early stage, you got the darshan of the Goddess and of Matsyendranath. Is it not so?" Gajanana then described the whole vision to Maharaj, who was highly pleased at hearing it.

Gajanana then asked for his blessings, saying, "Please give me this boon. Let my ego go away. One more boon for myself is that I should have the right knowledge of the Self. I have a yearning for Guru Darshan too. Please fullfil it, oh merciful one."

Maharaj caressed Gajanana and kissed him and uttered the following prophetic words, "Oh Gajanana, you will become famous in the world and many aspirants on the spiritual path will be benefited by you and you will always experience great joy and peace of mind." After bestowing this blessing Maharaj further said, "I shall always manifest myself to you in your breath." Thus Gajanana was made to realize himself in the company of his sadguru, which was unprecedented. After this all took the darshan of Maharaj and returned to their place. Food was then cooked and all had their meal.

A tiger visiting the samadhi

One day when all the members of the Gupte family were having the darshan of Maharaj, he said that a big tiger daily came for the darshan of the samadhi in the plaza and therefore no one should keep awake after 11 p.m., lest he might be terrified by the sight. That night others slept as usual, only Gajanana lay down pretending to sleep. His japa of Soham was going on and his mind was full of joy. In the meanwhile, the tiger as usual came there, took the darshan of the samadhi and of Maharaj and went away by the way it had come. Maharaj casually cast his eyes at Gajanana and finding him awake, said, "Child, are you still awake? Were you not afraid?" Gajanana replied, "I was awake, still by the grace of the sadguru I did not feel the least sense of fear." In the morning all others came to know about the incident at night. Everyone then said to Maharaj, "If Gajanana was awake, why were we also not awakened?" To this Maharaj replied, "Because you would have been frightened."

Visit to Borgaon: guru of Sri Narayana Saraswati

Some time later the day of the anniversary of the mahasamadhi of Maharaj's guru arrived. The samadhi of his guru was situated at Borgaon, and the road to it passed through jungles and was very difficult. By this road Sri Narayana Saraswati started with about two or three hundred disciples and about one hundred and fifty bullock carts. They reached the place on the seventh day. Borgaon is a small village. Maharaj was well-known in those parts. All persons took the darshan of the samadhi. They stayed there for fifteen days. Every day there were bhajan, worship, arati and processions. Dinners on a large scale were also given.

Guru's message to his disciples

There is a river near Borgaon. Maharaj pointed out the spot where his guru used to sit for meditation. One day while there, Maharaj narrated the following.

"My original name was Paramananda and my sadguru's name was Narayana Saraswati. When my sadguru knew that the time of his departure from this world was approaching, he called me near him as I was under his special favor and said, 'Paramananda, I am soon going to depart from this world. The tradition of my path must be continued as before. I do not see anyone more fitted for the task than yourself. You will be the only one to continue this tradition. Leave therefore, your name of

Paramananda and assume my name of Narayana Saraswati and carry on the tradition. Do not instruct anyone who is not a sincere aspirant and who has not trained himself in self-control. If you instruct a person and he later on acts thoughtlessly, withdraw yourself from him.' Soon after this my sadguru left his mortal coil."

Sri Narayana Saraswati as seen by his disciples

Sri Narayana Saraswati (Paramananda) was a saint of great powers. Many miracles performed by him were witnessed by Gajanana and his other devotees. He never allowed any one to take his likeness in a photograph. One Mr. Pendharkar, a drawing-master at Akola (Berar) and a photographer, had tried to take the photo of Maharaj about a hundred times but had failed in getting a likeness. Then he fell at the feet of Maharaj and prayed earnestly that Maharaj might be gracious enough to allow his likeness to be taken. Maharaj then consented and he succeeded in getting a likeness.

Many devotees of Maharaj once earnestly prayed to him to allow himself to be photographed. They begged earnestly for the favor, particularly urging that devotees living at a distance would thereby get something like his darshan and would be able to honor his image. When this earnest prayer was offered, then Maharaj willingly allowed himself to be photographed. If any of his devotees felt a keen desire to see him, Maharaj used to appear before him and ask, "Why have you called me?" Owing to such miracles his disciples were extremely delighted.

While he was at Antri or Jambore, thousands of pilgrims came for his darshan. To some he appeared to be sitting on a tree, to others he appeared sitting in meditation on the brink of a well. To some he appeared young, to others old. Sometimes he appeared jumping from one tree to another, sometimes weak and sometimes stout and strong. His form thus appeared as changing. He, however, told his disciples that such miracles happen naturally in the case of yogis, and undue importance should not be attached to them.

Sri Narayana Saraswati (Paramananda) left this world in November of 1910. His age was then one hundred and twenty-seven. His birthplace was Daithana on the banks of the Godavari at a distance of about forty miles from Paithana. The traditional trade of his family was that of a banker. His father died when Paramananda was very young. He was then brought up by his mother, and his thread ceremony was celebrated by her. When Paramananda was twelve years old, his mother also died and he took the bones of his mother's body after it was burnt to Nashik in order to put them into the Ramakunda there. He never returned home, but from Nashik went to the Punjab and remained there for a very long time.

Return of the Family to Akola

Gajanana, his brothers, aunt and others remained for some days at Antri and then took leave of Maharaj to return to Rambhau's place at Chikhli. Sri Narayana Saraswati placed his hand on the head of Gajanana and, having mercy in his mind, gave him this blessing: "If you follow yoga sadhana you will become known to worthy seekers. You will free souls just by your blessings. Oh, Yogadhikari [Fully Qualified in Yoga], now go back to your place. Show the path to the seekers. You will be a true Atmajnani."

Gajanana and others returned to Akola. Gajanana was educated up to the fourth standard Marathi at Akola. Narayanrao, his oldest brother, was then transferred to Washim, where Gajanana accompanied him for continuing his education. But in a month or two Gajanana stopped attending school.

Narayanrao was then again transferred to Akola, where he remained till his retirement. Gajanana also naturally stayed with Narayanrao at Akola. At the end of his stay at Akola, he succeeded in experiencing the over-flooding ecstasy of the bliss of the Self. He was always immersed in the awareness of "Soham" within. He was never entangled in material things, had a liking towards the company of spiritual people, was eager in the pursuit of spiritual ways and always wished to be with saints.

Meditation

About a quarter of a mile from the place where Gajanana Maharaj was living at Akola, there is an old abandoned fort. Gajanana Maharaj used to go to a secluded spot in the fort for meditation by day as well as by night. Nobody knew about this. Jackals came there at night and howled. Once or twice through fear of the jackals Gajanana Maharaj had to run away from the place. He, however, always went there for meditation.

Once while Gajanana Maharaj was sitting there in meditation he heard a voice saying, "Do not be afraid. After four or five days more you will never feel the sensation of fear in the least." Owing to this he gained great courage and continued his daily practice. After some time the howlings of jackals ceased altogether and at the time of meditation he began to be immersed in joy.

A friend of Gajanana Maharaj, named Shivrambhau Gupte, was then living in Gawalipura at Akola, and he alone knew about Gajanana Maharaj's place of meditation and about his going to and coming back from that place. Occasionally Gajanana Maharaj used to sleep in the house of this friend after returning at night from that place after meditation.

Sometimes in the house of this friend some miracles took place naturally at the hands of Gajanana Maharaj. When Gajanana Maharaj told him about his sitting for meditation in the fort and gave him an idea of his experiences, he advised him saying, "Child, you should not go at night to the fort." To which Gajanana Maharaj replied, "I do not go of my own accord. A superhuman power leads me there and I feel a wave of ecstasy surging in me and that power again brings me back safely. My sadguru is extremely kind. He guides my thoughts. As soon as the idea enters my mind, the mind itself begins to repeat Soham. I myself make no effort." Gajanana Maharaj later on began to sit for meditation in the house of Shivrambhau Gupte.

Miracles and the Anxiety Caused

Sometimes in Shivrambhau's house miracles took place spontaneously at the hands of Gajanana Maharaj quite naturally and without any conscious effort on his part. They all happened among his friends and were not revealed by them. On the contrary, efforts were made to keep them secret. As Gajanana Maharaj was then a young boy about eighteen or nineteen years old, a cripple, and did not observe all the rules of ritual purity and caste observance, they thought that if these miracles became known abroad people would ridicule them or think that they were tricks of ghosts and evil spirits.

Later on these miracles began to occur even in other places, when Gajanana Maharaj happened to visit the house of a barrister there or the houses of other acquaintances. Some people then asked Gajanana Maharaj whether they should communicate these miracles to the barrister and other people and whether he would perform some miracles in the presence of others. To this Maharaj replied, "I do not know anything about these miracles. I am not conscious of them. How can I then say anything regarding them? I do not know what these miracles are and why they occur. You know more about them than I. I just sit at one place in a state of meditation. How can I then throw light on these things?"

The members of Maharaj's family did not know anything about these miracles and no one had told them. When Gajanana Maharaj heard that these miracles were known by other people, he began to feel apprehensive that people would entertain various doubts regarding him, would blame him and would think that perhaps he was in league with evil spirits. This later on assumed the form of keen anxiety and he began to feel very uneasy.

Once when he was sitting in meditation he saw a vision in which it was made clear to him that such miracles often occurred in the case of yogis unconsciously without any effort on their part and there was no reason for being uneasy on account of them. When this elucidation was vouchsafed to him, Gajanana Maharaj became free from anxiety and was greatly delighted.

A boyish whim

Gajanana had seen the Shakti Puja [worship of a goddess according to tantrik rites] that was done by a Mr. Karnik, and according to his boyish mood he thought that he should also try the Shakti Puja in the manner he had seen. Mr. Karnik used to hold a pot of wine to be offered to the goddess and used to sit in meditation as if the goddess would come and take the wine from his hand.

Gajanana, taking all the puja material, shut himself up in a room in the house of Mr. Shivrambhau Gupte and started his experiment. He imitated Mr. Karnik in all his ways, solemnly offered his prayers and shut his eyes, but nothing came of this. The next night the same experiment was repeated, but with the same result. The third night, Gajanana persisted in the experiment and immediately went into an ecstatic state. And lo! he saw in his inner vision that the offerings were transformed from wine to milk and meat into rose flowers, and the garland offered to the deity was on his own person. When Gajanana regained his normal consciousness, to his surprise he found that there was an actual change in the puja material, as he had seen it in the state of meditation.

At this time, Mr. Shivrambhau who had been peeping through the chink of the door, rushed in and fell at the feet of Gajanana Maharaj, who blessed him and imparted to him instruction in the Soham Mantra.

Darshan of saints

After this Gajanana Maharaj's practice of meditation went on smoothly and he got the darshan of Riddhi and Siddhi (goddesses who are the presiding deities of the powers acquired by yoga practice), and of several saints. All the saints heartily gave him their blessings and said, "Your yoga is now complete. You will now be in a state of meditation ceaselessly. You have now become a siddha (a perfect yogi). Whatever mantra you will give to a spiritual aspirant, it will be attended with success. If you will touch an aspirant, he will make progress on the path of yoga." Then the saints disappeared.

Mental worship of the guru

One day at night, Gajanana Maharaj sat in meditation. His guru appeared before him, and Gajanana Maharaj worshipped him and offered him the naivedya (food offering). His sadguru thereupon smiled and said, "All this is not required, but the real truth is yourself–your devotion and faith. You yourself are the real bliss. Enjoy this bliss!" So saying, he disappeared.

From then on, at the time of meditation in his inner vision he would see Sri Narayana Saraswati sitting near him, and all the materials of worship, such as milk, shira (a sweet), garlands of flowers, etc., which were merely mentally conceived, were actually observed by others to be lying in front of Sri Gajanana Maharaj in the physical world. People often saw a garland of flowers appear round the neck of Gajanana Maharaj without anyone placing it there.

Disappearance of the Krishna Image

While Sri Gajanana Maharaj was at Akola a number of miracles occurred naturally at his hands. Only a few of them which were narrated by different eye-witnesses are given below.

While Gajanana Maharaj was at Akola, a wonderful miracle occurred at his hands. An old lady neighbor, an aunt of one Mr. Rambhau, was one day worshipping as usual a bronze image of Lord Krishna in her room. Gajanana, in company with some other boys of his age, had a whim to play a childish trick on her. He, therefore, asked her what she would do if he made her Balkrishna (Child Krishna) disappear from there. The old lady did not pay any attention to this silly boy. Gajanana therefore gave an order, quite innocently of course, to the image to go away from there. To the surprise of everybody the image of Sri Krishna

15

disappeared! The old lady was horrified at this jugglery and began to weep at the disappearance of her beloved image. She said that she would not eat or drink until the image was restored. At last Gajanana took pity on the old lady and asked her to spread out her palms. Gajanana then as innocently as before ordered the image to come back. To the pleasant surprise of her and the others present the little image reappeared in her palms. This was the first miraculous happening observed in the life of Gajanana Maharaj—at the early age of thirteen.

Mrs. Dighe's Account

Mrs. Dighe from Akola, a playmate of Gajanana in his boyhood, visited Gajanana Maharaj in the month of February, 1940. She narrated the following account of which she was an eye-witness.

It was the month of May. Gajanana, a boy of sixteen, was then sitting in the house of the clerk of Mr. Rambhau Gupte the attorney, which was close to Mr. Gupte's house. Most of the inmates of Mr. Gupte's house were assembled there. They requested Gajanana to procure for them some roses as he had obtained miraculous powers from evil spirits and they had heard of his having performed many miracles through their help.

Thereupon Gajanana remarked: "Do you wish that I should invoke the evil spirits and get myself killed by them? It is all sheer nonsense that I am possessed by evil spirits. The miracles which appear to occur at my hands are not done by me intentionally nor do I know at the time how they occur. They occur at the instance of some unknown Higher Power. I receive a strange shock and a light appears before me. This light later on takes the form of my sadguru and then sometimes such things occur. As they appear miraculous, people attribute them to the working of evil spirits."

"Anyhow, do anything you like, but do get some roses for us," was the persistent request of the people. Gajanana then went out of the room (though all the while the people could see his movements) and within a couple of minutes he came back into the room and threw twenty to thirty roses on the floor. Mr. Gupte's father, Mr. Martandrao Gupte, preserved some of these roses in a steel safe in order to test their their reality in case they were a kind of hypnotic illusion. To his surprise, however, he found the roses intact in the safe. None of them had disappeared. So his idea that they had been produced with the help of evil spirits proved to be erroneous.

[The foregoing needs some explanation. Evil spirits have an aversion to iron (and therefore steel) as it seems to burn them. Because of this many people in India wear small iron or steel bangles on a wrist to repel or neutralize any negative spirits or energy vibrations. If the roses had been produced by evil spirits and were either real or illusions, if put into an iron or steel receptacle they would disappear or be changed into something else. Since they remained intact, the men knew they had not been produced by any negative entities or energies. *Editor's note.*]

Mrs. Dighe also said that the young Gajanana always avoided taking a bath, but one day some people insisted upon his taking a bath. He then consented, and while he was bathing, the water gave out the fragrance of highly scented attar of khus. [Khus is vetiver, a grass whose essence is used in India both as flavoring and perfume.]

Cure of pneumonia

When Maharaj was at Akola, there was a gentleman named Mr. Santuram Gupte staying in the house where Maharaj lived. His wife had a serious attack of typhoid with pneumonia. Maharaj merely asked the people of the family to burn camphor near her, and she was cured.

Gajanana Maharaj in Bombay

After visiting many places of pilgrimage Sri Gajanana Maharaj went to stay with Mr. Narayanrao Samartha at Parel in Bombay. Mr. Samartha was his relative and had received instruction in the Soham Mantra from Maharaj.

One day Mr. Moreshwarrao Mathure came to visit Mr. Samartha. Mr. Mathure in his boyhood had been staying in the house of Mr. Gupte at Akola and was attending school. At that time Mr. Narayanrao Gupte (the poet "Bee") was also staying at Akola with his aunt and younger brothers as he was employed in government service there. Laxmanrao Gupte, one of the elder brothers of Gajanana Maharaj, was a class-fellow of Mr. Mathure and both of them were studying in the fourth standard Marathi. Gajanana Maharaj was then learning the first standard. Mr. Mathure, therefore, knew Gajanana Maharaj then.

More than fourteen years had passed when Mr. Mathure saw Gajanana Maharaj again at Parel. Maharaj was at the time sitting in meditation. Mr. Mathure asked Nana Samartha as to who the man was, to which Mr. Samartha replied that he was Gajanana, the youngest brother of Narayanrao Gupte of Akola and that he was called Gajanana Maharaj.

Mr. Mathure asked, "Is this Gajanana Murlidhar Gupte? When did he become a Maharaj? Some time ago Ramchandra Mahadeo Gupte, a barrister's clerk, had been to Bombay from Akola. He, too, told me about several miracles performed by this Gajanana in the house of Mr. Gupte, the barrister at Akola, in whose house I also was staying in my childhood. But I did not believe him, because this Gajanana in his childhood was a truant and a vagabond and was very mischievous. I know his brother Laxmanrao very well.

"You and I belong to the same place, Mahad, and are also related to each other. You, too, call him 'Maharaj' and I now see him sitting in meditation. I am, therefore, compelled to believe that he must have in him something special deserving of respect. Formerly Gajanana Maharaj of Shegaon used to come to Akola. This [present] Gajanana then used to go to take his darshan and spend time with him. I think that that Maharaj might have perhaps conferred his grace upon him. This Gajanana in his childhood was very fond of taking the darshan of saints. All right, it is now very late. I shall come to you again some time and then meet him at leisure."

Two or three days later Mr. Mathure again went to Mr. Samartha's place. Gajanana Maharaj was also there then but he did not recognize

Mr. Mathure. He, however, asked Maharaj several questions regarding practicing meditation, and Maharaj answered them.

When a question was raised about the use of reading religious books, Maharaj observed that the only use of books was to arouse a keen desire to know the Self. The reading of books did not deserve more credit than that. One should not, therefore, stick to books alone. If a person becomes addicted to the reading of books, his own powers of thinking and of discriminating between good and bad become weak and vacillating, and when this happens his whole life becomes futile and worthless. The most important thing in life is to get Self-experience.

After this conversation was over, Maharaj also asked Mr. Mathure his name, whereabouts, profession and other particulars. During these questions and answers Maharaj came to recognize his former acquaintance and having observed Mr. Mathure closely, and especially his eyes, remarked, "Mathure, do you practice pranayama?" Mr. Mathure was very much surprised and asked Maharaj how he could know that. Maharaj replied, "Quite naturally. By looking at your face, I could understand it by the grace of my guru." Mr. Mathure was greatly surprised at this and turning towards Mr. Nana Samartha said, "This is not the Gajanana of former days. Owing to the grace of his sadguru, a great transformation has taken place in his state."

Mr. Samartha replied, "Moroba, this Gajanana is now traversing the path of everlasting happiness. He has attained a very high stage owing to the grace of his guru. He is a great saint, but he does not wish this fact to be known and I, too, respecting his wishes, do not say anything about it to any one. As in the bazaar every one must test a coin himself and find out whether it is true or false, similarly in the case of saints everyone should find out for himself. Moroba, I am, however, glad that I have met a real saint."

Mr. Mathure then asked Nana Samartha whether he had gotten any spiritual experiences himself, and whether he would tell them to him. Mr. Samartha replied, "Maharaj told me to repeat the mantra Soham, which I have done continuously for four or five years. I had various experiences, but at present, however, all, these visions have disappeared and I go into the state of samadhi lasting for an hour or an hour and a half. The feeling of joy experienced in that state cannot be described in words.

"You know, I suffer from attacks of asthma very often. But I am glad to tell you that when in meditation I do not feel even the slightest pain from the malady. If you practice meditation as taught by Maharaj you, too, will get these experiences. It is not that everyone gets the same experiences. It all depends upon one's capacity and aptitude of mind. It is only necessary to carry on the practice steadily and perseveringly. Such is the power centered in the mantra Soham. I cannot say anything more."

Then Mr. Mathure said to Maharaj, "Gajananrao, now I must call you 'Maharaj.'"

To this Maharaj replied, "No, no. I am not a Maharaj. I am a servant of you all. That sadguru who conferred his grace upon me is the real Maharaj."

Mr. Mathure said, "I am very glad to see this humility of yours. I now request you to come to my place and give darshan to all the members of my family and bless me. I shall just call for a carriage."

Then Mathure brought a carriage and took Maharaj to his place. There Mathure's sister recognized Maharaj, and all talked together for some time. Then Mr. Mathure left the house and went to the market. During his absence his sister told Maharaj that Mr. Mathure was practicing pranayama, owing to which he had lost balance of mind and sometimes talked incoherently and at random and sometimes lay down for hours at a time in a state of semiconsciousness. She therefore requested Maharaj to take compassion on him and lead him to the right path.

When Mr. Mathure returned Maharaj made him sit near him and said, "Your practice of pranayama is not correct. You have learnt it from some novice in yoga and hence it is all wrong. You must now quit this pranayama. It is much better and also easier to get control over the mind instead of trying to get control over the breath. After getting control over the mind, if as a result you get control over your breath it will be extremely beneficial.

"In raja yoga, otherwise known as dhyana yoga, one who wishes to attain the spiritual goal must practice a good deal and that, too, regularly. Besides, one must to a certain extent be disgusted with worldly existence. Blind faith is harmful in raja yoga and is contrary to its principles. If a guru or a saint merely asks you to put your faith in him and he does not enable you to realize some experience within your Self, you should tell him plainly that there is nothing secret in raja yoga, which is not a mysterious science. All its practices are open.

[Whenever in this book Gajanana Maharaj speaks of "raja yoga" he means the yoga of Soham meditation, and not the system that employs pranayama as its central practice though it is often spoken of as raja yoga, also. *Editor's note.*]

"Those who merely rely on their guru without trying to get any Self-experience, weaken the power of themselves and will find themselves deluded in the end. Those who say that yoga is a secret lore are either deceivers and cheats or imperfect yogis, and it is better to keep at a distance from them because they bring a stigma on that celestial science and contribute to its decadence. Thousands of years have elapsed since the birth of the science of Yoga in this blessed land of India. Since then various sages have dived deep into it and given it the form of a definite science and explained it openly to various aspirants.

"Dear Mathure, you must have read various books on this subject, but I have told this to you in brief, not from what I have read but from what I have experienced in myself. You will be fully convinced of its truth when you also will get that Self-experience. You cannot be expected to put your faith in me, because we have stayed together in our childhood and known each other's character well, and it would be difficult for you to believe that I have acquired any great proficiency in yoga. Hence I had to explain to you at some length.

"In comparatively modern times, various modern learned men have written commentaries on the Yoga Shastra, but I have heard that they have committed many mistakes. The old commentators were much better because their commentaries are based more upon solid reasoning calculated to satisfy the intellect. But these latter commentators have covered the yogic lore with mystery and created an atmosphere of difficulty about it. These later commentators, instead of explaining all things more openly and on a scientific basis, have made the Yoga Shastra a bogey and rendered it more incomprehensible. The only advantage they got from doing so was the absolute power which they could exercise over their disciples, in their capacity as so-called 'gurus.'"

Mr. Mathure then said to Maharaj, "I shall stop pranayama, but you should kindly take me under your protection, bless me and lead me to the right path." He then immediately garlanded Maharaj and placed his head on Maharaj's feet.

Observing his keen desire, Maharaj told him the mantra Soham. Maharaj then told him that if he would practice meditation daily in the way shown, he would soon get Self-realization and attain the highest goal of human life.

Maharaj then added, "This path of meditation has been shown to you by me through my guru's grace and inspiration. I have up to this time shown this path to some of my friends and I shall show it to others in the future, only through the grace and by the order of my guru. But the result or success will depend upon everyone's keenness in practicing and his faith in the Self.

"Consider Self-experience as your real sadguru. Then there will be no necessity of relying upon the words of others, however great they be. Hence I say there is nothing secret in this path. What little I have told you has been told freely and with frankness. You should not pay any attention to miracles because they are absolutely useless.

"Every step in this path of yoga should be minutely scrutinized by the inner sight and tested by experience and reasoning. Where you cannot understand, shastras may be referred to. I would never tell you to place your blind faith in anyone, as I consider that to do so leads to self-ruin. Awaken your discriminating power, test everything in the light of your experience as you test gold in fire and on the touchstone. If you think that there is some sense in what I say, try to realize it in your experience. There is no cause of fear in this path. Truth can be proclaimed in broad daylight to thousands of people. There is no danger to it. You should, however, keep away from pseudo-saints."

In the course of conversation with Mr. Mathure, Maharaj had remarked that if Mr. Mathure would practice meditation as directed, in the course of time he would reach even the state of samadhi. Mathure thereupon asked Maharaj, "Do you go into samadhi? What is the nature of your practice?" Maharaj replied, "I was practicing meditation and going into the state of samadhi even when I was in my mother's womb. Now I do not do anything and I cannot do anything. Strictly speaking I do not do anything; whatever appears to be done by me is done by Rama (God). I am simply as it were playing in this world in a peaceful state of mind. I do not understand Vedanta and its theories. I am, however, seeking in myself my own Self which is one and beyond all these things, which is eternal, which is life and which is joy incarnate."

Mathure: "It is said that one must have the support (adhishthana) of God. Please explain to me what is meant by this.

Maharaj: Mathure, you have learnt too much Vedanta. I myself feel that there is no support of any thing to any other thing. Do not pay any attention to the above-mentioned saying regarding the support of God. Try to get the support of your own Self. Make the three things one: the meditator, the act of meditation and the entity to be meditated upon. And be absorbed into the state of joy. It will be of no use reading and discussing about what is written in thousands of books. In order to attain one's goal three things are necessary: association with saints, devotion towards one's guru and disgust with worldly life. If your conduct is pure, if you try to follow the principles of morality, and your mind is full of disinterested devotion and you repeat the mantra given by your guru, your mind is sure to be ultimately purified. He who experiences the joy of his own Self naturally and easily follows these rules of conduct!

"The real mission of saints in this world is to guide aspirants on the spiritual path. I am an humble servant of my sadguru. I am still in the sadhaka stage and am still carrying on the practice of yoga. I always tell my friends that I do not know anything about devotion [bhakti] or knowledge [jnana] or detachment [vairagya]. I, however, wish to impress upon you that while there are a few real saints who can be counted on one's fingers, there are thousands of hypocrites who merely imitate the outward behavior of real saints.

"People in the world cannot recognize real worth. They cannot recognize a real gem but are attracted by the tinsel luster of false diamonds. It is difficult under these circumstances to find out the worth of a genuine coin."

Mathure: Maharaj, from the time I was at Akola I have seen many pseudo-saints. Their method of testing the devotion of their followers was very peculiar. Some said, 'Serve me and then you will be purified.' Some asked their followers to keep their wives in their (saints') company and to devote their money, mind and body to their (saints') service. Some saints said, 'I was the husband of your sister in her former life, so keep her with me.' Some asked people to make their minds pure first of all and then go to the saints. Some said, 'You are not as yet fit for the reception of spiritual knowledge.'

"In this way they used to dispose of persons going to them for spiritual advice. Some Babas have amassed vast estates by accepting worship, and thousands of rupees as dakshina from their followers. Some are attended upon by women. Some Babas always propound Vedanta by their mouths. Some purposely put on a very shabby and dirty dress, while some even remain naked. But these are all tricks with a view to create an impression on the minds of aspirants. Some say, 'I have purposely been sent into this world by God for the uplift of women. I have undergone great endeavors from my childhood and went to the Himalayas and practiced severe tapasya in the caves there. Bhagavan Shankar [Shiva] then manifested himself to me and gave me the boon that I would be the savior of women. Hence I am fulfilling my mission.'

Maharaj: Moroba Mathure, I have carefully listened to what you have said. I, too, have heard about the various tricks practiced by many so-called saints, similar to those described by you. I say that perhaps God might have granted such a boon to some of these saints. Why should we not accept their word?

Mathure: Maharaj, I must say that you are misleading me by such words.

Maharaj: Mathure, I am not misleading you. Even in old times, when many great saints who had attained Self-realization flourished, there were also side-by-side hypocrites and pseudo-saints. At present, too, we have some "specialists" who have been given a boon to save only women. These things will always go on. Only we should not allow ourselves to be deceived and should learn to distinguish the true from the false coin. Sri Tukaram has remarked regarding such saints, "Tuka says that such (false) saints should be buried underground alive." Sri Ramdas has also remarked that crores [tens of millions] of such gurus can be had for a pice [one hundredth of a rupee]. When I was at Akola I, too, was for about four or five years going after such saints; but God saved me from their machinations and I was able to warn about twenty or twenty-five of my friends also. These saints were later on thoroughly exposed and we thanked God for having saved us from them.

Mathure: Maharaj, what you say is quite true. People who fall a prey to the various tricks of false saints and make efforts to stand the various tests laid down by them in many cases are ruined both from the worldly and the spiritual points of view. Your test on the contrary, that of concealing your greatness under the garb of vice, is much better. [Sri Gajanana Maharaj was a chain smoker–yet there was never the smell of burning tobacco, but rather the scent of the best incense! He also appeared to drink wine right from a bottle, but when he offered it to others they discovered that as they took it into their mouths it was changed into milk!] No crowds collect round you. There are no pictures of deities, there is no bhajana and there is no paraphernalia of materials of worship. You mix yourself in whatever is going on. He who does not know this fact may perhaps be misled by your drinking and abusing and may perhaps leave off coming to you. [Maharaj spoke very plainly and rebuked fools and fakes who came to pester him with silly and hypocritical questions and objections–as is very common in India. Naturally, such people considered his reprimands "abuse" and therefore unsaintly.] This, however, will not ruin him in any way. He, however, who has come in contact with you in his previous birth will, in spite of all these external appearances, stick to you and be surely benefited.

Now, Maharaj, I shall ask you one question. Many people, who are either atheists or pose as atheists, ask me questions regarding the existence of God and challenge me to prove it. Although I have firm faith in God, I get nonplussed at such questions, have to eat humble pie and say that it is a question of every one's belief and not a thing capable of proof. Will you kindly tell me how to answer such questions? Can the existence of God be proved by arguments?

Maharaj: I think the following is an easy and a scientific way of answering the question. Water may be produced by the chemical combination of hydrogen and oxygen, as the science of chemistry says, but the calculation of the proportion in which these two gases are to be combined can only be made by an intelligent agent to produce water. This faculty of calculating cannot dwell in unintelligent matter. There is such a vast expanse of water in this world. That intellect which calculated this proportion and produced this immense quantity of water could not belong to dull matter nor to any being of limited capacities. This universal intellect can only belong to a Being of universal power, who is none other than God.

If, however, any of your questioners say that matter has intelligence, then it is nothing but the doctrine of Vedanta that Brahman is all-pervading and is the only entity existing, only expressed in a different way. The distinction between matter and intelligence then disappears and one entity remains.

Thus whether you look at the question from a scientific or religious point of view, it cannot be doubted that God exists.

Mathure: Maharaj, you say that you are ignorant, that you have studied only Marathi and that too up to the Fourth Standard, that you have not read any shastras. Then how is it that you are able to answer such questions cleverly? Although I have read a good deal, I cannot answer such questions and find myself confounded.

Maharaj: I have heard educated men discussing among themselves and have learnt some facts mentioned in various books from educated men. I then thought over these things myself, and I can immediately remember things heard long ago and am able to give appropriate answers. In my childhood I always attended kirtans and purans [discourses on the Puranas] and carefully listened to any discussion on the shastras. Later on I read whatever religious books fell into my hands. I thus read some Upanishads and the Yoga Shastra of Patanjali. Some of these books I read myself and some I got explained to me by others. I have also read the lives of some saints. Hence I have been telling to my friends, brothers and sisters, whatever I have learnt from the lives of saints, only nowadays I have almost stopped doing so. At present I do not do anything, and make it appear as if I do not know anything. I find it necessary to let the world think that I am full of defects. To show off one's merits is to deceive others as well as oneself. Rishis in ancient times, too, tried to create the impression on people that they were full of defects.

Mathure: Maharaj, shall I be able to see my Self in the state of meditation? It has been said that the human Self is also the same as God.

Maharaj: Now enough of this Vedanta. You will be able to see your Self. I say so because I myself have some experience of it. I see that you are trying to pump out information from me. But it appears to me that this our meeting was decreed by fate, otherwise I would not have afforded you any opportunity to do so.

I have a feeling of great affection for Nana Samartha who told you of many miracles which occurred at my hand. That generated great faith in your mind towards me. Besides, Mr. Gupte of Akola also told you about me and the many miracles which happened at Akola at my hands. All this has swept off all dirt of doubt from your mind and it has become full of faith. Hence I am compelled to tell you.

Now just see. When your meditation will become ripe and developed, you will be able to see how the Self slowly enters the sushumna and is seen like a streak of lightning for a time before it enters the Brahmarandhra (the center of the brain). Only the attention must be quite alert. Otherwise it passes off so quickly that it is not noticed at all. All right. I have told you this particular sign. If you observe minutely with close attention, you will be able to see it. I had pointed this out to Mr. Shivrambhau at Akola.

Mathure: I wish to ask one more question. What is your opinion regarding miracles?

Maharaj: There are some mahatmas at whose hands miracles do occur. But these great saints do not care for the miracles in the least. There are also some real saints at whose hands miracles do not occur. But they should not on that account be considered as not being saints. A spiritual aspirant or a devotee is sure to attain the right path, provided he follows the right methods.

Now enough of all these discussions, Mathure. Nana Samartha must be waiting for me, I shall again visit you at some other time. You should now carry on the practice of meditation intensely. If you do so you will obtain real peace, although you may be leading a worldly life.

After this, Maharaj took leave of Mathure.

Mr. Mathure died at the age of fifty-eight, having reached the stage of samadhi.

An offer to take the position of a saint

At one time in his travels Sri Gajanana Maharaj met a very famous saint, Sri Rama Maruti, who received him very graciously and spoke of him extremely highly. When that saint left his body, some of his disciples were seeking Gajanana Maharaj to ask him to take over the ashram of the saint and become their spiritual guide. They had not previously met Maharaj, but came to the home of Mr. Nana Samartha seeking him. When they met Maharaj without knowing his identity, the following exchange took place between him and one of the group named Mr. Gupte.

Maharaj: What is the object of you all in coming here?

Mr. Gupte: We had to spend about a hour and a half to find out this place. We met one man below and we asked him where Mr. Samartha stayed. He told us to go upstairs and thus we arrived here.

Maharaj: That is all right. What is your work with me?

Mr. Gupte: We have no work with you. We want to see Gajanana Maharaj who stays here in Mr. Samartha's place.

Maharaj: Oh my God! But will you please tell me who gave you information about him? If you will tell me freely, I too will tell the whole truth to you, so that you might not be misled. Your purpose then will be properly fulfilled. Otherwise you might get yourselves into an awkward situation. In speaking thus, I have a sincere desire to help you. You will come to know by experience the truth or otherwise of what I will tell you.

Mr. Gupte: Sri Rama Maruti has left this world. I have a relative at Uran who is a virtuous and a sincere man. He is not a man to recommend any person, even though that person may be a mahatma, unless he is convinced of his greatness by his own personal experience. He is also not a man to be deceived by merely external appearances. He told me that the only person in our Kayastha caste who was worthy to occupy the place of Sri Rama Maruti was Sri Gajanana Maharaj, and that he was staying for many years with Mr. Samartha. Hence we have come here.

Maharaj: Now I understand. I shall tell you in short about Gaja-nana Maharaj. You may believe me or not. I leave it to you. Had your relative told you that Gajanana Maharaj has some bodily defect in his arms or feet?

Mr. Gupte: No. He has not told me anything about it.

Maharaj: All right. I won't ask any more questions. I shall tell you the opinion I hold about him. This opinion is based not on hearsay but on my own experience. He had almost dragged me into the meshes of the vice of drinking and it was only through sheer good fortune that I freed myself from it. He is an absolutely worthless man. He is a drunk-ard of the worst type. He abuses even women like a mawali [the lowest class of male street ruffians]. He does not care a bit for the world or for the opinions of other people. He rarely eats food. He taunts others in the presence of their friends or acquaintances by speaking about some awkward incident regarding them which might have occurred years ago. He repeats indecent sayings and proverbs, and when someone blames him about it, tries to give them a spiritual meaning. Some people say that he performs miracles. I cannot say whether he is a follower of the Aghora Pantha (the path of evil magic) or whether he has propitiated some evil spirit or whether they are tricks of hypnotism.

How can people like me say anything about him to Nana Samartha? First of all, he is a cripple. Secondly, he is related to Nana Samartha. Thirdly, Nana considers him as his guru and lastly all the members of his family, young and old, have full faith in him. They do not do anything without taking his advice and never transgress his orders. Of course this does not mean that every member of the family implicitly follows his advice in every matter but what I stated above is, broadly speaking, true. They all call him "Deva Mama" [Maternal Uncle]. This being so, how can I tell Nana that I do not like his conduct?

I am a resident of Akola from which place Gajanana Maharaj also comes. To place such a person in the position of a saint like Sri Rama Maruti would be an insult to the memory of that great saint. If such a thing is done the disciples of that great saint will become objects of contempt and ridicule in the eyes of the world.

Besides Gajanana is a cripple and he answers his calls of nature at the place where he is sitting even though women might be nearby. In short, all his external behavior at least is censurable from the ordinary worldly point of view. I cannot say anything about his internal spiritual progress, if any.

He has gone away from Bombay for the present temporarily. He will return in a day or two. You should yourselves personally see him and gather your impressions about him. I am leaving this place by tonight's train. If, however, I have to postpone my departure on some account, we shall all meet together in the presence of Gajanana Maharaj. Only I won't say anything in his presence. You should observe for yourselves and form your own opinion.

Now, therefore, all of you should go. Having heard from someone only about the good qualities of Gajanana Maharaj you have, in your minds, raised him to the position of a real saint. But please go now and when we meet again tell me what your opinion regarding him is after mature consideration. Please come over here again without fail.

As soon as Maharaj said this, one of those four or five disciples, who was a clever and keen-witted man, suddenly caught hold of Maharaj's feet and would not let go of them, saying, "You yourself are Gajanana Maharaj."

Maharaj had ultimately to admit the fact and said, "I am not really a Maharaj; but some few persons call me so. Well, now you know me as Gajanana Maharaj, what have you to say?"

They replied, "Not much. You are worthy to succeed Sri Rama Maruti."

Maharaj told them, "I am exactly as I described Gajanana Maharaj to be, neither more nor less." All of them laughed at this.

They were then given tea. After tea Maharaj said to them, "Really I am not worthy of the honor. Even supposing I leave off all my bad habits, still I am as yet a sadhaka. I also have not much knowledge. Whatever I appear to know is not my own knowledge, but my guru makes me his mouthpiece and speaks through me. I only repeat the japa in my mind without others knowing about it, as has been advised by saints. Through my sadguru's grace, I contemplate upon and repeat 'Soham' internally. My internal dirt has not been swept off. When it will be entirely swept off by means of some broom, then I will not mind being placed in any saint's position. Even if I then do not occupy any 'seat,' still I will be able to instruct aspirants and guide them on the spiritual path through the order and grace of my guru.

"All right. It is now nearly five o'clock and you have to catch your train. If all of you really wish that I should succeed Sri Rama Maruti, come again a week or so hence after mature consideration and then we shall see."

They never returned or made any communication with Maharaj, nor was he ever even invited to attend the annual anniversary festival of Sri Rama Maruti.

When Nana Samartha came to know about this, he asked Maharaj why he had not accepted their offer. He said that it was a very good offer and it would be a credit to the Kayastha caste also.

Maharaj said, "I personally have no objection to sit on the seat of Sri Rama Maruti. He was a great saint. Through his grace I should be able to carry on his work. But there is one thing. You people will lose the pleasure of my company. I shall be there surrounded by many people. Many rich persons will visit me and pay their respects to me. Who knows, I may also get a little feeling of pride and perhaps would find it a little derogatory to my dignity to be on friendly terms with people like you! Would you like it? Consider."

Nana Samartha then said to Maharaj: "Please remain as you are. If we were to lose you, nothing could compensate us for such loss."

Some time later this incident was narrated by Maharaj himself to a friend. After narrating the incident, Maharaj remarked, "That is as it should have been. Everything further may happen as it may."

Humility, mercy and grace

[This account centers around the proposed visitation of a woman to her family whom she had not seen for four or five years. For some reason, in India this matter of a woman going to her husband's household, or returning to her parent's household for a visit, is very often a source of conflict, mutual recrimination and all-around ill feeling, usually with no basis at all except ego. *Editor's note.*]

When Maharaj was at Bombay he was often asked by his brother, Mr. Narayanrao, to go to Pen and other places where their family had their landed property for receiving land rents which amounted to about five to eight hundred rupees per year. During one of his visits to Pen, a friend of Gajanana Maharaj, Mr. Trimbakrao Shikekar, went to him and requested him to accompany him to the village Nate via Roha. He said he had to bring his sister Kerubai from Roha, where her husband was living. As Maharaj was not acquainted with anyone at Roha, he hesitated to accompany him. But as Trimbakrao insisted upon Maharaj's accompanying him, he at last consented.

The next day Trimbakrao, his friend and Maharaj started in a bullock cart in the morning and reached Roha in the evening. Maharaj was at that time dressed rather shabbily, and he asked Trimbakrao to tell the people there that he was his servant. Trimbakrao was unwilling to do so. But the occasion was such that it was necessary for Maharaj to remain incognito.

On arriving at Roha, Trimbakrao went to his sister and told her how Maharaj had asked himself to be represented. She did not like the idea, as she had heard about Maharaj being a saint. But when she came to know that these persons had come to take her with them, she was glad, and she hoped that her husband's people would consent to her going.

The family consisted of Kerubai's husband Wamanrao, his father Narayanrao, his mother, children and other near relatives. Kerubai, however, had no child although nearly eight years had elapsed since her coming of age. Some said that she was possessed of some evil spirits and so had no issue.

When these guests arrived, Narayanrao, Wamanrao's father, was at home. He received the guests and Maharaj being a stranger to him, asked him the following questions.

Narayanrao: What is your caste?

Maharaj: We people have no caste.

Narayanrao: What is your father's name?

Maharaj: They say it is Murlidhar.

Narayanrao: What is your surname?

Maharaj: Gupte.

He asked him no further questions. [This was because his family name indicated his family's place of origin and his caste.] In the meantime, Wamanrao returned home and without taking any notice of the guests went straight into the house. He was told in the house that the guests had come to take Kerubai with them to her father's.

At the time of dinner in the evening, Maharaj was served outside in the verandah as he was supposedly a servant brought by the guests for driving the cart.

After dinner, arrangements for sleeping were made for the guests. Trimbakrao asked Maharaj to open the topic regarding his sister, and if her people consented to her going with them, they would start early next morning. Maharaj accordingly opened the topic with Wamanrao, but he did not say anything in reply. Some time later the same night, Kerubai asked her husband for permission to go with her brother. Wamanrao became so enraged that she was absolutely silenced. Maharaj tried to pacify him but it was of no avail. Before going to sleep Maharaj told Trimbakrao that he would see his way next morning and that he should not yoke the bullocks till 10 o'clock.

Next morning, Maharaj told Trimbakrao and his friends to go out and that he would again open the topic with Wamanrao. Maharaj then joined Narayanrao, the old father of Wamanrao, near the hearth. Immediately

Wamanrao came out and Maharaj asked him whether he was willing to send his wife with them, as she had not seen her parents for four or five years. Her father was also then ill. Maharaj gave these reasons and assured him that she would be sent back in a week and that they would be highly obliged if she were allowed to accompany them. Wamanrao got excited and told them to go away–he was not going to send his wife to her father at all. Maharaj then asked him not to lose his temper and said that though he was a servant he made himself bold to make those casual inquiries. Wamanrao became a little mollified at this and after drinking tea began to explain the reasons for not sending his wife to her father's. He said that whenever she went to her parents, people there blamed him as she was possessed by evil spirits and consequently had no issue.

Thereupon, Maharaj, casting a glance at him, asked him whether he observed any fast, to which he replied in the affirmative. Wamanrao used to observe a fast every Tuesday, having been told to do so by an astrologer who had come to Roha and of whose proficiency in that science he had been convinced. The astrologer had directed Wamanrao to observe fasts for thirty-six Tuesdays. It was then the third Tuesday.

Maharaj then asked him whether he had full faith in astrology. As this question was put, Wamanrao began to think that it was rather peculiar for a person who was merely a servant to speak in that calm, dignified and thoughtful tone. Maharaj again asked him the same question and inquired whether he had faith in astrology and would put faith in whatever Maharaj would tell him. To this he replied that it all depended upon his being convinced about the truth of what Maharaj would tell him. Then Wamanrao went inside and brought the Panchang (astrological almanac) and gave it to Maharaj. While he went inside he was becoming comparatively calmer and calmer and he began to wonder how that man, a mere servant, was influencing him in that manner.

Maharaj looked at the Panchang and said that he did not know how to read it, but asked him to write down on a piece of paper the questions which he had a wish to ask–without showing them to him. Maharaj made a show of counting on his fingers and then correctly gave him the answers to all his questions.

Wamanrao was extremely surprised and he at once placed his head upon Maharaj's feet and caught them firmly. He felt that Maharaj was not a servant or an astrologer, but a saint. He asked Maharaj to give him guru upadesh (instructions given by a guru to a disciple), and said that he would not leave Maharaj's feet until he granted his request. Maharaj granted his request and gave him the Soham Mantra and conferred upon him the internal sight. He made Wamanrao sit in front of him for half an hour repeating Soham in his mind. Wamanrao asked Maharaj to tell him exactly who he was, for he knew he was not a servant as he feigned to be.

He did not allow Maharaj to go that day. He himself took a day's leave and remained at home to attend upon the guests. Maharaj told him who he was and said that he was only a crippled child of God. Owing to the grace of his guru he was able to benefit people on the path of Self-realization. All were delighted and begged Maharaj's pardon for having treated him as a servant. Maharaj replied that he looked upon respect or disrespect as one.

The guests remained there for a day and started next day, accompanied by Kerubai. Maharaj assured Wamanrao that he would cure his wife of her complaint and that she would have an issue. Maharaj's words came true and Kerubai gave birth to a son.

Wamanrao progressed well on the path of Yoga. He occasionally visited Parel (a suburb of Bombay) to see Maharaj while he was there.

A vegetarian miracle

In the next trip of Maharaj to his landed property for collection of rents, he happened to be at Mahad. There was a friend of Maharaj, Mr. Randive, who was of a believing nature. He had been introduced to Maharaj some time before this by Mr. Vamanrao Kulkarni of Roha. Their camp was about three miles away from Mahad. Mr. Randive requested Maharaj to be with them in the camp that night. Maharaj had another doctor friend, Wamanrao Mathure, who was a devotee of Sri Rama. Maharaj went to him and requested him to accompany him to the camp as he had been invited there by Mr. Randive. They started in the doctor's bullock cart and though the river Gandhari near Mahad was in flood they reached the camp by about 10 p.m.

All those in the camp were waiting for Maharaj for dinner. Among the camp there were some Brahmins and some Kayasthas also. Dishes of meat were served. Maharaj and the doctor protested that they were unaccustomed to such a meal and that they ought to have been served with vegetarian food along with the Brahmins. The Kayasthas who knew Maharaj began to joke and said that he being a Kayastha should not find anything unusual in the dishes, and charged Maharaj that he was making an unnecessary show. [Actually, in Maharaj's family, even before his was born, no meat was ever eaten.] Maharaj said that if they persisted, he would partake of any dish which was given to him. Maharaj then offered the food to God and lo! The meat served to all was immediately transformed into vadas in broth. [Vadas are a kind of deep-fried savory doughnut.] All were struck with wonder. Some said it was jugglery and some that it was hypnotism.

Mr. Randive, who had invited Maharaj to the camp and was originally of a believing nature, was convinced of the greatness of Maharaj as a saint and sent the same broth as prasad to his family at Alibag. And the wonder of it was that the broth remained unspoiled for eight or ten days.

Some days later Mr. Randive appeared for the higher standard examination of the Revenue Department. Before his writing the papers he brought Maharaj to mind, and he succeeded in passing the examination and later on became a high official.

It is, however, sad to relate that although Mr. Randive had gotten such decisive proofs regarding Maharaj's greatness as a saint, some mischievous persons duped him into the belief that Maharaj was either a clever conjurer or a follower of the Aghora Panth (path of black magic).

Mr. Randive fell a victim to these evil suggestions and as it were surrendered his own reasoning power to the makers of these suggestions. May we all beware!

Mr. Raje of Dhulia

In 1924 Sri Gajanana Maharaj became acquainted with a Mr. Raje who lived at Dhulia. On the Gokul Ashtami day [the birth day of Krishna] of that year, Mr. Raje and all the members of his family were in their house with Maharaj, who was reclining on an easy chair in the verandah, seemingly asleep. Mr. Raje, in another room, smelled a fragrance as though hundreds of perfumed incense sticks were being burned. He looked everywhere in the house but could not discover whence the fragrant smell was proceeding. He came to the place where Maharaj was reclining on the easy chair. The smell was coming from there! Mr. Raje then awakened Maharaj and told him of it. Maharaj laughed loudly and only remarked that he himself had been absorbed in a feeling of joy, and that he could not explain it. [We can see from various accounts that miracles were often the result of supernormal states being experienced by Gajanana Maharaj.] All the members of Mr. Raje's family then came there.

Later, on two or three occasions at about four or five o'clock in the early morning, all of a sudden there was spread everywhere an exquisite and almost celestial fragrance of flowers.

Mr. Raje also observed on some occasions Maharaj's whole body besmeared with ashes and his forehead marked with sandal paste without any apparent physical cause. Maharaj, when asked about it, kept silent.

As Mr. Raje had published several books on astrology, many educated men used to visit him. These persons would see Maharaj sitting on a cot in the outer apartment. One day some of them asked Mr. Raje as to who the lame man was. It is not known what Mr. Raje told them.

The next day, some of these persons said to Maharaj, "Maharaj, where do you generally stay?"

To this Maharaj replied, "I am neither a saint nor a Maharaj. I am just like a member of Mr. Raje's family and have come to him as a guest. I am only a poor ignorant member of the universal family of human beings. Some people call me Maharaj. This name has been given to me by others. My real name is Gajanana. I am a resident of Akola. For the present I am staying at Bombay with Mr. Nana Samartha, who is a friend and relative of mine. I am returning to Bombay in a week or so."

These persons, however, thought that Maharaj was purposely giving them evasive replies, and said, "We have perfectly understood that you are a saint."

Upon this Maharaj said, "I do not know what has been told to you about me and by whom. I do not know anything else except the two syllables which have been granted to me by my sadguru. [By this he meant the two syllables of Soham.] I have not the ability and worthiness to instruct any one. I myself am still a student. I also do things which are not done by others. I drink wine almost the whole day and night. What would be the use of such a guru to you?"

But the people were not convinced by this reasoning and persisted in their request that he should instruct them. Maharaj, therefore, granted to them the Soham Mantra.

Miracle of Bukka (Incense Powder)

Once Mr. Raje and Mr. Saswadkar came to Nashik. While there they told about many miracles of Maharaj which had occurred at Dhulia. Mr. Saswadkar recounted a miracle in the following actual words.

"It was the month of Bhadrapada and the day was Anant Chaturdashi day, the last day of the Ganapati Festival. All of us had gone to the house of Mr. Sule, a barrister, at about 6 p.m. After seeing the dioramas and Ganapatis there we, Messrs. Raje, Madhavrao Vaidya, Pradhan and myself, went to the place of Mr. Pradhan and sat there casually talking about various matters.

"The talk turned upon saints and miracles performed by them. Many miracles were described by their disciples as having been performed by certain so-called saints, and these saints were later on exposed in the newspapers as hypocrites and charlatans. Many educated people who also were of a believing nature were deceived by these miracles, which later on were proved to be false. I myself had seen a sadhu in a village where thousands of people were coming for his darshan. But that sadhu later on committed suicide and instead of light spread darkness on the village. I remarked that I, owing to such instances, had no faith in any of these latter day saints. Sri Gajanana Maharaj was there, and I said to Maharaj, 'Why don't you say anything?'

"Maharaj said, 'What can I say in the matter? Every one describes the things seen by him and the actions of saints observed by him. I am an ignorant person. I do not do anything. I do not know Vedanta or its principles. I have no knowledge of books. There is, however, one thing–the Supreme Brahman–which is beyond all these things. Earlier saints like Tukarama, Ramadas and Ekanatha, and modern saints like Sri Ramakrishna Paramahansa, Vivekananda, Sri Gulabrao Maharaj and Sri Rama Maruti have pointed out the path of reaching that Supreme thing, Brahman, and of realizing It within oneself.

"'My Sadguru Mother has pointed out the same path to me and has given me the mantra of Soham. If you ask me anything about it, I might be able to say something. If you people, however, begin raising fanciful doubts, the whole night might be spent without coming to any conclusion. If you say that all saints are hypocrites and all miracles are false, what sort of reply can I give?'

"I said, 'I do not mean to say that all saints are hypocrites and all miracles are false but I only say that in these days false saints predominate.'

"Maharaj thereupon replied, 'It may be so, but it cannot be helped. If five or ten saints are true, there are hundreds of hypocrites who merely imitate these true saints and try to pass themselves off as true ones. Hence people are misled. Some married women abandon their husband

and families, but have people on that account given up marrying? Accidents occur to railway trains, motors and airplanes. Have people on that account stopped using those things? Similarly there may be many false saints but that does not mean that an aspirant on the spiritual path should not try to seek for a real sadguru. I can only say that one should act carefully in the matter.'

"While Maharaj was speaking, my eyes had been fixed upon his face. I saw a halo of light encircling his face and then a shower of bukka began to fall from above on the bodies, faces and coats of all persons sitting there, including Maharaj—and also on the carpet. Maharaj was crying out, 'Sadguru Narayana Maharaj Ki Jai! Ganapati Maharaj Ki Jai!' All there were highly delighted.

"Mr. Pradhan then took Maharaj to the terrace, where bukka fell on the head and body of Mr. Pradhan. He made Maharaj sit on a pata (wooden board used as a seat/asan) and gave him tea. All persons in the house then came upstairs and took the darshan of Maharaj. Raosaheb Gupte also was there. All present took a little of that Bukka and kept it in a small box.

"This miracle became known to many people in Dhulia. Maharaj, however, soon after this left for Bombay. He requested that the miracle should not be made known to others as far as possible."

A conversation

Next day Messrs. Saswadkar and Madhavrao Vaidya came to see Maharaj, and the following conversation took place.

Mr. Vaidya said: "Maharaj, I had asked some questions to one or two saints at Pune and one of them had said, 'We send various dreams to our disciples and also give them advice on spiritual matters. Those who act according to our orders are saved by us at the time of their death, and after death they are born again and become saints like ourselves, and God actually speaks with them. But the disciple must have implicit faith in us and must freely give us whatever we ask for. If, however, he does not serve us properly, we never look to his welfare, because we have to give a portion of our merit to the disciple and we many a time have to suffer from diseases for the sake of our disciples.' I and some of my friends agreed to follow the advice of the saint. We were told to write down the name of Rama one lakh [one hundred thousand] times on separate pieces of paper, then roll each piece of paper in a pill of wheat flour and give these pills to fish to eat. If we would do this, we were told that we would get the darshan of God.

"Another saint told us, 'We save a disciple after his death. You should first try to make your minds pure and should repeat the Name of God.'

"Another saint said that his particular mission was to save women."

Maharaj pressed Mr. Vaidya to tell the name of the last-mentioned saint. But he said that the name of that saint was well known and that some time in the future such false saints would be fully exposed in newspapers.

Maharaj then said, "All right. What have I to do with his name? I must see that my own house is swept quite clean. It is true that one should have a discerning mind. What is not wanted is the tendency to raise unnecessary and baseless doubts and suspicions. If a spiritual aspirant has real insight, he will not be deceived. You are like brothers to me. I shall try to explain to you in a few words what I think about these things. I, too, have many bad qualities in me. I do not find a single habit of mine which I think to be good. It is you who must really judge what is good and what is bad in me.

"Many saints have flourished in past times, there are some living at present and there will be saints in the future, also. All real saints have said that the source of real joy is in ourselves. In order to understand how to experience this internal joy of the Self, it is necessary to go to a sadguru and act according to his instructions. If once you know the real path leading to this Self-experience, you can enjoy the bliss of the Self even though you may be leading a worldly life.

"If any saint says that he has a special mission to save women only, he may be considered a specialist. Whatever a devotee asks for is granted to him by God. This saint might have asked for such a boon from God and God might have granted it. Great saints like Jnaneshwar, Tukaram and Ekanath, however, have said that they had come into this world to save all human souls and not women only. Female saints like Mirabai, Muktabai, Janabai or Bahinabai, did never say that they were in this world to save male persons only. Nothing like this has been mentioned in the lives of the ancient rishis or in the Upanishads or in the Yoga Shastra of Patanjali. It appears that God has created such 'specialists' among the present day saints only.

"In the ocean of this worldly existence, I have been thrown like a log of wood, and you call me a saint. How am I, then, to close your mouths? I tell you that I am not a Maharaj; still you persist in calling me Maharaj. You are simply besmearing a stone with red pigment and calling it a god. [This is a common practice in India. *Editor's note.*]"

Madhavrao Vaidya thereupon said, "Maharaj, is it ever necessary to gild gold? Can a real gem be hidden even in darkness? Can the fragrance of a rose or a champak flower or of musk be ever concealed?"

Maharaj said, "What is the use of discussing such senseless questions? Every person will get the fruit of his actions. Never again indulge in the censure of any saint. There might be sometimes among them a real saint who has realized the highest bliss and you might be incurring sin in censuring him also among the others."

Madhavrao said, "I shall ask only one final question. Is it not the duty of parents to teach ignorant children?"

Maharaj said that it has been prohibited by the shastras to shake the faith of other people, ignorant though they may be.

Madhavrao said that that did not hold good in the case of educated people.

Maharaj asked Madhavrao whether he was ever deceived, to which he replied that he had never been deceived although during the previous ten years he had taken the darshan of many saints, and that he was sure that he would not be deceived in the future also. He added,

"It is the mission of real saints to teach wisdom to people. Great saints like Tukaram, Ramdas, Eknath and Gulabrao Maharaj have written in severe terms of censure regarding hypocrites and false gurus in order that ignorant people might not be misled. Were these great men not saints? Then why did they criticize others? They really saw God everywhere. Then why should they have done so?"

Maharaj said, "Madhav, you are wrong. Those great saints had authority to do so. Such great personages have authority over the whole world. How would it be proper for us to imitate them? My sadguru has given me the shining torch of Soham. I do everything in my mind: bath, sandhya, japa, etc. I sit among people and talk with them. Whatever good things I see in saints or even in ordinary educated people of good conduct, I try to take a lesson from them and I sweep off myself whatever bad things there may be in my mind. I do not allow bad ideas to enter my mind again.

"I, however, cannot tell you why miracles occur at my hands, although that they sometimes occur is true. Mr. Raje might have told you about many miracles which occurred here. But I do not know how they occur. I, however, feel sorry when they occur. I go into an ecstatic mood, I see light before me and the form of my guru in that light, and then sometimes a miracle occurs which is observed by other people. I, however, attach no importance to miracles and pray that they should not occur. Please go away now. I shall not come here again. If you want to see me, you will have to come to Parel, Bombay, when we shall talk further."

"Adventures" of Mr. Saswadkar in his own words

I was transferred to Dhulia in 1926. Soon after that I got information that a great saint known as Gajanana Maharaj, and who was a cripple, was staying with a Mr. Raje who was the postmaster there. I also came to know that he came to be recognized as a saint some months after he arrived at Dhulia, although he never gave any sign of his greatness and did not permit anyone to praise him or to describe his greatness. His external appearance and his dress also belied the idea of his being a saint. Whenever people came to see Mr. Raje, this saintly guest always left the place and went inside the house, where he sat alone.

Mr. Damodar Martand Chitnis, who was then living at Nandgaon, had come up for a visit to his brother-in-law, Mr. Raje. I took Mr. Chitnis for a walk to the railway station. On the way I began asking him searching questions regarding the saint. He, however, appeared extremely reluctant to answer them. I thought that Mr. Chitnis was reluctant to give any information regarding him because the external conduct, dress, talk and the habit of abusing indulged in by the personage were such that to describe him as a saint would provoke only ridicule. I, therefore, told him a fib. I said, "Why are you not answering my questions? Only yesterday Maharaj himself told me that you know everything about him and that if asked you would give me all information about him. Then where is the objection?"

Then Mr. Chitnis began to speak and said, "I first met Maharaj in 1924 in Nashik. He had then come on a visit from Bombay to one of his relatives, Mr. Bhise, whom I often visited. I asked various questions to Maharaj and pestered him with various doubts and objections. In the beginning he kept quiet, but ultimately he acted as if he was angry and began to answer the questions. By taking worldly and homely illustrations he turned my mind towards spiritual matters and gave me an idea about what real happiness was.

"A few days later I had a dream in which I was told to go to Maharaj and take his upadesha. I accordingly was instructed by him and I was shown the path of dhyana yoga. I saw various visions, and could see Maharaj himself in my state of meditation, and in that state would know if Maharaj went anywhere in the physical world from one place to another. Later these visions began to disappear and I began to experience a state of extreme joy in which I was entirely unconscious of my body, and which lasted sometimes for more than an hour. This is the present stage of my progress."

As by this time it was nearly 8 p.m., we returned and Mr. Chitnis went to Mr. Raje's house and I went home. I was feeling a little bit afraid, as I had obtained all this information by telling a lie.

The next day was a Sunday. Mr. Chitnis came to me in the morning and said that Maharaj had taken him severely to task for having told me about him, and that Maharaj had forbidden Mr. Chitnis to see him when he would be visiting Nashik. In short, Maharaj had been very angry with him.

Mr. Chitnis appeared to be greatly troubled and said, "You told me a lie–that Maharaj had asked you to get all information about him from me–and hence I gave the information. I have now come into trouble for it. I was unwilling to give you any information regarding him, as it was his desire that we should not say anything about him to others. He wants everything left to the course of circumstances.

"Nowadays almost all people want worldly happiness and they want saints who will give them worldly happiness. They consider spiritual knowledge as all bosh and to spend time in trying to get it as mere waste of energy and a sure sign of future poverty and adversity. They want saints who will give them wealth, children and worldly prosperity, and they will bow down to such saints. They do not want spiritual happiness, which they regard as chimerical. They want a life full of worldly pleasures.

"Hence Maharaj is known to very few people. Only someone will go to a real saint and ask for lasting happiness who has realized that all worldly pleasures are perishable and ultimately lead to misery. Really speaking, poor and rich persons stand equally in need of real saints who have attained Self-realization. But who wants real saints?"

Then I said to him, "Chitnis, please do not be angry. I asked you in the capacity of a friend, and although I told you a lie I had no bad intention in doing so. Nowadays many pseudo-saints are flourishing in this world and we see even educated and big persons falling a prey to their machinations. It has, therefore, become very difficult to recognize a real saint. I do not mean to say that at present there are no real saints at all, but if at all they are there they are very rare. Newspapers and magazines are full of descriptions of such false saints and are warning people to beware of them. Still we find even learned men getting into the clutches of such false saints and offering their estates and even their wives to them by putting blind faith in their words.

"Instead of being thankful to the writers in newspapers and magazines, they on the contrary run them down as blasphemers of saints saying, 'What do they know? They do not admit the existence of God. How can they then believe in saints? They do not want either God or religion. They have no idea of what is meant by devotion. The only thing they can do is to spread scandals regarding saints and to increase the number of their subscribers.'

"I asked you for information so that I might not be deceived, because some of these false saints have powers of hypnotism owing to which they produce an impression upon others and catch them in their snares. My only point is that genuine coins and counterfeit coins are mixed in the bazaar, and it is the duty of every one to test the coin and find out whether it is true or false. I again request you not to be angry.

"If you know from your experience that Maharaj is a real saint, then where is the cause for anger? I fully believe what you have told me regarding him. But please remember that I will not rely simply on your words, but shall try to find out the truth for myself, although I shall not do so in a spirit of fault-finding and opposition, but in the spirit of a real seeker of truth."

Mr. Chitnis then gave me additional information. "Gajanana Maharaj does not accept any worship from anyone. He treats all equally, young or old, rich or poor. The mantra, Soham, which he gives is to be repeated, keeping time with the incoming and outgoing breath. I, after some time, obtained the gift of internal vision and easily I went up to the sahasradala [the sahasrara, the thousand-petalled lotus of the brain]. Maharaj for some days made me sit near him and practice meditation.

"Then he told me to practice at home and said that there was no necessity of going to him. He thus remains aloof even from those who have taken his upadesha and hence it is that he has remained so unknown.

"If anyone goes to him, he finds only two or three persons near him and hence no one can think him to be a saint or Maharaj unless he is specially told about him by somebody. I am, however, fully convinced that he is one of those very rare real saints who have realized the Self themselves and are prepared to show the path of Self-realization to others. I cannot say anything further.

"I have read several letters written by some of his disciples to Maharaj, which contain a description of their spiritual experiences which they obtained after having fully tested the correctness of the path shown to them by practice for a year or two. What more proof do you want? He has more disciples among Brahmins than among persons of our Kayastha Prabhu Caste and they are far advanced in their spiritual experiences." I then gave tea to Mr. Chitnis and accompanied him to Mr. Raje's house. Mr. Chitnis left the same night for Nandgaon.

Later on I personally asked Mr. Raje about the saint and Mr. Raie also told me everything that he knew about him. He said that he himself had no faith in modern saints but his mother being an aspirant on the spiritual path, he had brought Maharaj there. He personally liked Maharaj as his conduct was very pure, he was witty, humorous and mixed freely with children and there was nothing reserved or awe-striking about him. He never left the house, and unless particularly questioned rarely talked with any one.

After having obtained the above information I went to Maharaj in order to take his darshan. He was then sitting on a stool. He was a very lean man and his hands and feet appeared to be very weak and emaciated. I took his darshan and asked him some questions. He, however, gave evasive replies.

He said, "I am a poor man. I go to anyone who invites me affectionately and is glad to receive me as a relative. I am a fakir [wandering sadhu] in mind and consider myself as an humble member of the universal human family. I go wherever I am invited sincerely and stay there as long as I please."

I then began to visit him daily for about seven or eight days. Whenever he was in a joyful mood, he talked with me freely.

I once said to him, "Maharaj, please do not be angry. When we are sitting near you we occasionally experience various kinds of beautiful fragrances. What is the use of exhibiting such miracles?

"I have heard that there are eight kinds of siddhis (powers) which tempt a yogi and interfere in his spiritual progress. Only those yogis who are of an exceptionally strong mind are not tempted by these siddhis. They turn aside from them and steadily reach the highest goal.

"You, on the contrary, perform these miracles by using these siddhis. How then can it be said that you have really accomplished yoga? We, too, can go to the bazaar and bring various kinds of highly scented attars or sweetmeats or other things. Whether you get these things by means of powers (siddhis) acquired by practicing yoga in this birth or you get these things by means of money obtained in this birth as the fruit of merit done in previous births, the result is the same. I myself attach no importance to these miracles.

"If a yogi practices yoga and tapasya for years together, obtains these siddhis and gets himself entangled in them, I do not attach the slightest importance to him. Such yogis ruin themselves and also others. Please excuse me if I have spoken too much. But is it not simply deceiving ignorant people? If I am wrong, please correct me and explain to me and satisfy my doubts.

"In all spiritual matters, in yoga, in all the different religions, tenets and books, the only real thing that matters is experience. I have read the works of many philosophers, the sayings of many saints such as Ramakrishna Paramahansa, books of Vivekananda, Jnaneshwari and Yoga Vashishtha, and tried to understand their meaning. I have nowhere found any importance attached to such miracles. Ancient sages also in explaining the characteristics of a sadguru have always criticized yogis who indulge in miracles, and have definitely warned people not to place themselves under the spiritual guidance of such miracle mongers.

"There is nothing secret in raja yoga or in the other yoga paths, and I am not prepared to believe anyone who says that there is something secret or mysterious in yoga. A real saint or yogi will never ask any aspirant on the spiritual path to put blind faith in him, without having shown him the path of at least a little Self-experience."

By speaking in this manner I pestered Maharaj to a great extent.

Raosaheb Gupte and Mr. Madhavrao Vaidya were then with me. Maharaj did not speak a single word but was smiling quietly to himself, being greatly amused. We then went to our respective houses.

All of us three were, however, greatly perturbed and became very anxious to know something further about Maharaj.

The next day we three again went to him a little earlier. Maharaj appeared glad to see us and said, "My dear brothers, you have told me a great deal about Vedanta, but I am an uneducated man and do not know anything about Vedanta. I have learnt only up to the second or third standard in Marathi.

"But what is the use of raising objections and arguments before me and making me non-plussed? I have not come here for exhibiting myself as a saint and for deceiving ignorant men and women by displaying miracles. Miracles are inherent in every one. They are not required to be procured from outside. If you practice meditation you also will be able to bring about such fragrant smells. When a person practices meditation, as his concentration increases these smells naturally come out. These experiences are got merely on the lower steps of Yoga. They only show that one is proceeding on the right path.

"I casually got acquainted with Mr. Raje, and as I learned that Mr. Raje's mother and my aunt knew each other from childhood, I have stayed here, being pressed by Mr. Raje's mother to do so. Then why do you bother me? What advantage or benefit do you get from it?

"There is another thing. If a person keeps a parrot and teaches it to speak and the parrot speaks cleverly, would you give real credit to that person or the parrot? It is obvious that real credit is due to that person. I say these arguments of yours are like words spoken by a parrot. You have read many books and shastras. Suppose I also tell you something and you merely listen to it. What benefit would you get from it? You repeat things learned from books, but just as a parrot does not understand the meaning of the words he utters, similarly you do not understand the real meaning of what you say. It is all words and nothing else.

"Dear friends, I urge upon you to practice meditation and get actual experience. If after practicing for some time you do not get any experience then say that everything is false. Real saints will always urge you to get actual experience because they love all human beings heartily and sincerely. Tukaram has said, 'I cannot bear to see people sinking in ignorance, and a feeling of tender pity rises in me.' Such outbursts of feeling on the part of real saints will give you an idea as to how deeply they love all human beings and what great and keen interest they feel in their welfare.

"Now you have seen certain miracles and have heard of others. But have you any personal experience regarding them? Absolutely nil. I tell you, my dear friends, that if the mind gets internal sight and is concentrated in meditation, every person who practices meditation will, in the course of nature, experience such fragrant smells. There is absolutely nothing wonderful in this." After this talk we all went home.

Next day I again went to Maharaj accompanied by three or four others. At that time I had applied highly scented attar (perfume oil) to my hands and clothes and had placed small pieces of cotton soaked in attar in my ears. Some other men also were then sitting with Maharaj.

One of them said to me, "Well, you have come besmeared with attar scent today. Do you celebrate your Diwali today?"

I replied, "Maharaj gives out various fragrant smells. I thought I would do the same by means of merely attar."

Upon this Maharaj remarked that he himself was not smelling the fragrance of attar, but on the contrary the bad smell of ordinary oil. Other persons, on being told by Maharaj to do so, actually smelt my clothes and they too experienced the smell of ordinary oil. Then a big laugh burst from all the people there. I alone felt a sensation of shame and immediately begged the pardon of Maharaj.

All the people then said to me, "If at all you want to test a saint, it should be done with all humility. It is much better not to undertake such a difficult task. If we do not find our way to put faith in a saint, we should salute him from a distance, but should never find fault with him. Now this Maharaj is here for the last eight or nine months, but very few people know about him. It does not appear proper to us that any one should try to test this great saint. However, whatever has happened, has happened for the best." After this all went away.

Mr. Saswadkar tells about an incident involving an attar [perfume oil] seller

One or two days after the above, Gajanana Maharaj came to my place at about 9 a. m., and we both sat talking with each other.

A vendor of attars, who had been to Dhulia from Kanouj, came there. He had sold attars to many rich and important personages in the town, and he had made a list of them. He showed the list to me and said, "I have come to you, having heard about you. You must buy at least two or three tolas of attars. [A tola is about one third of an ounce.] I said that I was not fond of attars and wanted to send him away, but somehow I had to purchase attars from him worth two or three rupees. I then went inside for taking my bath. When I came out I heard some talk going on between the attarwalla [attar salesman] and Maharaj.

The attarwalla said, "I never give samples gratis. Pay money and I shall give you a piece of cotton soaked in attar. My attars are not of an inferior quality costing eight or twelve annas per tola. [There were sixteen annas in a rupee.] I take eight annas for a small piece of cotton soaked in the attar."

Maharaj thereupon said, "I am a poor man, my good sir; merely apply a little attar to the back of my palm. I do not want a piece of cotton soaked in attar. Show me Hina [a fragrance prized in India] or Mogra [Jasmine] attar." Still the attarwalla refused to show Maharaj samples.

I then told the attarwalla to show samples to Maharaj. I had an idea that Maharaj would work some miracle. I therefore again pressed the attarwalla and said, "Do show your samples to him, he will purchase your attars."

But the attarwalla seemed to be an obstinate fellow and said "My attars are very costly. How can this gentleman purchase them?"

Ultimately, however, he applied two different kinds of attar to Maharaj's hand. Maharaj asked him about the price of those attars. He said that it was ten rupees per tola, but that he would give them at the same rate to him as he had given to me—eight rupees per tola.

Maharaj then inhaled the smell of the attar and remarked that the smell was like that of ordinary oil which we use in our cooking for frying things. The attarwalla got angry and began to sputter and fume.

I then said to him, "You cannot understand the real worth of persons, just as some persons cannot understand the real worth of attars."

Maharaj then turned to me and said, "Bhausaheb, pay this man five rupees and ask him to show samples of all his attars."

Accordingly the attarwalla began showing the samples of all attars which he had with him. But every sample that was shown had the bad smell of ordinary oil. Even the costliest attars smelt likewise. The attarwalla himself and myself smelt the attars and both of us were convinced that what Maharaj said was true.

Then the attarwalla got frightened and he began to think that the man wearing the shabby coat was some great saint. He fell at the feet of Maharaj and prayed for pardon. We then burst into a laugh.

Maharaj said to the attarwalla, "I have done nothing in this matter. For all attars you use ordinary oil. A least I have heard that you do so. Hence the attars went back to their original form of ordinary oil. What is there to wonder at?" Maharaj, however, again transformed all his attars into their sweet-smelling state as before.

Mr. Saswadkar continues…

Since that time, however, I began to feel an extremely anxious longing for obtaining Maharaj's grace. Then Rao Saheb Gupte, Madhavrao Vaidya and myself consulted together and came to the conclusion that it would be very unwise not to get ourselves instructed by such a saint.

Madhavrao Vaidya was the first. He begged Maharaj's pardon for having taken part in and helping me in my attempt to ridicule Maharaj, and having taken him to his house garlanded him and got instruction from him. Maharaj had him practice meditation which developed his internal sight. He described his experiences to me. I was greatly delighted to hear all this and whatever doubts had been still lurking in my mind were entirely dispelled and I became full of repentance for having entertained doubts regarding such a saint.

Madhavrao Vaidya said to me, "Bhau Saheb, I feel I must have acquired great merit in my previous birth, as I have the good fortune of obtaining the grace of such a saint, who not only has spiritual experiences himself but also can show them to others. Such saints are very rare. Besides, Maharaj is absolutely selfless. Even the food which he takes is as small in quantity as that taken by a small child and he merely makes as it were a show of sitting for dinner.

"Some years ago Annasaheb Patwardhan of Pune had come here. He had told me that I should not be anxious, and that I would get initiation at the hands of a great saint. His prediction has been fulfilled. Maharaj gave me these experiences and showed me the path. He then told me not to put my faith in him but in the things experienced by me."

Two or three days later Raosaheb Gupte and myself got ourselves instructed. Maharaj gave me the mantra of Soham and told me to practice meditation. He conferred the grace of internal sight upon me and I began to see various wonderful visions in the internal world. For a year or two I continued practicing meditation according to my convenience and leisure. I then began to feel calmness of mind and a sensation that the japa was proceeding from all parts of my body. At any time the japa would automatically proceed. Sometimes I felt someone giving me pushes while I was sleeping and asking me to carry on the japa. After a pretty long time had passed in this manner and after Maharaj had gone back to Bombay, I communicated to him all my experiences by means of letters.

Two or three years later I personally went to see Maharaj and mentioned all these experiences to him in the presence of some of his disciples, who jotted them down. I then asked the following to Maharaj: "These visions which are seen during meditation are also sometimes seen in dreams. What is the difference between the two?"

Maharaj replied, "Things seen in a dream have no luster, that is to say they are not of light. But things seen in meditation are full of light and are really made of light. Brahman is just behind these appearances. Hence when all these appearances disappear, what remains behind is pure bliss. Although these appearances are not real things, still they are external manifestations of the real thing.

"This was the path followed by all the great saints like Jnaneshwar, Tukaram and Ramdas and by all the ancient rishis. This was the path which was pointed out to me by my guru, and the same path has been shown by me to you. All these appearances are as it were sign-posts on the way leading towards the highest goal: Brahman. When they disappear, the person practicing meditation enters the state of samadhi. This is the real experience in raja yoga. If you are prepared to say that all those old saints were fooled by hallucinations, then suppose me to be one of those fools.

"I, however, am still a student. Even though you may call me a siddha (one who has attained perfection), it will have no effect upon me."

In this manner Maharaj solved my doubts. During the last two or three years, all visions have disappeared, and for the space of an hour or an hour and a half I remain in a state of pure joy without any thoughts or ideas. Since then the whole tendency of my mind has been changed and I feel a sort of peace pervading everywhere. I feel as if the whole world is inside me. In this state of peace the Atmarama inside–the real Self–appears to repeat the japa of Soham. I can only say, Glory be to my sadguru who has made me realize these things in myself!

Restoring the Ashes

In May of 1928 when Mr. Saswadkar was at Talegaon Dhamdhere in the Pune District, Maharaj accompanied by Mr. Nana Samartha and Bala Maharaj Ramshejkar went to him on a visit. There is a holy place by the name of Vithal Vadi at a distance of about ten miles from Talegaon, and one day Mr. Saswadkar took his guests there in a bullock cart.

Mr. Saswadkar gave a bath to Maharaj in the river there and Mr. Nana Samartha similarly gave a bath to Bala Maharaj. He also washed Bala Maharaj's zoli (a square piece of cloth with the two ends on each side tied into a knot, used by sadhus to keep their things in) in the river without noticing what it contained. That zoli contained sacred ashes and sundry other articles belonging to Bala Maharaj. All these things had flowed away into the river Bhima and the zoli was clean washed, dried and handed over to Bala Maharaj, who felt very sorry for the loss of his sacred ashes as he wanted to besmear his body with them after his bath.

Bala Maharaj said, "Maharaj, what is this? Mr. Saswadkar and Mr. Samartha did not take care to see what was in my zoli, and have thrown away the things in it. Especially I am sorry for the loss of the sacred ashes."

Maharaj said, "Don't worry, these people have no sense. I, however, ask you why you are so very upset. Why don't you ask your favorite deity, Dattatreya, to give the things back to you? You have for such a long time served your deity faithfully on the hill known as Ramasheja. Will he not take pity on you? And now you are actually sitting in the temple of Shiva, who is fond of these ashes. All right. Tell me how much ashes do you want. Do you want a sackful or only as much as your zoli will hold? Because that much will suffice you for about two or three months."

In the meanwhile Messrs. Saswadkar and Samartha came to that temple of Shiva where Gajanana Maharaj and Bala Maharaj were sitting, and they heard most of this conversation.

Gajanana Maharaj said, "Oh Samartha and Saswadkar, how is it that you have no sense at all? You have thrown away the sacred ashes of Bala Maharaj contained in the zoli!"

Then Saswadkar and Samartha begged the pardon of Sri Gajanana Maharaj and Bala Maharaj, and fell at their feet.

Bala Maharaj said, "What is the use of all this talk? Give me ashes to besmear my body." Gajanana Maharaj again asked him how much he wanted, a sackful or as much as the zoli would hold. Bala Maharaj then got a little irritated and said, "You are simply talking and talking. You have not as yet produced as much ashes as would be held in two fingers. You simply talk about devotees and their gods. You have also taunted me about my tapasya and asked me to invoke my deity."

There was a great laugh at this and Gajanana Maharaj said, "Bala Maharaj, please do not be angry. I do not possess the merit of tapasya, I have no soul-force (atmabala), I have no knowledge of spiritual or worldly matters. I am simply a sweeper at the door of saints and my duty is to do menial work there. I only take a dose of Soham and that suffices for me. Oh Dattatreya, run for my assistance, run for my assistance and give ashes to my friend Bala Maharaj here."

With these words Gajanana Maharaj put his hands near the pindi [stand for the Shiva linga] and began taking out handfuls of ashes and besmearing the bodies of Bala Maharaj, Samartha, Saswadkar and on himself. Then he stopped, and Bala Maharaj fell at the feet of Sri Gajanana Maharaj and asked his pardon, saying "I am your child, kindly pardon me for my mistakes." Then Gajanana Maharaj and Bala Maharaj embraced each other. The cart was yoked and all started from that place at about 2 p.m.

On the way they saw a garden of orange trees. They got down there, purchased some oranges and ate them and drank cool water from the well there.

Gajanana Maharaj remarked, "It is worth observing how wealth and women lead to ruin. If we leave Brahmajnana (knowledge of the Supreme Self), devotion to God (bhakti) and detachment (vairagya) aside, it is difficult to say in this world what virtue is or what constitutes vice. If fortune is favorable, a man of originally bad disposition becomes virtuous so far as his worldly actions are concerned. If, on the contrary, fortune is unfavorable, even a person of originally virtuous disposition sometimes does questionable actions. But one thing appears to me to be clear. Just as gold, even though thrown into the dust, does not become dirty, similarly the virtues of a really virtuous man, even though he may be undergoing adversity of fortune, are sure to spread their luster all around and attract the attention of other people." (These remarks, which appear to be uncalled for and unconnected with any previous topic, we think were made in reply to the thoughts of Bala Maharaj).

They then started again and reached Talegaon at about 9 p.m. Gajanana Maharaj, Samartha and Bala Maharaj then went to Bombay.

Curing Meningitis

In 1934 in Mr. Bhise's house at Nashik, Mr. Appasaheb Vaidya, Mr. Walawalkar and one or two others were sitting talking with Maharaj, when Maharaj suddenly exclaimed, "He is lying ill on my bedstead in my room in my house. I must go to Parel." As no letter or telegram had been received from Parel regarding anybody's illness, people were wondering about Maharaj's sudden exclamation, when to the surprise of all a telegram was received from Parel that Shankar, the nephew of Mr. Samartha, was seriously ill and requesting Maharaj to come immediately.

Maharaj started by the first train available which was in the afternoon and reached Parel in the evening. The children of the family came running to the place where Maharaj's motor had stopped crying aloud, "Deva Mama has come." Maharaj made inquiries with them regarding the illness and then went upstairs. Shankar being almost unconscious did not recognize Maharaj at first but after some time did so.

Doctor Dabholkar was the family doctor of Mr. Samartha. He was a very good man, benevolent and successful in his profession. In the beginning the case could not be properly diagnosed as it was the first case of meningitis in Bombay. It was only after four or five days since the illness had begun, when the patient showed signs of delirium, that a proper diagnosis was arrived at. Shankar was examined by a committee of doctors consisting of Doctors Bharucha, Mulgaonkar and Mistry, all MDs.

Neighbors and relatives and friends were coming morning and evening to see how the patient was doing. Every day about forty to fifty persons visited. Shankarrao was a store-keeper in the office of the *Times of India* and people from his office also used to come for making inquiries regarding him.

Nearly a month passed, during which doctors were paying their visits. Religious ceremonies such as japa and other things were also performed. Whatever was suggested by anyone was done.

Maharaj visited Shankar only twice or thrice in the beginning and at last when his critical time came. Outsiders began to ask the members of the Samartha family, "What has your Maharaj to say about the illness?" To which they replied, "We only know that everything depends upon his grace."

In this manner two months passed and still there were no signs of any improvement in the patient's condition. The eyes of the patient became swollen and there was pus in his ears and he began to stammer incoherently in English, Urdu and Gujarati. His fever was 103 or 104 degrees continuously.

Shankar's superior officer had told all clerks to make inquiries regarding his health every evening and give him a detailed report next morning. The officer had sent a message to Nana Samartha, Shankar's uncle, that he would remove Shankar to a hospital and arrange for his special treatment there. The officer himself then came with his wife to see Shankar, but Shankar could not recognize him. The officer felt very sorry and after seeing Shankar's condition was convinced that Shankar would not live for more than five or six days. He therefore left, thinking that it was useless to remove him to a hospital.

The next day Shankar saw a vision which he afterwards described as follows: "I saw a black Yamaduta (Messenger of Yama, the God of Death) putting his noose around my neck. There was a funeral pyre burning nearby and a widow was ceaselessly crying. I myself was also crying loudly and shouting, "Oh Deva Mama, Deva Mama, save me, save me!" Then somebody went and brought Sri Gajanana Maharaj near me. He saw me crying and said, 'Do not cry; from tomorrow you will feel better.' Still I could not be consoled. Then he told me to repeat Soham continuously. I began to do so with my eyes shut."

At this time almost all people had gone away. Only four or five persons were sitting near Shankar's bed and were continuously burning camphor near the head of the bed. Shankar began to speak and said, "Have all run away? I see here a big snake and Sri Krishna upon it, who has placed his hand upon my head. See they have gone." All felt glad at hearing this. [Vishnu is often portrayed as reclining upon the great serpent Ananta which symbolizes Infinity. In this instance Krishna, the avatar of Vishnu, was seen instead. *Editor's note.*]

From that night Shankar's fever began to subside slowly. Three months later he became all right and regained his former strength. He then resumed his employment.

Healing paralysis

Raosaheb Shankar Sitaram Gupte, was associated with Maharaj after he received instruction from Maharaj at Dhulia. His wife, Mrs. Anandibai Gupte, also received instruction from Maharaj. At one time she was suffering from paralysis for about six or seven months and was confined to her bed. Raosaheb Gupte had been staying at Nashik since 1927 for getting the benefit of Maharaj's company. But somehow or other he never thought of taking Maharaj to his house, as perhaps he did not like to give trouble to Maharaj regarding his worldly affairs and thought that one must try to bear one's own afflictions sent by fate. One day, however, Raosaheb Gupte casually said to Maharaj, "I am tired of giving doctor's medicines to my wife. It would be better if you would kindly come over to my house and give her your blessing."

Maharaj replied, "Only doctors can cure such diseases. You ignorant people wish them to be cured by the blessings of saints. Of course the blessings of saints can accomplish anything, but I am not a saint of that sort. If I could cure diseases, why should I not be able to cure my own? As you know, in a month I am generally ill and suffering for nearly twenty days. Your wife is now about sixty years of age. Such ills of the body are quite natural." Although Maharaj said this and Raosaheb Gupte thought that the matter would rest there, Maharaj suddenly changed his mind and agreed to accompany Raosaheb to his house.

Maharaj then went to Raosaheb Gupte's house and took hold of Anandibai's hand and had her stand up and then said, "Meditate, while standing, upon that upon which you meditate every day. Direct your mind upon all your senses and carry on the japa." Mrs. Gupte was greatly delighted as she had not had the darshan of Maharaj for eight months, and she felt that the Great God Himself had brought about this meeting with Maharaj. She then did as she was told to do by Maharaj and could move a few steps. This was repeated two or three times during the period of two or three hours. She then was able to go into the inner house and again come out. Maharaj then returned home. In a day or two more she became all right as if she had never suffered from paralysis.

The look of grace

Vishwanath Patankar was never religious or spiritual. Rather, he was an atheist. But due to his past life karma he happened to suddenly meet Maharaj at Mumbai. When Maharaj looked at him lovingly, his mind took a complete turnabout and he prostrated at Maharaj's feet, saying, "Now you need to save me!" Spontaneously he began both praising and praying to Maharaj as though he had known him always. Understanding his good intentions Maharaj readily blessed him, then gave him the Soham Mantra and showed him how to meditate.

Mr. Bhave

Mr. Bhave after his retirement was living at Nashik as a tenant in the Shringeri Math of Sri Shankaracharya. He had been doing various religious practices, but had not obtained peace of mind. In November of 1937 Mr. Bhave learned of Sri Gajanana Maharaj through a letter from one of his friends. One day Mr. Bhave found out the location of the house of Maharaj and went there at about two o'clock in the afternoon. Mr. Bhave saluted Maharaj, who asked him about his name, etc., and as to how he happened to come there. Mr. Bhave mentioned everything in detail unreservedly and said, "Maharaj, teach me yoga and take me under your protection."

Maharaj at first tried to put him off, but as Mr. Bhave continued to come successively for some days, he ultimately conferred his grace upon him.

Sri Gajanan Maharaj said to him, "I have told you something in the capacity of a friend as I have been telling some others also. As those others are enjoying spiritual joy, you also may enjoy it. The only thing is that you must continue the practice. I do not wish to lead anyone astray, as I do not possess that art. You have to convince yourself by experience. From the worldly point of view, you are like parents to me and from the spiritual point of view I am like a father to you. Worldly transactions are to be carried on according to the worldly point of view and spiritual things according to the spiritual standpoint.

"All saints in the world are objects of reverence to me. But nowadays many false saints are flourishing. These false saints on the strength of the sayings of old saints say to their disciples, 'Miracles are worthless. True saints have considered the performance of miracles as unworthy. We are real saints, who have gone beyond the stage of performing miracles. Real saints never make a display of any miracles.' With such words they delude their disciples and conceal their own falsity and unworthiness. Simple people are deceived thereby and accept upadesh from these Babas and become their devotees. Both the Babas and their disciples are thus carried away by the flood of ignorance and sin. These Babas had committed many sins in their previous births, and in this birth also they commit many sins. They deceive people and enrich themselves at their expense. When they themselves have no idea of what is real purity of mind, how would they be able to save their disciples? If there is no water in the well, how can you take a bucket of water out of the well? Though saints of old have considered miracles as unworthy, still on certain occasions miracles have occurred at the hands of saints. Real saints who had reached the stage of complete Self-realization have performed miracles on proper occasions. They only say that it is merely a primary stage and aspirants on the spiritual path should not allow themselves to be tempted by them. They should not allow their attention to be diverted from their goal by such miracles."

On the Dattatreya Jayanti day Mr. Bhave came with sweetmeats and garlands of flowers and said to Maharaj, "Today is the day of Dattatreya Jayanti [Birth Day of Dattatreya]. It is a very good day according to the shastras. Kindly confer your grace upon me today."

Maharaj replied, "What you say is correct according to the shastras. But to saints all days are equally good. They do not look to auspicious or inauspicious days or times. This does not mean that I am a great saint. You are like a father to me. I shall willingly learn from you. The true knowledge which is really in you, but of which you are not conscious, will manifest itself to you."

Mr. Bhave appreciated the true meaning of this conversation and was greatly delighted. Maharaj then told him to come on the next Thursday, when he promised to tell Mr. Bhave what had been told to Maharaj by his guru. Mr. Bhave then garlanded Maharaj, took prasad and went away.

The next day Maharaj made him sit for meditation before him in an erect posture, and asked him to concentrate. For about ten minutes he became absolutely void of thought, and he told Maharaj about this state. Maharaj said that he himself had taken his thought process under his own control.

On Thursday he went to Maharaj again. Seeing that he had firm faith, Maharaj gave him the mantra Soham and also asked him to practice meditation. Mr. Bhave carried on meditation with great devotion and concentration of mind, owing to which his mind became absorbed. In the mental worship which he used to perform, Maharaj appeared before him and solved all his doubts and difficulties by explaining all things in detail by apt illustrations.

He used often to complain to Maharaj that he did not see light as other disciples did. Maharaj told him directly and indirectly that he should proceed according to his own way and get whatever experiences are to be obtained in that path. If he would look to the experiences of others or to what is told in the shastras, he would place himself in a state of doubt and difficulty. There are different ways in the case of different persons. Some see various visions and some hear different kinds of sounds. There is expansion or restriction of the pranavayu in different parts of the body in the cases of some. Some have to pass through all the six chakras. Various saints have got various experiences. After this conversation Mr. Bhave continued his own practice and left off asking such questions.

A few months ago, while Mr. Bhave was sitting in his house, he happened to shut his eyes for a moment and he saw Gajanana Maharaj standing near him. This was not merely an illusion, but an actual fact, except the form of Maharaj was of light. Mr. Bhave carried on the practice of meditation with full faith and self-confidence, and he began to see various wonderful things in his body. He felt that his body became as light as a flower and as if it was moving in the air. He felt that his strength was increasing of itself. He began to practice meditation for longer periods at a time, and with greater concentration. He sat in the padmasana posture, slowly began to lose consciousness of his body, and others could actually see that his limbs were becoming contracted as it were. He felt his whole body became as light as cotton and feared that it would be blown away if a strong breeze came. It appears clear from this that owing to his great faith, persevering practice, and merit acquired in his previous births, he has secured the full grace of Maharaj.

Mr. Ghanekar's child

Mr. Dattopant Ghanekar of Nashik has been intimately connected with Maharaj for about the last fourteen years. He visits Maharaj occasionally. Maharaj sometimes used to speak harshly to him, but that had no effect upon him. He did not discontinue his visits on that account. On the contrary, he has firm faith in Maharaj. He has never asked Maharaj for worldly happiness, and is not likely to do so in the future.

One time his wife and his child, four years of age, also visited Maharaj for darshana. Thereafter she used to visit Maharaj with the child very often. This child appeared to have acquired great merit in his previous birth, because while sitting near Maharaj he used to go into the state of samadhi. He used to describe his visions in that state, saying that he got the darshana of many saints who gave him their blessings, and that he felt a sense of deep joy.

Maharaj once said, "This boy will be a great saint in his next three or four births; but you should not expect that he will live long."

The child died at the age of about six years. Mr. Ghanekar visits Maharaj every Thursday. When time permits the couple both go to have the darshana of the Maharaj.

Basic Teachings recorded by an unnamed disciple

"If a person has any defects, the responsibility for them lies upon him. You may come to me or not as you like. I do not insist on your listening to my advice and acting according to it. It is a matter which should be left to everybody's conscience. Really, people like you should not associate with persons like me. You will thereby render yourselves objects of censure and obloquy. Of course I have no objection to your coming to me. The world will naturally censure things which appear bad to it. If people will censure, you must be prepared to listen to it with equanimity. The only thing to be remembered is that appearances are not always true and are not permanent. Real saints are beyond all censure."

In short, one should not form one's opinion without experience of longstanding and should never put blind faith in anyone. Maharaj says, "I have to say this to you as you are people who have to lead worldly lives. To me, either censure or praise is entirely worthless and meaningless. But I have to speak to people according to the worldly standards."

The only thing Maharaj persistently lays stress upon is that a person should day and night repeat Soham in his mind and direct all his senses towards it. He will then become one with it.

He sometimes says, "I have not made any efforts to obtain the siddhi of speech (the power which is gained by a saint by which whatever words come out of his mouth prove to be true, and events occur accordingly). I have also no great merit acquired in previous births. There are many learned and meritorious saints and mahatmas whose words carry influence with people, and hence people flock to them. Such saints are highly esteemed, and they will be able to effect cures and other things. I am a simple man like yourselves; only owing to keeping company with good men I have acquired the qualities of a real human being. I am always trying to take a lesson from whatever good I find in others. I am an ignorant child in the universal family. I am just like water which takes on the color of the thing with which it comes in contact."

Sometimes when Maharaj is in a joyous mood, he gives discourses useful to a person practicing meditation, and illustrates his remarks by apt worldly illustrations and stories. Once he said, "Varkaries [members of a Vaishnava sect] often say that the body is the temple and the Self is Panduranga (Krishna). But only those will know the truth of this statement who try to get inner spiritual experience. If anybody would ask me as to my experience regarding the above, I would say that I am not merely quoting the sayings of saints. Merely giving quotations is the business of learned men who explain to others without having any real experience themselves. If a person has really experienced these things in himself, and he says that he has done so, he should not be blamed as showing pride. There is nothing blamable in such a sattwic ahankar (ego). If a person is rich, is the master of thousands of rupees, and he actually gives you one thousand rupees at the time of your need and then says to somebody else that he has given you one thousand rupees, will you blame him for being proud of his wealth? No.

"If, however, a man having nothing says that he will give a thousand rupees to anyone, then he deserves only censure. Similarly, a saint who instead of merely saying that he has found God and known him, has really realized him in his Self, is a fitting guide to all aspirants on the spiritual path.

"The mantra Soham reveals the same principle. He alone is a true saint who has thoroughly realized the truth of Soham (I am He). His mind, intellect and his senses, and even the hair on his body, are full of the true meaning of Soham. He may or may not do any outward actions. Even though he may do certain actions, he is detached from them. He is videhi (apart from the body), like King Janaka. He looks upon worldly and spiritual things equally, and goes beyond the states of pain and pleasure. He knows the only true Being, and is always experiencing the state of unlimited joy.

"Some people say that meditating upon the Nirakara (Formless) is difficult. But in my opinion it is very easy and in addition it is natural. A man easily gets into the state of samadhi by meditating upon the Nirakara. The path of doing so is, however, concealed and secret. Once you are established in it, you can be in that state although outwardly you may be talking, laughing, playing or sleeping. This power is concealed like the river Saraswati. [The sacred Saraswati river which once flowed above ground, has for centuries been only flowing underground. *Editor's note*.] As some people have not understood this secret path, therefore they mistakenly say that it is difficult and that it would require the passing of many lives to obtain success in it.

"Not to see anything in meditation shows a state of concentration. When seeing is turned into non-seeing, then there is the real state of samadhi. The state of complete samadhi is like the state of death, but it is a state of life after having conquered death. The state of sleep is also a kind of death, and he really knows the secret of Dhyana Yoga whose sleep is nothing but samadhi.

"I therefore, say that if you have learnt Dhyana Yoga it is all well with you. If not, try to learn it. Stop learning shastras and do not entangle yourselves in discussions. If you merely learn shastras and try to acquire mere learning, you will spend lives after lives uselessly. You might get a reputation for saintliness and deceive others and yourselves, but in your innermost Self you will know your real worth, and will have to wander through cycles of births and deaths.

"Strictly speaking, God is none else than our own Self. Every one should try to see this Self by the torch of Soham, and obtain the internal sight. Saints have said, 'People who have obtained the internal vision are saved, while those who have only the external vision are drowned.' I do not say that you should not meditate upon a deity. I only say that you should obtain the internal vision. Do not meditate merely upon the form, but upon the internal power (shakti) which pervades that form.

"It does not matter whether you can do external actions correctly, or not. If you really enter inside, your true guru who is inside will automatically lead you to the right path. Otherwise you will not be able to understand clearly who is leading you on. Kabir has said, 'If you want to know the Eternal, you will not find Him in the Vedas, the shastras or in the Koran, in the temples or in the mosques. Tapasya, pilgrimage, breath-control, or living only on neem leaves will not lead you to him. You can find him only in your breath (Soham: *So* when naturally and spontaneously breathing in, and *Ham* when naturally and spontaneously breathing out).'

"All human beings on this earth are really gods, but only those who know themselves enjoy peace and joy. They alone are entitled to say to an aspirant, 'Whomsoever you think of as an incarnation of God, he is really an incarnation.' I only wish to warn false saints that they should not represent themselves to be incarnations of Rama, Krishna, Dattatreya or the Goddess, and deceive ignorant people.

"If your life is not pure, what can soap do? Your mind must be internally merged in the divine joy. Do not put on merely the outward dress of a saint, such as orange-colored robes or garlands of rudraksha beads, and deceive others as well as yourselves.

"Do not entertain evil thoughts. If, however they arise in your mind, check them then and there by the mantra Soham. Then your mind gradually will become void of thoughts. But you must be very careful then. Because siddhis will then tempt you. Do not succumb to them, but disregard and discard them, and go straight to your goal and be one with your Self. Then duality will disappear, and you will enjoy the real bliss of the Self.

"The real mission of great saints is to teach ignorant persons how to turn inside towards their real Self. They make the human being realize that he is not insignificant and worthless, but he is really the beloved child of God. Those who have received modern education cannot appreciate this. However, I have tried to explain in my own way certain things so that they may be acceptable to all, ignorant as well as learned."

Concluding remarks

All people who have seen Maharaj or observed miracles performed by him, even though they may be his worst enemies, can be sure in their minds that Maharaj has never taken even a single pice from others and that he has no wish to do so. Then what would be the purpose of displaying false miracles? Maharaj has visited several places. Not a single individual in all these places could ever say that Maharaj has in any case deceived anyone or obtained money from him.

It is true that he has no learning of Vedanta and does not perform worship of gods with flowers and other outward materials. Whatever he says in his simple words is his Vedanta which is based on Self-experience and not on books. This Vedanta is such that ordinary people can understand and appreciate it.

Although there are some of Maharaj's disciples staying at Nashik, Maharaj generally does not go to their houses for years together unless there is some special reason. It depends upon his will. He never goes to some at all, while he goes to others of his own accord without being called.

Sri Gajanana Maharaj is at present staying at Nashik and a small number of persons who are aspirants on the spiritual path are his disciples. To these persons who have attained actual experiences in Dhyana Yoga, the publication of this life sketch is a matter of indifference. Without putting blind faith in anyone, these persons have got actual experiences, and they are enjoying peace of mind and joy.

Maharaj's personality is very genial and witty, and by his affectionate dealings with all who come in contact with him he attracts people to himself. Aspirants are sure to be benefited by the company of such a saint.

His personality

We shall conclude this life-sketch of Sri Gajanana Maharaj with a brief description of his personality.

He was one of the most unostentatious persons—such as one so rarely meets with in these days of reckless egoism and spiritual bankruptcy. Though a cripple and lame in the right leg and rather lean and emaciated in his general constitution, one never found him gloomy or morose in his dealings with the world and the people in it. In fact he had an inexhaustible fund of sparkling humor on his lips.

He was a bachelor in the strict sense of the term and looked upon all women as his mothers or sisters. He had all the appearance of a worldly man about himself. He liked to dress well, was clean and tidy, and his stiff collar, golden pin and white speckled tie were typical of his dress.

His food habits were of the simplest kind. He ate only once or twice in a week—a piece of chapati with some unspiced vegetables. Usually he drank tea five or six times daily.

He smoked cigarettes almost continuously. But it was the experience of his disciples and friends that there was no smell of tobacco, but rather a powerful sweet fragrance of burning incense sticks, particularly at moments when he withdrew his mind into an ecstatic mood.

In his external appearance and mode of life there was very little that would reveal the great yogi hidden within. In fact nearly all those who came in contact got the first impression of his being an ordinary person with worldly habits and earthly ideas. It was only more intimate contact with him that convinced others of the presence of a mighty soul residing in that frail body. Not that there was any dubiousness about him, but it was all due to his instinctive virtue of self-effacement so characteristic of him since his childhood.

It is noteworthy to mention here, that whenever he wrote to others he invariably styled himself as "Your humble sweeper or broom." Curiously enough that word "broom" is very significant. It unmistakably indicates his mission in this life. It appears he was charged by destiny to serve as a sweeper of the minds of men who happened to come to him.

The human mind often gets clouded and eclipsed by a false and deceitful valuation of material things. It becomes dirty and unclean and cannot therefore see the beacon light within. In the absence of a guiding star it becomes miserable, despondent and diseased. Modern medical science may cure physical disabilities and alleviate bodily sufferings, but it is absolutely helpless in regard to mental disorders, particularly of the type mentioned above. The only science that will render effective and lasting cure to the human mind under such conditions is the science of dhyana yoga.

Sri Gajanana Maharaj by continuous practice in his previous births and by the grace of his guru in this life was an adept in that science. He often said that he had yet to climb many a step, but that whatever he had learned so far, it was his bounden duty to give it to others in the name of his guru and thus help deserving humanity to see and realize the divine light inside each and every individual. His principal mission therefore was to sweep the human mind of its dirt, render it an effective reflector of the inner light and thus establish harmony or equilibrium between spirit and matter. One fact however needs special mention here. Though his mission had a positive background, Sri Gajanana Maharaj being by nature a strictly non-advertising person never allowed himself to be brought into the limelight of this world like so many other con-temporary saints. He in fact left it to the seekers of truth first to seek him out of obscurity and then to attain their salvation through his guidance. This is exactly in keeping with his tendency towards self-effacement and absolute humility.

In this quality of humility and absence of egotism Sri Gajanana Maharaj stood on a very high level. His disciple Mr. Vaidya wrote, "Maharaj said to me that in the outward world I should behave towards him as if I was his elder and he (Maharaj) was a youngster." He further wrote, "Sri Guru Gajanana Maharaj is a great personality and knows worldly as well as spiritual matters thoroughly well. If any one bows to him as a sadguru he bows to him in return. He addresses old men as fathers, young men as brothers and women as mothers or sisters, calling himself their child. His words are full of affection. He does not treat anyone as his disciple and does not accept service from anyone, but loves one and all."

Sri Gajanana Maharaj stayed at Parel with one of his relatives for sixteen years. He remained there unknown. Nobody had the least idea that he was a yogi or a Maharaj. At Nashik, too, he was known to very few persons, and he never came into celebrity.

Words of a devotee

Gajanana Maharaj was a great saint; he knew spirituality as well as material transactions. If someone prostrated to him as a sadguru, he in turn prostrated to that person. He respectfully told old people, "You are my parents." He lovingly addressed young people as his siblings. All women for him were his mothers and sisters. He addressed them as if he was their own child. Such was the speech of sadguruji that those to whom he spoke in this way could not control their loving tears. The love that flowed from his speech, made everyone very moved.

Maharaji gave the Soham Mantra, telling the newly-instructed to repeat Soham as japa. When they did so, he asked them to describe their experiences. In this way was new wisdom gained every day. He asked them to write their perceptions down to help in remembering them.

Thus was the method of Maharaj. He was in all things and at all times a Meditation Yogi. He made all the desires and various longings vanish and made the mind very pure. He spoke very nicely, sweetly with young and old, and showed respect to one and all.

This Maharaj was an authority on spirituality. He never accepted any acknowledgement of his greatness. He respected close people, friends, society and everyone in general. This great man did not desire any relationship of guru and disciple with anyone. He never accepted any service from any person, but had love for everyone within himself.

The path to attainment of spirituality is very easy. He gave the Soham Mantra which should be constantly repeated within. By the blessings of

God meditation became like the drinking of heavenly nectar (amrita) here on earth for his friends.

As soon as he was alone, he was immersed in Atma Swarup, the Vision of the Self. Only those who, impelled by their seeking in previous births, had mastered yoga themselves could realize the greatness of Sri Gajanana Maharaj.

When Maharaj was immersed in Self-Attainment, true miracles happened spontaneously, as others witnessed. In the first years after his meeting with Sri Narayana Saraswati, Maharaj lived in Akola. There he did his yoga sadhana in solitude. He also mentally did worship of his guru, Sri Narayana Saraswati. When only in his mind he gave a bath to his guru, his body would actually become cleansed as from a bath. [*Editor's note.* Because of this he rarely took an ordinary bath and thus was scorned by many ritualists as being ashuddh–impure.] Offerings he made only mentally were often seen to appear physically in a miraculous manner. For example, a flower garland he offered mentally would suddenly appear around his neck in physical reality. Wonderful fragrances would be experienced around him. Sadguruji did not like any importance to be given to these things. He also did not want them to happen and said to God, "I don't want such things." Then he heard a voice saying, "Though you do not like this, nevertheless it is happening by itself. When the worship in the mind is complete then everything is merged with the Self. Worshipper, worshipped and worship itself become one. That is when such things happen." Hearing this voice, Guruji felt happy. Doubt was cleared and he became at peace in his mind from then on.

During yoga practice miracles may result, but beyond such miracles is that of Self-Realization. Maharaj said himself, "Material or external miracles do not matter. What is important is that which is happening during the meditation of the yogi. Never reveal such miracles, as this will only result in unnecessary trouble with the worldlings."

Whenever he heard that a mahatma was somewhere, he would go there, have their darshan and be in their company to confirm his Self attainment. He would live with them for a few days to learn from them. He sought many saints and mahatmas and thus confirmed his Self-attainment.

He had never read Vedas or Srutis (Hindu Scriptures), never studied the Atma Vidya (Science of Spirituality) yet experienced the Supreme Being due to his previous tapasya.

Childhood, youth, and old age are the three stages of the human body. Having taken birth as a human being it is better to go through everything that is accumulated due to one's karma. Unless this karma is exhausted, even the saints and other seekers suffer also, so what is so surprising in that? Similarly this Gajanana Maharaj, crippled since childhood, was paying off the karma. There is no escape from this.

Because he was crippled he was dependent. He lived at his niece's husband's home where his niece Kamalabai used to look after him. Both Kamalabai and Sitaram Bhise, her husband, were relatives of Maharaj, therefore he lived there. Previously Kamalabai's mother at the time of her death had prostrated to Maharaj and entreated him, "I am your god-daughter. I would love to do good things for my only daughter Kamala, but my life will be over in just a few more moments. Therefore I am asking you to bless her." Maharaj replied, "Don't worry my dear sister, God will bless."

Maharaj left Akola at that time and came to Mumbai where he lived at Narayan Lakshman Samarth's home and meditated. After living there for years he imparted knowledge to the believers. Then he came to Nashik and lived at his nephew-in-law's home. Again he went to Mumbai and then to Dhule where he lived at the postmaster's home.

He became Self-realization personified. To those who desired the same realization he gave the Soham Mantra.

There are many saints, mahatmas and sadhus in the world. Many follow the path of rituals, and many follow the path of mantra. In every place, including households, mantras which are written in the scriptures are given and repeated over and over, but all that is to no avail. Unless the mantra is empowered or awakened, there is no use of repeating it. Certainly it is only empowered or awakened by the practice of yoga meditation. The siddha purushas (perfected souls) perform external actions, but they are always done while immersed in the Name of the Lord. Anyone who can do and teach this type of mantra siddhi is a guru. Others are just businessmen filled with ego and a dozen a penny.

Maharaj was once ill with high fever and suffered with pain in his eyes. Allopathic and Ayurvedic doctors administered medicines, but nothing worked. Maharaj himself told them, "This is just suffering of the body due to karma. It will not go away without being undergone. This is according the scriptures."

Maharaj was very peaceful at all times. Peacefulness was his very nature.

Maharaj was very natural in his moods. Sometimes he would be very happy, sometimes very quiet, sometimes he would discourse on sadhana and sometimes he would be quite jovial. He respected everyone. He spoke very softly. He frequently drank tea, but rarely ate food. This was his daily routine.

When Maharaj wrote letters to his disciples, he used to sign as "Your Broom" Seeing this devotees were puzzled as to why he was using this name. One devotee, understood the deeper meaning in this and wrote a poem which he sent to Maharaj as an offering. In this poem he set forth these ideas:

"Broom" is the name of that which cleans from dirt. It cleans the dirt of karma, then gives the inner sight.

This is the the condition called turiya. It is the basis of all forms of knowledge.

It is Maharaja's work to keep his disciples engaged with the only true japa: the japa of Soham.

I prostrate to my sadguru–not to his physical body but to his instructions for the attainment of Self Knowledge, which are easy.

The essence is the constant repetition of the Soham Mantra by which we cross through this material world. Therefore salutations to it!

If we always hold on to the truth with faith and trust, and stay detached from this material world, then what more does a person need?

The greatest benefactor is the sadguru. Prostrations always to this Broom, Hail always to Gajanana Maharaj.

A broom which cleans the house and removes all the dirt from the home, is always treated as a lowest object but is happy with it, and always stays in a corner all alone. But the ignorant do not know its properties. Therefore Maharaj adopted that name.

Words of another devotee

Early in 1938, my friend Mr. Kamat saw Gajanana Maharaj, who expressed a wish that I should come to see him. That a yogi like Gajanana Maharaj should express such a wish was in my opinion a great compliment which I hardly deserved. Towards the middle of last July (1939), I went to Thana for some business and thence I went to Nashik on the weekend and saw Gajanana Maharaj and prostrated at his feet. I was most cordially received and welcomed by Gajanana Maharaj and all the disciples, for which I thank them all most heartily.

As Gajanana Maharaj has not the least paraphernalia of a yogi or saint, and as he dresses well, wearing a shirt, coat and necktie, and looks more or less stylish, many people mistake him for an ordinary man. But on closer contact with him, his due worth and merit stand out prominently and are recognized.

Gajanana Maharaj looks very simple and unostentatious, but he is original and full of wit and humor. He always talks freely and without any reserve with all. But with regard to his disciples, he criticizes them openly and does not spare them in the least. If his jokes and criticisms are closely observed they are seen to have a truly positive effect on the persons to whom they are addressed.

As Gajanana Maharaj is perfectly egoless and guileless, he soon endears himself to all, who when they come to know his real worth hold him in high esteem. He styles himself and signs as Kersuni (Broom), and his principal mission in life is therefore to sweep the minds of his disciples clean and render them fit for Self-realization.

His life habits are very simple. He takes meals very rarely. Whenever there is a guest with him, he sits down with him for meals when any special dish is prepared, but he partakes very little of the things served. Otherwise he goes without food for days altogether. He drinks tea many times a day. Like a true yogi he is not fond of wealth, women or fame. If any coins are offered, he tosses them back. He is a true bachelor, as he does not care a jot for the fair sex. He has got very few women disciples. As he is by nature selfless and unassuming, he shuns the limelight of fame and publicity and likes to work out his mission in secret.

A Bow To That Broom Always

In consonance with the mission stated above Sri Gajanana Maharaj instructed aspirants into the science of dhyana yoga. Some of these people were arta [seeker of earthly welfare], while others were real jijnasus [seekers of spiritual knowledge]. Whatever their nature, whosoever approached him with a sincerity of heart and firmness of purpose was gladly shown the way to spiritual realization and eternal bliss. The experiences of some of these aspirants in the process of their spiritual enlightenment have been given in this account about this great, though unassuming, saint of Nashik. It may be that these experiences, though varied in their exposition according to the mental make-up of each individual aspirant, will induce other seekers of truth to find a source of solace and a way to salvation by his holy teachings.

The final phase

Sri Gajanana Maharaj for the remainder of his life stayed at Nashik and only a small number of persons who were aspirants on the spiritual path became his disciples. Most of those persons came in contact with Sri Gajanana Maharaj during the last dozen or so years of his life.

Without blind faith these persons obtained actual spiritual experiences and peace of mind and joy.

Sri Gajanana Maharaja left the mortal coil of his physical body and entered into mahasamadhi at Nashik on the 28th of September, 1946.

SRI GAJANANA MAHARAJ
THE GREAT SAINT AT NASHIK

by
A Peace Seeker

This tribute to Sri Gajanana Maharaj was an introductory essay in Atma Prabha, *but I have put it here as it fits as a kind of summary of Maharaj's life. The Editor.*

Pseudo-saint worship is a kind of disease ever and anon attacking the people of India. This disease is constantly carrying away such a vast number of the Indian population that even plague and cholera together have never done it so far. Particularly our moral and economic exploitation has never been carried out in such a ruthlessly alarming proportion as is done by the following of false sadhus. Illiteracy campaigns alone will never be able to eradicate this evil, as even many of the literate, educated and intelligent people have been found falling an easy prey to false sadhus. The angle of vision towards life itself must be changed, and the inner life must be made morally stronger than what it is today.

The market-monks that we often come across are in fact void of that selflessness which is the prime factor of saintliness. In a crore [ten million] of ascetics, perhaps only one may be found worth the worship which the great soul Sri Gajanana Maharaj of Nashik deserves. He can be easily approached by those who wish to do so with a pure and sincere heart, without which he cannot at all be found even after a good deal of effort on the part of the seeker!

There are Hindus, Muslims and Christians amongst those who hold Sri Gajanana Maharaj in high esteem and respect and take delight in paying homage to him.

For more than twenty years Sri Gajanana Maharaj has been continuously staying at Nashik and yet, out of those who annually spend their summer or even of those who live throughout their lives there, not even a score of men know him! People living within the radius of a couple of homes around his residence cannot tell his correct address to a newcomer.

Sri Gajanana Maharaj never calls any one his disciple, but calls all his "friends." Such is the degree of his humility.

Today, in 1946, Sri Gajanana Maharaj is about fifty-five. Schooling he had barely for one year or two, and yet he can best the most intellectual man in talks on any subject, all the while complaining that he himself is an ignorant man! By nature he is as simple and innocent as a baby!

His dress and needs are of a more simple standard than that of a middle class Indian gentleman. A sip or two of tea is enough to sustain him for the whole day, while rarely during some weeks he takes a morsel of dry bread. He never needs a square meal.

He never shows miracles to order or by previous intimation and intention. Sometimes miracles do take place in his presence, but he at once declares that their origin is not himself but his Master, Sri Narayana Saraswati. He says they take place without his efforts and knowledge.

Healing physical pains, foretelling births or deaths or increments of pay and wealth, are subjects outside the domain of his discussions and discourses. He never asks for even a farthing, nor does he accept anything offered without sincerity. On rare occasions he has asked some people to do something for him or bring him certain articles. But those who brought something at his request in this way found that somebody else had already supplied the same to him. Thus, by the grace of the great God, he has no wants whatsoever, and it is only to give an aspirant a chance of selfless service that he may request someone to do something for him. His personal expenses do not exceed the amount of ten or twelve rupees per month.

This demonstrates that Sri Gajanana Maharaj belongs to a higher rank of saints than we ordinarily come across in everyday life. He has no tricks and paraphernalia that deceive masses. Hundreds of people never find his abode unless he so wills it, and this alone is saying enough. One day the writer observed the servant of a well-known Nashik merchant searching for his house for not less than an hour just in the neighborhood, with coconuts sent for the marriage ceremony of the merchant's niece.

How could he reach such a high order of spiritual grace? Only because he is an adept in the science and art of yoga or spiritual union with God. He is one with Him. This science of yoga is far superior to ordinary jugglery which so many of the so-called monks make use of to squeeze out others' money and weaken their minds. Yoga is a science well-established in society by the rishis of olden times. They have taken the utmost pains to put it in the most scientific and practical form for the generations that followed them and that are still to follow. Anyone can practice it and get one's self lifted high up to God! Sri Gajanana Maharaj is here to help men in realizing the highest goal of life, to distribute amongst us freely the everlasting joy that he himself has acquired through the grace of his guru.

While still a boy, Sri Gajanana Maharaj was directed by his guru to guide aspirants on this path. He selects them and freely gives them the Soham mantra. Some approach him intentionally, others come accidentally in contact with him, and yet there is not the least doubt about the fact that it is a sheer impossibility for souls that seek only materialism to meet with such an eminent director on this path. Only one who is earnest can obtain his grace. His followers, though not materially very prosperous, have all the same acquired profound spiritual experiences by practice.

The man of the world is generally in need of that mental peace and tranquility which lead to an equilibrium of mind in pleasure and pain. Without that peace many cannot even bear to live in this world. The saints of old have shown the way of repetition of mantra: the name of someone or some principle. Concentration is another step further. Then comes meditation and lastly realization. Sri Gajanana Maharaj directs his friends with his divine love. In this book his methods are described and explained to help pilgrims progress. The book shows the reader his undoubted ability to do it.

His everyday life is absolutely simple and methodical. Images and ceremonies exhibiting unnecessary show have no place in his room. He has nothing of decorations belonging to any religion, caste or cult. All are welcome to him and can meet him as man to man. He directs all who approach him in the simplest way and language through the spiritual realm without performing any miracles or practicing any deceptions. No selfishness, no snobbery. To lead the soul onward is the only mission of his life. He explains things so convincingly and in such a masterly manner that even the most intelligent man that goes to him is entirely satisfied. Anyone can have this experience of peace and satisfaction from him in the first, or at the most the second, visit and keep it for life.

There is not even the idea of any dependence on him. Rather he makes us independent and free. It is the raising of the Self [Atman] through self-effort.

At the feet of this Master soul, who is a self-sacrificing, developed being of authority and intelligence and who is a fine jewel in our land, we beg to lay our heads with deep devotion and love.

Om Peace! Peace!! Peace!!!

CHAPTER TWO

CONVERSATIONS OF SRI GAJANANA MAHARAJ

I

One day a man who was very proud of his shastric learning–which was only superficial–came to Maharaj and began with the words, "Maharaj, having heard about your great renown, I have come to you with the full hope that all my doubts and difficulties will be dispelled and solved by you. I have firm faith in you. Two or three days ago I came here, but on that day you were ill. Hence I have come today." Maharaj intently looked at his face and at once understood that the man must have been directed to him by someone with the object of making him non-plussed and an object of ridicule.

Maharaj said to him, "My good sir, who told you that I am a Maharaj? Everybody knows that I do not know anything about the shastras and that I can never explain anything from the shastras. How can I solve your difficulties? You said that you have firm faith in me. Did you see any miracle performed by me or did you get any special experience so that faith was generated in your mind? Or were you a relative or a school fellow or a very dear friend of mine so that the previous relationship unwillingly attracted you towards me?

"You see at present I am often very ill. Through the grace of my guru I have been seeking to know the nature of death, and in doing so I have actually approached it. Once I know what is death, I shall then find out God by means of the mantra Soham. I shall then know who I am and will begin to enjoy the bliss of the Self. The whole world will then appear to me as nothing but Brahman. Then only through the order of my guru shall I be able to explain all the shastras. Until I reach that stage, how can I, an ignorant and uneducated man as I am, presume to tell anything to a learned pundit like you?

"What I think, however, is this. When a person, whether educated or ignorant, wants to go to a saint for the purpose of obtaining from him success in the accomplishment of worldly objects or any guidance on the spiritual path, he should first of all make full inquiries regarding the conduct of the saint in his dealings with the world, and after being fully convinced that his conduct is pure, should go to him. He should not merely depend upon hearsay reports regarding his great spiritual powers.

"He should also read carefully the lives of the great saints of the past and ponder deeply over them. He should then think things out for himself and come to a conclusion regarding what is right and what is wrong. After that he should approach a saint with a feeling of due humility, after purging his mind of all pride of learning, of all doubts and of all misgivings. If this is done then the Siddhi Vinayak (Ganesha, the Lord of all Powers) will grant him all happiness in worldly life as well as spiritual bliss in his own Self.

"This is my candid opinion, which I have arrived at through the grace of my guru and of my own inner Self. A person gets pleasures and pains in this world according to the good or bad actions of his previous lives. Though saints and mahatmas have all powers, still everyone has to suffer the results of his own previous karma. Saints do not interfere with the working of this law. Their mission in this world is to point out the way leading to everlasting happiness and thus to make persons going to them blessed in the real sense of the term. They pay very little heed to worldly pleasures and pains which are after all of an ephemeral nature.

"The great saint Tukaram, who had realized God, has proclaimed with a loud voice in words worth their weight in gold his great anxiety regarding worldly people who are groping in the darkness of ignorance. He says with deep feelings of love and care, 'I cannot bear to see all these people floundering in the mire of ignorance and hence my heart overflows with pity. I shall try to save all these souls.'

"Oh, my good sir, you are learned in shastras. I request you to leave off the reading of the shastras and giving dry advice to others, and especially to leave off trying to ridicule saints who should be approached with feelings of reverence and humility. You appear to be about sixty years old. Merely performing sandhya, worshipping gods with flowers and garlands and marking your forehead with sandal paste will be of no real use to you. You must have a real feeling of devotion and learn to see the one God in all these various external objects. My earnest request to you is that you should go to a real saint and learn how to obtain this kind of devotion at his feet."

These words of Maharaj had a great effect on that man's mind, and he said, "Maharaj, you have really swept off all dirt from my mind with your broom of Soham, and I am now thoroughly satisfied. I had indeed come to make you non-plussed and then to ridicule you. I had once before seen you and at that time formed an unfavorable opinion about you. Hence I had come today with the fixed object of putting you to ridicule. But you understood this state of my mind and gave me this sincere, excellent and disinterested advice, for which I am deeply grateful to you. I accept your advice with bowed head. What is the use of advanced age? I am sure that you will be a real guru and will save many people like me by initiating them into the path of spiritual knowledge."

Maharaj replied, "You are a learned Brahmin. It is my duty to pay you respect. You are like a guru to me. I tell you one last thing. Whenever a person, big or small, male or female, feels the want of anything, whether worldly or spiritual, he approaches God and begs Him for granting his desire. We go to a temple. The idol there is of stone. But we, through faith, attribute to it the divine powers of Sri Rama or Sri Krishna and pray to the idol to grant our desires; and we get the fruit of these prayers at some time or other. This is true in the case of all human beings. Whenever a person entertains a desire to obtain some worldly object or to attain spiritual progress, he obtains the fruit of his desire as a result of his efforts in this life or of his karma in previous lives, or owing to fate or destiny–call it anything you like. No astrologer or saint or God is required for that.

"Men and women go to a saint, whether a true one or a false one, for getting their desires fulfilled. Some want employment, some are in want of progeny and some want the curing of their diseases. An aspirant on the spiritual path desires to obtain the bliss of the Self or the vision of God. I wish to say with all the earnestness at my command that every person should internally repeat the mantra Soham and should bear in mind that he himself will be able to fulfill his desires. Only it must be borne in mind that he must keep his conduct pure, should have at least a little vairagya and should have firm faith in Soham. When once a person obtains this self-confidence, he is sure to get Self-experience and will meet with his real guru. Evil thoughts will then cease to rise.

"One thing regarding this japa must be remembered. The japa of Soham must be repeated continuously in the mind. It should not be allowed to be known to others that you are repeating the japa. If such a person then prays to this God of internal light to grant his desires, he can be absolutely sure of his prayers being granted.

"This method is a hundred times superior to that of praying for favors to God who is outside ourselves. Not only will the desires be granted, but either in this or in the next birth according to the person's present efforts and previous karma, a person is sure to attain the highest bliss of the Self. But if all my brothers and sisters will do as I have just told you, they will be able to enjoy real happiness and will never fall into the clutches of false saints. Well, my good sir, I hope that you will spread the knowledge of what I have just now told you among others and so make the lives of many happy and contented.

II

One day a gentleman came to Maharaj for his darshana, having come to know about him from someone. He was a well-read man and had visited various saints. The following discourse then took place between him and Maharaj, which we give below as it throws light on many interesting points in religious and spiritual matters.

Maharaj: You are referring to the shastras. Will you please tell me what religious books you have read?

Gentleman: I have read the Upanishads, Yoga Vashishtha, Panchadasi, Bhagavad Gita, Jnaneshwari and others.

Maharaj: I have not even heard the names of some of these, nor have I read any of them. But will you tell me whether you understood them and whether these books solved all your doubts and difficulties?

Gentleman: No. I then began to think that all this reading is useless without guidance from a sadguru and put these books aside.

Maharaj: I think you did a very good thing. When I was in school I learned a verse to the effect that life is too short for studying what is contained in all the shastras. Well, I now know that you have read a good deal of Vedanta. Have you read the lives of any of the saints?

Gentleman: Yes. I have read the lives of Sri Ramdas and of Swami Maharaj of Akkalkot. I have also read the life and letters of Sri Gulabrao Maharaj and some of the books written by him which have been published. I, however, remember only a little of the principles explained by Sri Gulabrao Maharaj in his letters and books.

Maharaj: All right. Do you remember that Sri Gulabrao Maharaj has dealt with the subject of "dosha-drishti" (faultfinding tendency) and its different kinds? And will you be able to tell me what you remember of the subject?

Gentleman: I do not remember anything about it.

Maharaj: All right. I shall tell you about it. Sri Gulabrao Maharaj has divided the tendency to find faults into three categories: (1)

Individualistic; (2) Social; and (3) Scriptural. He says that if a father tells his son that he is going to get him married, the son will be pleased no doubt, but this pleasure is quite of a different nature from the pleasure which he will get from the actual marriage to a wife. The same sort of difference is that between a jnani, one who has realized Brahman, and a vadi, one who merely discusses Vedanta. A blind man delivering hundreds of lectures on the different colors, red, blue or green, would be but an object of ridicule in the eyes of a person who can actually see the colors. To talk about Vedanta without any real Self-experience is equally ridiculous.

That guru alone is a true guru who will lead a disciple to the path of Self-experience. But many aspirants fall into the clutches of pseudo-saints who tempt them by holding forth before them the bait that they will get Self-experience, but ultimately they are disappointed. They then leave off all Vedanta and religious matters and remain content with merely ordinary morality. Their angle of vision of looking at things and persons entirely changes and they begin to see faults in almost every person.

In my opinion the tendency to find faults is bad from one point of view and good from another. This tendency will be very useful for the purpose of not getting entangled in the snares of hypocrites and pseudo-saints. But if it leads a person to find faults even in real mahatmas, it is certainly reprehensible. Even food, if not properly taken, may act like poison and do harm, while even poison properly administered in minute quantities sometimes acts like a tonic and cures diseases.

Before trying to find faults a person must make himself sure that he has acquired a correct insight and acumen to find out real faults. He must make himself sure that he will not mistake apparent faults for real ones. If a person while examining rice throws away a grain of rice mistaking it for a grain of sand, he cannot be called a wise person. Hence a person must acquire clear insight; otherwise while trying to find out faults, he might discard virtues also, mistaking them for faults.

To consider everything which is against our ideas as a fault is what I mean by the individualistic tendency to find faults. This tendency is very bad and leads to disastrous results. It is at the root of all disturbances in domestic, national and religious life. A person in fortunate and affluent circumstances looks down even upon a virtuous man who is in adverse circumstances, and considers him as full of faults. This is the result of this individualistic tendency. A false saint having obtained vast sums of money from others under false pretenses, feeds thousands of people, makes a show of his charity and looks down upon a real saint who passes his days in calm contemplation in solitude apart from the haunts of men, and taunts him about his poverty. Thus it will be clearly seen that this individualistic tendency to find faults is very bad and leads to ruin. Wise persons should, therefore, take scrupulous care not to fall a prey to it.

The second kind is what I call Social. It is good to a certain extent, but on the whole it is more bad than good. Whatever is opposed to the views of a particular society or community is looked upon as a fault by its members. But as the constitution and the underlying principles of every society are different, it is but natural that every society is considered as full of faults by other societies. Besides, every individual has some faults in the eyes of his society. Some sociologists tried to make an equal distribution of property among all the members of the society but these attempts signally failed. If a person models his actions on the principle of sacrificing his interests for the good of the society, he is blamed by the members of his family; if on the contrary he looks too much to the interests of his family, he is blamed by the society. Hence the angle of vision, which I have called Social, is very nebulous and puts an individual into a very awkward position—on the horns of a dilemma as it were. This method of finding faults, however, affords opportunities to some persons for posing as social workers and philanthropists.

The third kind I have called Scriptural or Shastric. This is the best, and it conduces to the real welfare of a spiritual aspirant. It consists in considering anything which is opposed to the shastras as bad. A person who has acquired this angle of vision will never fall a prey to the machinations of self-seeking hypocrites and pseudo-saints, will never allow himself to be overpowered by his society and will ultimately attain the real goal of human life himself and will also help to raise the moral and spiritual standard of the society of which he is a member.

Merely by reading the shastras or by carrying on discussions regarding them, a person can never ascertain what is opposed to the shastras and what is in consonance with them. If a person reads the shastras merely in the light of his own reasoning and views, it is but natural that he will accept only those sayings in the shastras which are favorable to him or interpret them so as to be conformable to his own views. Suppose a prostitute reads the Bhagavatam and draws a lesson from the account given of the gopis there that the shastras permit unchastity on the part of women, is there any hope of the character of the prostitute being ever improved by this sort of reading? If the shastras do not make a change in our views and angle of vision, how can they be said to teach us anything? If guests are served with stale food can it be said that they are treated as guests?

Hence it is necessary to learn what is told in the shastras at the feet of a sadguru. It is, however, difficult to know who is a real sadguru. We find that even many educated men have fallen into the clutches of self-seeking pseudo-saints. The ways of outward conduct, too, of even really great saints differ on account of the difference of surroundings and of prarabdha (destiny). Hence superficial observers are not likely to recognize the greatness of even real saints. Some persons posing as saints are very clever in giving learned and impressive discourses on Vedanta, while internally they are seeking opportunities to cheat their gullible followers. Real aspirants meeting such saints are ultimately disappointed, because they find that they asked for bread and got a stone instead. They had wanted real Vedanta and instead they had as it were a lecture on the science of sexual love.

Hence it has been said in the Yoga-Vashishtha that without the grace of God it is not possible to meet with a real sadguru. Even to get affectionate parents entirely depends upon the favor of fate. Instances of mothers selling their children for obtaining money for drinking liquor, though rare in India, are not quite uncommon in other countries. A sad-guru must teach yoga not merely by words but must lead an aspirant to the path of Self-experience. The disciple, too, must know what questions to ask and how to ask them, otherwise everything will be futile. This is in short what Sri Gulabrao Maharaj has said, and I entirely agree with him. A great poet has remarked that it is very difficult to understand the minds of great persons because they are sometimes harder than adamant and sometimes softer than flowers.

Now I shall tell you in brief what Sri Gulabrao Maharaj has said regarding raja yoga. You might say I am not telling you anything of my own, but only what has been said by other saints. My reply to that is that it is so. My guru did not teach me Vedanta and the principles established by it and the arguments adduced in books on Vedanta to establish them. He only gave me the mantra Soham and showed me the path leading to Brahman which is beyond all Vedanta and arguments. He made me realize the truth of Tat Twam Asi (Thou Art That) and said that nothing else was required to be told. Hence I am telling you what other saints have said. It might be even said that my guru is speaking through my mouth.

Look at it from another point of view also. It has been said that whatever has been said by any one else in the three worlds has been borrowed from Vyasa. If that is so, then what wonder is there that an uneducated and unintelligent person like me should borrow from what other saints have said? I have read a few books on spiritual subjects and tell others a little out of them. I possess no power of words but my real strength lies in understanding the true sense behind the words. Saints like Tukaram and Eknath also did not possess the power of words to an eminent degree, but their strength lay in their thorough grasp of the sense behind the words.

Regarding raja yoga, Sri Gulabrao Maharaj says raja yoga is the best of all yoga practices. The practice of raja yoga can control the impressions produced by a person's ignorance and negative experience and wipe them out. All this controlling is possible only through two things (1) practice and (2) vairagya (detachment). A person who merely carries on practice without having vairagya, does not go to the end and has to leave it in the middle, because every now and then he is attracted by sensual objects and he gets tired of trying again and again and leaves off the practice. Perfect control can be accomplished only with the help of both practice and vairagya.

The tamasic power (shakti) is brought under control by carefully reading the principles of Vedanta and contemplating upon them. This is known as shravana, and forms part of yogic niyama. Through the practice of yama and niyama, the rajasic power of the action of the organs is controlled. Asana (posture) leads to the steadiness of the limbs and through pranayama all power of motion is controlled. When this stage is reached the mudhawastha—the state of infatuation—of the mind disappears. The state of distraction is controlled by dharana and dhyana and the sadhaka then enters the state of samprajñata or savikalpa samadhi by concentration. This state later on develops into nirvikalpa samadhi.

This in brief is the full course as described in the Yoga Shastra. But this requires great preparation of the mind. Only those who have left attachment to sensual objects can be the recipients of this knowledge. He alone who first of all subdues the desires of the mind regarding sensual objects, understands their comparative importance or unimportance, keeps his mind in a state of quietude even when enjoying pleasures allowed by the shastras and ultimately leaves off all sense of enjoyment of pleasures, succeeds in ascending to the summit of yoga. He who understands how to dispel thoughts which arise in succession in the mind, he who understands what particular thoughts must first of all be subdued, so also he who understands how to contemplate upon Brahman alone succeeds in arriving at the end of yoga and becoming a master.

Many persons think that bhakti (devotion) is easier than yoga, owing to the fear for the body which the yogi has to conquer. But Sri Jnaneshwar says, "Is there anything as easy as yoga?" I also think that bhakti which depends upon some external object, is not so easy as Yoga which depends on one's own Self. If a person thinks on these questions deeply and gets explanations for himself, and then leaves off contemplation of things which fetter him and contemplates upon the opposite, he will succeed in putting an end to all pain and obtain the highest bliss. He should fix his mind upon and thoroughly grasp the principle of the Sankhya Shastra that the Self is absolutely free from attachments, and then by means of yoga he should practice meditation.

Ordinarily no one likes pain, hence every one desires to end it. We ourselves are dearer to us than any other thing. Things which come in the way of our happiness are disliked by us. We, however, have never any dislike respecting ourselves. Hence it is clear that real bliss lies in ourselves and not in any extraneous thing. Sri Gulabrao Maharaj has also said something about how to subjugate the mind and ultimately to annihilate it. He says that Sri Vashishtha mentions two means of annihilating the mind. One is to control thoughts of the mind by yoga and the other is to observe ourself by ourself being the observer. This second is a little bit difficult. The thoughts of the mind can be controlled by the practice of yoga and by vairagya. Vairagya can be obtained by getting into the habit of looking upon all worldly things and pursuits as full of faults and troubles.

Suppose a person sees a rope in the darkness and thinking it to he a serpent, runs away from that place. He will not then be able to see it, but the impression will still remain upon his mind that he has seen a serpent. If, however, he stays at the place, brings a lamp and satisfies himself that it is a rope and not a serpent, all fear vanishes and no impression of the fear remains on his mind. Thus knowledge alone is capable of dispelling the fears of worldly existence. For obtaining this knowledge it is necessary to read religious books, to listen to discourses on them, then to think over them in solitude, and when the mind is thoroughly satisfied about the truth of the principles, to ponder over them again and again. The realization of Brahman is to be obtained only by the method of Self-experience.

If some people say that they cannot put any faith in yoga, they may be asked why they then put faith in morality, because morality also does not conduce to success in this worldly life. Its fruit also is to be obtained not in this life but in a future life.

Well, my good sir, as I have not been educated and have also very little natural intelligence, I have to borrow from the sayings of other saints and learned men, who are far superior to me in knowledge and erudition. If I explain things in my own simple way as inspired by my guru, people will not put faith in me. Hence I tell people a little of what has been told to me by others or of what I have read myself. To listen to it or to give any importance to it entirely lies with those people. I myself am not a Maharaj, but an ignorant fool.

Looking to the sayings of great saints, I am absolutely convinced that it is not at all necessary that I should perform miracles or that people should call me a saint. Hence I say to my friends that if anybody censures me in their presence, they should not be pained. A story is told regarding Tukaram Maharaj that a widow in the village became pregnant and the fatherhood of the child was attributed to him. So he was made by the people to sit upon a donkey with garlands of old shoes round his neck and taken in procession through the streets, and he was abused and censured by many people. I have not as yet been put to that test, but through the grace of God I wish that I might be. I do not know when this desirable event will happen. I am waiting for it.

III

One morning Mr. Ambadas Gopal Paithankar went to Maharaj's house. Maharaj was then ill and was lying down. Mr Paithankar related the conversation as follows.

Maharaj: Whom do you wish to see?

Myself: Yourself.

Maharaj: What is your business with me?

Myself: I have not any particular business. I only wanted to have your darshana.

Maharaj: Do you ever practice meditation or worship any particular deity?

Myself: I do not worship any particular deity or meditate upon any. For about three years I worshipped Sri Ganapati, then for about two years the Goddess. For some days I was trying to concentrate my attention on a particular point (bindu). Then I stopped that also. As I had no desire to obtain any particular object in doing all these things, I naturally quit them in the course of time.

Maharaj: How is it that you worship one deity for some time and then leave it for another and then leave that for a third? Are you going to do so till the end of your life? And are you going to continue this process in your future lives also?

Myself: I can't fix my mind anywhere. I have got to look after my family and children. I have also to work as a priest. Hence I cannot fix my mind on a particular course or deity. Therefore I have come to a saint like you. The desire to have your darshana might have been generated in me by the good company of my father, or perhaps it might have been generated by some sudden rise of faith in my mind through God's grace. Although I cannot account for it exactly, I have come to you and I earnestly request you to confer your grace upon me. I have not come to you through mere blind faith because it is not in my nature to put such blind faith in anyone. I have tested my feelings on the touchstone of deep thought and it was only when I was fully confident of myself that I ventured to come to you.

Maharaj, I am now thoroughly convinced that a knowledge of the shastras only teaches a man to enter into endless discussions and to raise innumerable doubts. I now firmly believe that the only true shastra is that of Self-experience. Maharaj, will you grant me the vision of God?

Maharaj: Just see. Suppose you have a lighted lantern in your house and I ask you to bring its light and show it to me here. Will you be able to bring the light here and show it to me?

Myself: No. The light cannot be brought here.

Maharaj: Then you would say to me, "I shall at the most be able to tell you what particular means are required and what particular action is to be done in order to generate the light." You would ask me to purchase a lantern, fix a wick in it, put kerosene oil in it, to strike a match, to ignite the wick, etc. Then there would be light.

Paithankar, similarly it is not an easy thing to show God. I may tell you in what way you should conduct yourself. When you will be endowed with all the four sadhanas [(1) the discrimination between eternal and non-eternal things; (2) disinterestedness regarding enjoyments in this as well as the next world; (3) possession of self-control, peace of mind, etc.; (4) a keen desire for liberation or moksha], or when your desires have vanished, or when you are full of devotion, or when your mind is fully detached from all worldly objects and you get knowledge of spiritual matters, you will be able to realize the presence of God who is really without form. You will then be able to see the light of the Self and be one with that Reality which is Self-existent, which is Life and which is Bliss. That is the real God.

God is not an external object which can be shown by simply pointing a finger towards it. A person must get instruction from a sadguru by obtaining his grace. Then when he gets the internal sight, he can see God—not by the physical eyes but by this internal sight which is known as the eye of knowledge. A person's egoism must entirely disappear, his desires must all vanish, he must have complete vairagya (detachment) and he must feel that he is one with God. Then quite naturally he attains everlasting peace and joy. His whole worldly life will be nothing but Brahman. He will go beyond pain and pleasure.

I shall give you an everyday illustration. Suppose some night you get very sound sleep. When you get up next morning you say to others, "For the last month or so I did not get good sleep. But last night I got such a sound and deep sleep that I was greatly delighted." Now just see. If you were in deep sleep, how can you say that you got sound sleep? Who was awake in that state? Had you seen who was awake in that state? Who enjoyed the bliss of sleep, and who is now describing his feelings in that state?

Myself: I myself.

Maharaj: This "I" is present in each and everything, even in the minutest atom of dust. It is your Self. Know it. Through continuous meditation on Soham be one with that Self which itself is the Supreme Self. I cannot tell you anything beyond this. This God is in my heart, similarly he is in your heart also. When through the grace of guru and through the japa of Soham you will get the internal sight, you will be able to understand everything.

Myself: Maharaj, I see in you what I have never seen before and I hear things explained by you in a manner never heard by me before.

Maharaj: What you say is true. Move aside the curtain of fear. Leave all doubts and misgivings and fall at the feet of saints with feelings of taking entire refuge. If an ignorant and uneducated man goes to a saint of Self-realization, he quietly turns towards him and becomes one with him. That means that his jiva quickly merges in Siva. He recognizes that his own Self [jivatman] is nothing but the Supreme Self [Paramatman] by continuous practice of meditation, and experiences unlimited bliss and joy.

The case of a learned and educated man, on the other hand, is different. There are many doubts and arguments warring in his mind and he takes a long time in becoming one with Shiva. He is doubtful whether this is true or that is true. His mind is, therefore, fickle. If, however, he turns from all doubts and practices with intensity what has been taught to him by his guru, he also without difficulty will attain everlasting happiness. In that stage all distinction between an educated and an uneducated man disappears. This distinction is there as long as doubts and misgivings are there.

Myself: I have an intense desire that you will confer your grace upon me and instruct me and take me under your protection.

Maharaj: Through the grace of my guru I got the Soham mantra and I am at present in the sadhaka state. I am not authorized to advise Brahmins like you. But my guru speaks through my mouth. The words that I utter are not really mine.

My sadguru told me to repeat Soham internally and then to get Soham merged into the Supreme Self and enjoy eternal peace and joy. If that was done I myself would become one with the self-existent, eternal and blissful Principle (Tattwa) and experience the presence of that Supreme Self everywhere. I would then become perfect, leave behind all egoism and realize the true "I."

I have been ordered by my guru to instruct anyone, educated or ignorant, rich or poor, fit or unfit, who happens to come to me, to preach openly in the presence of all and at any time. He told me that I would meet different kinds of souls having different desires and different impressions (samskaras) from previous lives, but all would be benefited by me in spiritual or worldly matters according to their attitude and their faith, without any conscious efforts on my part.

Even if I know everything, I have been ordered by him not to allow my thoughts to dwell upon the knowledge but to keep myself entirely detached. I have, therefore, laid all pain and pleasure at the feet of my guru. I, however, tell what I know to those who come to me and I do that according to the orders of my guru. If a sadhaka practices dhyana yoga with intensity, I am sure that in this very life he will reach the state of perfection through the power of the Soham mantra.

(*Mr. Paithankar continues:*) I was listening to these nectar-like words of Maharaj with avidity and rapt attention. My mind experienced a feeling of deep calm. Two days later Maharaj granted me the Soham mantra and took me under his protection. Since then I go for Maharaj's darshana almost every day. Having a curiosity to know many things, I have asked Maharaj various questions and he has given very lucid explanations regarding them. Some of these discourses are given here as I found them very instructive.

Maharaj: When a disciple gets initiation at the hands of his sadguru and begins to practice meditation, he sees various visions which are as it were sign-posts on the path of Self-realization. As he proceeds he goes beyond these visions and realizes the infinite Brahman which is behind these visions.

Myself: We many a time see people calling themselves raja yogis. My idea of a raja yogi is that his mind has turned inwards and he is full of bliss in every state, whether he is in a state of contemplation or is doing external worldly and physical actions. Please tell me your ideas about this point.

Maharaj: What you say is quite correct. At present, however, raja yoga has been given an altogether different meaning. This is a typical instance of how things are misinterpreted. Present day saints obtain vast amounts of money from ignorant people through various pretexts, build bungalows for themselves, acquire estates, wear costly clothes, eat sumptuous dishes, are surrounded by groups of beautiful female devotees—in short, indulge in unrestrained behavior and call themselves raja yogis. I can only say that it is a sad misfortune of the people that such persons of reprehensible conduct pass off as raja yogis.

Myself: Maharaj, I am thoroughly satisfied with the explanation given by you. I wish to ask a question regarding the practice of meditation. Books propounding methods of the practice of meditation lay down that an aspirant should bring before his mind's eye Sri Krishna or Om or a small point and worship it mentally.

Maharaj: What you say is true. But this direction is given to mere beginners. I have explained this subject to many of my friends up to this time and the topic is not a new one. Still I must satisfy you and solve your doubts. Many non-believers used to ask the same sort of questions to some of my friends who, not being well read, could not answer the questions satisfactorily. My friends had real experiences, but got rather non-plussed by such questions and used to come to me for the solution of the difficulty. I told them that if any one asked them such questions they should keep quiet saying that they did not know anything or should leave the place, but that they should not allow their minds to be disturbed or confounded by such questions.

Now the real answer to such a question is this. It is true, no doubt, that deities which have been imagined are perishable. They will disappear after some time. All these visions, even though seen by the internal sight, are after all a play of ideas. The aspirant needs to enter into the state of nirvikalpa samadhi. All ideas are absent in that state and the object of dhyana yoga is to acquire this state in which ideas or thoughts are entirely absent. When all ideas stop Brahman is experienced. There is then no necessity of making any further conscious efforts but this state is automatically reached.

The following illustration will give you a clear idea of what I say. As long as the musk-deer does not know that the musk is in its own navel, it runs here and there trying to find the source of the fragrant smell. If the deer would meet someone who would point out that the source of the smell is in the deer's own navel, would the deer then run here and there? Similarly, ultimately the internal visions also disappear, the aspirant gets the experience that he himself is Brahman and becomes merged in the bliss of the Self.

The ignorant human soul takes its birth and questions, "Who am I?" But originally this human soul was full of knowledge and was one with the Supreme Self. A sadguru gives the answer to the human soul's question, "Who am I?" by telling him the mantra Soham (I am He) which, having thoroughly convinced the human soul that it is one with the Supreme Self, takes the human soul back to its original state of knowledge and bliss.

Myself: Maharaj, all my doubts have now been solved.

Maharaj: Paithankar, now go on practicing meditation as you have been told. Do not, like the musk-deer, wander about seeking outside for what is really in yourself. Do not ask any further questions. You have now only to get Self-experience by carrying on the practice of meditation steadily. If, however, after practicing meditation as told by me, you do not get any experience, you may go to any other guru who might be able to give you proper guidance and help you attain the goal of human life. I only want to urge that you should now leave off all doubts and begin to practice meditation.

Myself: Maharaj, on the very day on which I came to you, I decided to make you my guru. That decision still holds and is not likely to be changed.

Maharaj: Paithankar, I have firm faith in my sadguru and I have got full experience in this very body of the power of Soham. I, therefore, never tell any of my friends to bring the forms of deities before their mind's eye, but give them the mantra Soham and turn their minds inwards, owing to which all ideas become merged in the sahasradala. [the sahasrara, the thousand-petalled lotus of the brain].

While going towards the sahasradala, some visions in the form of light do manifest themselves. All these visions appear without any effort and they are full of light. After some time all these visions merge into the Self and the aspirant gets for a short time into the state of samadhi, and experiences great joy. Saints of old like Jnaneshwar, Eknath, Tukaram and others and comparatively modern saints who had all realized the Self, enjoyed the state of sahaja samadhi even while carrying on worldly actions. My friends experience the same state of sahaja samadhi, though for a short time, for a minute or two. As the practice of meditation increases in intensity, this state of samadhi lasts longer and longer, and ultimately becomes continuous without any limitation of time or space.

Myself: Do all your disciples to whom you have given the mantra of Soham see visions of light?

Maharaj: Some do see them while some do not. Those who repeat Soham with very great intensity become at once merged in the sound of the inner repetition of the mantra. Hence they are unconscious of any visions of light. Some of my friends, therefore, who get merged in the sound do not see any visions. If you do not see any visions, you should not on that account entertain any doubts regarding the efficacy of Soham. For this purpose I have made this point clear.

Myself: Among all your disciples, who are the best?

Maharaj: Paithankar, I can only say that as I do not consider myself as anybody's guru, I do not look upon anyone as my disciple. Some of my young and old friends, owing to their merit acquired in previous lives and owing to the practice of meditation have reached the state of samadhi. But I do not consider any of them as my disciples.

When a real mumukshu who is thoroughly disgusted with the worldly existence will come to me, I shall be his guru and he will be my real disciple. At present, however, through the grace of my sadguru, I simply give the mantra of Soham to my friends and ask them to practice meditation.

Myself: Supposing that through the reading of religious books or through some other cause a person gets the actual darshana of Sri Krishna, or of the Goddess or of any other deity, is it of any benefit to him?

Maharaj: It is not of any real use. As long as the mind is not turned inwards, and as long as desires have not entirely vanished, these external appearances are of very little use. All these appearances are illusory like a mirage. So even if a person actually sees Sri Krishna or any other deity, it is merely an appearance and not of much use. Paithankar, carry on the repetition of Soham. It will be sufficient for you.

Myself: Maharaj, I have read about Sat, Chit and Ananda. But I have a great desire to hear an explanation of these three terms from the mouth of a saint like you. Your explanations are so very simple and clear that I understand them very easily and they also get fixed in my mind. Besides, whatever has been written in the shastras should, in my opinion, be got explained by saints who really know the shastras.

Maharaj: Well done. It appears that you are well versed in the tricks of priests and pundits and have caught me in my own words. I have been telling all that I am an uneducated person and that I am just approaching the state of a siddha through the stage of a sadhaka. But as you are my friend and have faith in me, I have to tell you. Although I am not a siddha but merely a servant of humanity, still, whatever I tell you will be beneficial to you owing to your faith.

Sat means that which is never destroyed, which always exists. It is nothing but Brahman. Chit means that it is self-effulgent as consciousness in all the three states, the waking, the dreaming and the sleeping states. Ananda means bliss. A thing is dear to us not for the sake of that thing but for the sake of our Self, which is the real object of all our love and is therefore the only entity which is dear to us. The Self is, therefore, bliss: Ananda. You are the Self and the Self is essentially Brahman. This principle should be thoroughly grasped by means of arguments, the authority of the Vedas and lastly through Self-experience.

Some Vedantins say that "I" (*i.e.,* the Self) is present always at the time when passions rise as well as when there are no passions. This principle, "I," exists independently of the passions. Hence the "I" is really not fettered but is mukta (free). But the true Vedanta doctrine is that at the time of death only all ideas become entirely merged in the Self. This sort of merging of ideas cannot be brought about by merely self-control. If that is so, then how would the doctrine, that the "I" is present both at the time when passions rise as well as when they are absent, help a sadhaka in catching hold of the Self which can be grasped only when the flow of ideas has altogether stopped? On the contrary when the sadhaka is in the waking and therefore in the discriminating state, he will surely be conscious of the existence of "this" and "that."

Myself: I know that concentration is absolutely necessary for spiritual progress. Will you kindly tell me how a sadhaka should try to get the habit of concentration?

Maharaj: Although the mind has always a tendency to leave the object of meditation and run away to other things, the only remedy is to bring it back again and to fix it on the object of meditation. If we try to give a bend to the branch of a tree, in the beginning as soon as we remove our hand from it, it again becomes straight and assumes its original position. But by continuous efforts of bending it and also by tying the bent parts by means of a rope, etc., we succeed in giving it a permanent bend. Similarly, if a person while repeating his japa finds that his mind has wandered away, the only remedy is to forcibly bring it back and to fix it again on the japa. This must be practiced for some days at least.

Control over the mind is not obtained merely by such practice. Vairagya (detachment) is also necessary. The mind naturally runs towards those objects for which it has an attraction. By abhyasa (practice) the fickleness of the mind may be controlled. But its attachment cannot be done away with by mere practice. Pranayama may help towards concentration, but undue importance should not be attached to it. Pranayama, too, will only be useful in removing the fickleness of mind. It cannot remove its attachment.

The saying, "As long as the breath is moving or unsteady, the mind is also unsteady," is not an absolute truth. The vice versa is also true. Breath becomes unsteady when the mind becomes unsteady. In grief or anger breath becomes more quick. It is not, therefore, safe to expect that mind will be brought under control when the breath is controlled. Hence mind-control and breath-control must be carried on side by side. Hence it has been said by Sri Krishna in the sixth chapter of the Gita: "Wherever the fickle and unsteady mind runs away it should be brought back therefrom and made to fix itself on the Self" (verse 26).

Myself: It is so. I have asked all these things in order to make it clear that in coming to you I was not actuated by any blind faith. I came to you because I was convinced of the great unseen powers which you possess.

If through the force of some karma in the previous life a sadhaka commits a sinful act in this life, what would be the result in his case?

Maharaj: If a sadhaka commits a sinful act once, in a way it might be explained away as the result of his karma in a previous life or lives designated as prarabdha or sanchita. But if such sinful acts are committed over and over again, and he tries to explain them away by attributing them to his prarabdha, he should certainly be considered as a base man.

Just consider a homely illustration. Suppose there is a live charcoal. You see it, and although you are warned by your friend not to place your foot upon it you, out of a feeling of pride and arrogance, do not heed the warning and place your foot upon it. You are sure to suffer pain. This is something like prarabdha. But would you ever again place your foot upon a fire even if you are asked to do so by a friend? No. Where has prarabdha gone now? That means that when a person is full of repentance, he does not commit the sin again, nor does he quote shastras and the doctrines of prarabdha and sanchita for justifying the commission of the sin.

A sadhaka, therefore, should exercise his powers of reasoning and discrimination at the time of doing acts. Gradually all his fetters will fall off as he progresses in the practice of meditation.

Look at our present-day "saints." Their jivanmukti consists in not doing anything for their maintenance. They have, therefore, to practice tricks for getting their livelihood. They practice more deceits and do more low acts than persons who maintain themselves by labor ever dream of doing. These so-called saints have thrown off all social restrictions.

If I, for instance, find some other saint is more respected as a guru and has more disciples, I am sure to spread scandals about him among my disciples and his disciples also. Even if these saints do not know anything they can conceal their ignorance by assuming an attitude of being above discussions and arguments and of being merged in everlasting tranquility.

I therefore say that in my opinion there is no class of scoundrels in this world worse than such saints who profit themselves by deceiving their followers. Whenever such saints are actually observed doing a sinful act, they attribute their sin to their prarabdha and seek protection under its wings. This "prarabdha" many a time saves them, because they do not suffer for their sins in this world. Of course, the punishment meted out to them by God hereafter will be beyond the knowledge of people in this world. All this argument of prarabdha has been trotted out from the inexhaustible store of Vedanta. All actions which a follower of Charvaka [see the Glossary] would do can safely be done by these saints on the authority of the doctrine that saints are beyond sin and virtue, and that they are above all principles of morality which are meant for ordinary people. The only wonder is that these saints have learnt no real lessons from reading works on true Vedanta. I do not mean to say that Vedanta is to be blamed for this. I should not be considered as belonging to that class of social reformers who have attacked Vedanta and have attributed many of the evils in our social system to its doctrines.

What I want to say is this. Without performing the duties of his varna [caste] and ashrama [stage of life], without devotion and without acquiring the four sadhanas, a person can study books on Vedanta like a school or college student and repeat its doctrines like a parrot. What is the use of all this? But perhaps I am wrong. If a person acquires all the four sadhanas and then begins to think about Vedanta, a sentence or two from all these works will be quite sufficient to illuminate his mind and to enable him to attain moksha. Then where would be the use of all these big books? Who would read them and save them from oblivion? Such persons who merely read all these books must therefore at least be credited with a desire to save these works from oblivion. They, however, only partially follow the doctrines of Vedanta as explained in these books. Many of the present-day saints are similarly followers of Vedanta only partially.

Now if we look to the doctrine of samata (looking upon every thing equally), even an ass may be credited with following this doctrine as it rolls in the dust. Even a dog may be said to follow samata as it has sexual connection with its mother or sister; even a fly may be given credit for following the doctrine because it eats good food as well as dung and is equally delighted with both. These creatures also are partially followers of Vedanta! Most of the present day so-called saints have in them some external characteristics of jivanmuktas and thus fall into the category of one or other of the above-mentioned animals.

A story is told in the Chandogya Upanishad of a sage who asked a king for his daughter in marriage. In the Brihadaranyaka Upanishad there is a story of a sage who had two wives. These stories perhaps go to show that even sages and Vedantins are fettered by prarabdha. But these sages clearly admitted that they were victims of certain passions. It is quite a different matter that notwithstanding this admission many people put their faith in these sages. But the present day saints conceal the fact that they have passions and remain unmarried. When, however, their passions are exposed in the case of the sisters or wives of their disciples, they explain them away and give them a garb of virtue by resorting to the argument of prarabdha. They represent that that particular woman was their wife in their previous life and that it had been predetermined by prarabdha that they should have sexual connection with her.

Those who are real followers of Vedanta, however, are always sorry for any sinful action that occurs at their hands, even though it might have been brought about by the force of prarabdha, and they are always prepared to make a full admission of their faults. They always pray to the Almighty that they may be freed from the clutches of their passions without being required by prarabdha to do bad actions. They generally never find fault with others who might have succumbed to their passions. If, however, they blame others, they also blame themselves.

Although it is very difficult to define in words as to who should be regarded as a saint, still it can be very easily understood that a person who comes forward as a guru must at least not be a man whose actions are without any moral restrictions.

If saints are of different sorts and their external actions are also of different kinds, it is but natural that people also should treat different saints in different ways. If a saint's outward actions are morally bad, there is nothing to complain of if people blame him or treat him with disrespect. The present day saints pose as if they are like Sukhadeva [a sage who was the embodiment of purity] as long as their passions are not exposed, and when they are exposed they represent that they are, like Sri Krishna, beyond all moral restrictions and that they are quite detached from all sense of enjoyment.

Myself: Maharaj, I want to ask a question regarding the light I see. Now I see a big circle of light around you. I saw it for the first time at Mr. Bhat's house. There I saw your form encircled in a halo of light. What is this light and how is it seen? Can an ordinary person see this light?

Maharaj: Every person since his birth has a circle of light surrounding his body. It is known as the "aura." It is slightly bluish in color and is oval in shape, broader towards the head than towards the feet. When a person is in good health and his intellectual powers are keen, this circle appears more distinct and more blue. Electricity or a magnet produces no effect upon it. Hence it cannot be supposed to be made of any material substance. The intensity of the light and its colors differ in different individuals according to their spiritual, moral and intellectual progress. Even in the same individual the intensity and colors change from time to time according to the state of his body, mind or intellect.

The scientist Bagnal at first doubted the very existence of this light-circle or aura, but after many experiments he was convinced of its existence. He was convinced that these circles of light surrounding human bodies were not phantom images, nor could they be explained as the result of fluorescence or phosphorescence. He, however, thought that these circles of light were quite natural and that there was nothing mysterious or spiritual about them. He explained why they cannot be seen by the ordinary eye by saying that they are made up of ultraviolet rays. He has also mentioned the method of how to nullify the activities of certain nerves in the retina and to quicken the activities of certain other nerves in order to be able to see these circles of light. With all these experiments, however, he was later on convinced that his guru, Dr. Kilner, possessed clairvoyance as he could see these circles of light without having recourse to any method of nullifying and quickening the activities of any nerves.

This clairvoyance or divya-drishti [divine sight] is possessed by some great personages from their birth, while some get it by their own efforts, by tapasya and meditation. Although these circles of light are natural, they are not made of inanimate electricity. Those great-souled personages who have an extraordinary quantity of this light can impart some of it to others who possess less and can cure them of bodily and mental ills. It, therefore, appears that your divya-drishti has been opened and hence you have been able to see this circle of light.

There is however, another kind of light which is actually seen by sadhakas who practice dhyana yoga. They see it in themselves by the internal sight. It is the light of the Self and it cannot be seen unless the power of internal sight has been awakened by sadhana.

IV

The following are words of Sri Gajanana Maharaj spoken to Mr. Vaman Keshav Mahegaonkar at various times.

You have seen many visions, and more will come. But ultimately there is only one Chitshakti (Consciousness and Power of the Ultimate

Being), which is without any form and constant. That is where you should become steady. Continue to practice.

See every being as the same, this is what we profess.

Conceit or pride, happiness or sorrow, are the states of consciousness in this physical body. We do not need them at all.

If you think that your physical body is "I" then you are doomed. Then you will go through lakhs [hundreds of thousands] of birth cycles, just due to the infatuation for this body. Therefore forget the attachment to this body and concentrate on Ultimate Being. That is how you are going to cross over this material world. Then you will know the Almighty. You will worship him with faith. You will have happiness in the mind which will be always immersed in unwavering happiness.

The physical body and such material things are not the Atman. The life of the body is you, the Atman. When you realize this then you will become one with The Ultimate Being. You will comprehend the nature of Self-realization. You will see the entire world as your Self. The illusion of dwaita (duality) will be banished. You yourself will be Brahman.

With meditation alone, you will understand everything one after another. No other effort is required. This alone is the practice you need to continue.

You do not need to go to the mountains and forests, and do not need to hold your breath till you are uncomfortable by doing pranayama. Do not get confused by such things.

The Atman residing in your heart is great, he is always filling the universe. He can be seen only with the inner eye, as you can experience for yourself.

The chitshakti (power of mind) is not understood by the ignorant. Other gurus may tell you differently, but you will realize by yourself who is this "I"?

You have to ask your own mind this question: Since the "I" is neither the physical body, neither the prana, nor the trishudhi (the combination of mind, intellect and body), then who is this "I"? This has to be searched out first. The one who has created this body, made the breath work, gave vision to the eyes–who is he? The ears are enabled to hear, the tongue made capable of speech–similarly our other organs are made to perform predesignated functions with whose power? All this is not done by us. The one making this happen is within this body itself. It is his power, he is the doer and the one getting it done. How much more need I tell you? The Indestructible Power is this. It does not have any color or shape. That is atma swarupa, the form of the Self; you need to understand this. That is the mother of the five elements, space, earth, fire, wind and water. She is the one who creates, maintains and destroys this universe. She is all-encompassing. That is chitshakti, the power residing in the mind. Understand this. Now what remains? She is the mother of universe; if you understand her then you are Brahman. You will not be separate from anything else. THAT will be God. That will be Sadguru. He will reveal Aham Brahman–I am Brahman. Therefore concentration comes first. Steadiness of mind and other elements come later. You will acquire it gradually. Repeat Soham within your mind.

You have to comprehend the One Principle in all this. You need to concentrate either on saguna (with form) or nirguna (without form). Consider everything as the Atma Tattwa, the Principle of the Atman, whether saguna or nirguna. This physical body is the temple of God. The prana is the form of Lord Shiva.

Leaving behind all remaining ignorance, just repeat Soham. In the eagerness of your mind, desiring Soham experience [Soham Bhava], you want it right now. But that is not appropriate. A great deal of practice is required for this. You will have to follow a great deal of strict discipline. That kind of tapasya is very difficult to carry on. "If you want to be in the state of Brahman then you have to endeavor intensely," is very easy to read, but to bring it into reality is a very difficult task.

You might say, "If there is the blessings of the guru, then that person can achieve anything." But there is no shortcut to the practice. The importance of practice is that you will get experiences gradually and in the right order. This cannot be achieved in just one birth without spiritual merit from previous births.

All the accumulation of good or bad karma has to be enjoyed or suffered by all beings. Your accumulation of some good karma was there, therefore you have come on this path. You know all this. Then why are you harboring doubts? You need to just practice the path of Soham that I have shown you. This is the path which will take you across the sea of samsara; you will get what you wished for. You have to keep this this in mind for sure.

With meditation, all anxieties and doubts vanish. With meditation comes peace. With meditation, knowledge becomes pure. With meditation the intellect (buddhi) becomes pure.

Take the lamp of knowledge of the Self (atmajnana) in your hand. You are neither any god, goddess or any other being. You are the Original Form (Adi Rupa). You are yourself Brahma Prakash (Brahman in the form of light). Brahman does not admit of any differentiation. This is the play of Atma Sukha (Happiness of the Self). No one apart from you is playing this. It is a constant, pure Essence. That is Adi Brahman, the Ultimate Being. To realize the Atman you need the inner sight.

Come to your senses. Understand my words. Store them in your mind. Become fortunate. First you must follow the path. The path to Brahman the Source is full of mind-boggling insights. You have to be steady, so make the resolve to be so.

The Absolute is knowable. Yogis become immortal by always repeating Soham. Holding the Soham Sudarshana in mind, regain your true form: the Self. Through this Soham you will be able to attain Self-realization. You will easily hold the Ida, Pingala and Sushumna in your hand and control them. If you can control them by one hand (i.e., easily) then you will attain Self-realization as surely as the sun shines in the sky.

Go after the Soham Sushumna [the Sushumna awakened by Soham japa in time with the breath]. Having taken a human birth, this is the bhakti (devotion) you should be pursuing. There is just one Atman (Self) which is the same in every being. If you are holding the chakras, then you will easily be freed from the cycle of birth and death.

While in the material world repeat and meditate on Soham, which will save all beings provided they constantly remember it.

Absolutely unparalleled and unequaled is this Soham Yoga, which makes the material world disappear from the mind and the Self appear. When you use other means like rituals and asceticism they do not give you what you wish for.

(Thus the sadguru blessed me, lit the lamp of knowledge within me and erased my ignorance by giving me knowledge. Thus he taught me, and it became etched on my mind.)

The following paragraphs are translations from a poetic form known as Ovis which Mr. Mahegaonkar wrote for inclusion in Atmaprabha, *a book of Sri Gajanana Maharaj's reflections on spiritual life. (See Chapter Four of this book.) They embody the teachings he was given by Maharaj.*

Be attentive and understand the six centers (chakras or plexuses) in which the Sudarshana Chakra is revolving twenty-one thousand and six hundred times (in a day). [A human being breathes approximately 22,600 times in a day. The breath to which the Soham mantra is joined in time with its inhalation and exhalation–*So* when inhaling and *Ham* when exhaling–is the Sudarshana Chakra referred to here. *Editor's note.*] You should take the Sudarshana Chakra of Soham in your hand and conquer the six enemies (the six passions). …and the Paramatman will bless you with His darshan.

You should at once begin to tread the path of Soham and Sushumna. This is the path of real devotion, which everyone who is born as a human being should follow.

Concentrate your mind. If you steadfastly stick to the mantra Soham, you will yourself be one with the Paramatman. Soham tells you how to acquire the nirguna state. Soham reveals that everything is Brahman.

Soham is the Shabda Brahman (Brahman manifested in the form of sound). It itself is the Paramatman, it itself is the Megha-Shyam (God). It is nothing but the "I" pervading everywhere.

The real greatness of Pandharpur [the famous Vithoba (Vithala) Temple of Lord Krishna] resides in Soham.

The four Vedas are nothing but Soham, which is the expression of Brahman in words. Soham is the pure Sudarshana, which removes all distinctions and gives the experience of unity in diversity.

Soham is the Nirguna Brahman, Soham is the Saguna Brahman,

If a person obtains Soham samadhi, he gets complete Brahmajnana. Death itself bows before it. It is the original seed of Shunya (Void). God Brahma and God Vishnu worship really this Deity. You should meditate upon this Soham Brahman. Thereby you will be one with it and will attain perfection.

Soham gives salvation (mukti). Soham is the Brahman described in the Mahabharata and the Bhagavata.

Soham gives Brahmajnana and the main teaching of the Gita is nothing but Soham.

Soham is punya (virtue).

When the mind becomes unmana (loses consciousness) in the contemplation of Soham, the unmani state is reached. Shiva, Vishnu and Brahma have obtained the samadhi state through this very meditation. All troubles cease when this stage is attained. So this Soham is the secret test of all.

By the contemplation of Soham attachment to sensual objects is destroyed, the effect of karma (actions) is nullified, the chain of births and deaths is cut off and a person becomes immortal.

Soham is the Atmatattwa (the principle of the Self). To obtain realization of this Soham, great merits accumulated in many lives are required. Rishis, munis, siddhas, Sri Dattatreya, Gorakshanath and others always contemplated upon this Soham.

The Nine Nathas (the first Siddhas of the Nath Tradition) contemplated upon this Soham and transmitted their knowledge to the Eighty-four Siddhas.

Soham is the seed which later on sprouts into the tree of samadhi, oneness with, and the realization of, God. All the Siddhas meditate upon this, which is obtained only through great merit. They become holy owing to this and obtain the ultimate liberation.

The ajapa japa is automatically going on in the breath (*So* in taking the breath in, and *Ham* in giving out). When one repeats this japa of Soham consciously then it is called ajapa japa. If one fixes his attention on the sound (of the japa of Soham) in time with the breath, the three nadis—Ida, Sushumna, and Pingala—become free in their actions.

The yogi as it were plays (sports) in the Turiya in the company of the three nadis, Ida, Pingala, and Sushumna, to the accompaniment of the sound of Soham.

The yogi hears the sound of Soham and gets merged in it.

The practice should be continuously carried on keeping the attention fixed on Soham. Complete and unchangeable bliss then envelops the sadhaka quite naturally of its own accord.

V

The following are words of Sri Gajanana Maharaj spoken to Mr. Vishwanath Gopal Vaidya at various times.

Disciples ask the guru, "Where is the 'Soham Sudarshana'? Please explain it to me." Listening to the disciple's query, the guru says, "The Soham Sudarshana is in the breath, which eliminates the three types of anxieties, namely: those pertaining to this physical body, those pertaining to this material world and those pertaining to the attainment of moksha. Soham Sudarshana is when the mind is moving in the interior ajapa by the repetition of Soham in time with the breath.

When the jiva, the individual Self, and Shiva, the Supreme Self, merge inwardly through the japa of Soham, that is the means whereby you can become immortal when perfectly established in that state. Understand that this Soham Hansa (Swan of Soham) state is the ultimate state in yoga.

Meditate on the sounds of the inner, mental repetition of Soham until they reveal the Self.

Listen to my words with full attention. Soham is a Purna [complete, All-encompassing] Mantra. With this you will become a Self-realized person, an Atmajnani. Soham is Brahmajnana [knowledge-experience of Brahman]. Soham is the Nirguna Brahman. Soham is the Only Guru. Everything is Soham Brahman, Soham Shabda, Soham Atmaram [Self], Soham Vishnu, Soham the All-pervading, Soham Shiva, Soham Shakti, Soham Krishna, Soham Brahma, Soham Veda, Soham Shabda Brahman, and Soham Sudarshana.

One who attains Soham Sudarshana is the same as the Lord Krishna.

The Shastras have been expounding the Soham Sudarshana for ages.

Soham Sudarshana is Nirguna (without attributes) and Saguna (with attributes).

Soham is the state of an Avadhuta.

Soham Brahman is attained by practicing meditation on Soham.

Attain Soham Brahmajnana, and even death will prostrate before you.

Soham is the essence of ritual worship.

Meditate with the Soham Brahman.

Soham is the Muktidata [one who gives Moksha/Liberation].

Soham is the Brahma Bhagavad Bharata [the Divine Scripture for India].

Soham is the giver of Brahmajnana [knowledge of Brahman].

Soham is the meaning of the Bhagavad Gita.

Soham is the Gayatri.

Soham is all that is sacred.

Soham Sadhana is complete in itself.

Meditating on Soham makes the mind still, and in that stillness is the first stage of samadhi. This meditation is itself samadhi.

Soham eliminates all obstacles.

Soham meditation should be done quietly and privately.

Soham meditation will eliminate all desires and karmas and will break the cycle of birth and death.

Soham meditation makes you imperishable and immovable.

Soham is the Self, and one learns of it only after many births.

Soham is the seed of Self-realization.

All the siddhas meditate on Soham.

With Soham meditation, one is purified.

Soham meditation gives the ultimate state of moksha.

Through Soham the adept sadhaka is able to do anything and abide in Self-knowledge.

To what I am going to tell you, listen carefully. Keep your awareness within the head [the brain, the sahasrara chakra, the thousand-petalled lotus]. There you will find the Gurupada, the feet of the Inner Guru, the Self. Be absorbed in the subtle sound of your mental intonations of Soham in time with the breath. [In *Soham Yoga: The Yoga of the Self*, there is a citation in the third chapter from a talk by Swami Muktananda in which he speaks of this very same teaching of the Nath Yogis about the Gurupada in the sahasrara. *Editor's note.*]

Meditation Yoga is mild and clear.

The world, Brahman and the Self should all be merged. That is the true Brahmajnana, there is nothing else besides this.

When [the sense of] "you" and "him" merge, that is the real Veda.

The main factor in sadhana is the sattwa guna. Understand that through practice.

Yoga is primary. Understand that as the truth.

A Self-realized person thinks nothing of the material world. "I" and "You" does not touch his mind.

A Self-realized person escapes from hundreds of thousands of birth and death cycles. A Self-realized person attains liberation from rebirth. That, too, through and in this physical body.

Make this as your routine: meditate at least for an hour or so. Thus you will quickly have experience.

By right behavior, right thoughts, philanthropy and reading spiritual books, understand what is truth and what is not.

Consider anyone as a child of the Almighty; salute them lovingly and create for yourself peace on earth.

Do not have attachments in the material world, and restrain all attraction. Then there will be no differentiation between people, and your mind will be centered in the Self.

This concludes the teachings of Sri Gajanana Maharaj as recorded by Mr. Vaidya. What follows are the words of Mr. Vaidya himself which I include here because of his worthy character and attainment as a Soham Yogi.

If you desire permanent bliss, then attain spirituality without blemish. Experience the Self and the Almighty merging into each other without doubt. This is the permanent indestructible bliss. Other types of happiness are false and destructible. What seems happiness to the mind is the root cause of sorrow. There is absolutely no happiness in the material world. You struggle for happiness, but happiness and sorrow is predestined by your karma, so why do you get entangled in this illusion on a daily basis?

There is no true happiness between birth and death. Therefore do such deeds as will certainly not propel you into rebirth. It is birth that is difficult to get again, then why have sorrow over death? Therefore be intent on the path to spirituality, for by this road only can liberation be attained.

Without the blessings of a sadguru the path to permanent bliss is not to be found. Who is a sadguru? How can you recognize him? He is the one who will help you to break the most difficult attachment to this material world.

Guru or initiation need not always be visible. This is not an exam of a school class. He is the one who will help you attain Self-attainment.

Someone may be wearing tilak (marks on the forehead), strings of beads, be smeared with bhasma (sacred ashes), wearing gerua clothes, and having a big jata bandhan (tied-up uncombed long hair), but his mind is polluted and not pure or spiritual. Some [grihasta gurus] have sacred images, pictures of saints and deities, and small temple shrines in their household; they worship and give mantra and ashes. They will tell stories and sing in praise of the Lord, but all this is done only for gaining money. Many are affluent, they have excellent clothes and even jewelry, and call it Raja Yoga and cheat the rich.

All spiritual people are absolutely pure. Their heart is always pure. No vested interest can ever be there for them. For them the Self is the only Almighty which is present in every being, and to It they render service.

There are many types of gurus in the world. They also have various kinds of initiations. They accumulate many disciples. And through that they become famous.

Some gurus have good intellects, some have vast learning, but all are greedy for money. There are many such sadgurus.

Some are "oceans of peace," are soft-spoken and show dignity in their manner, but inside there is ego. There are many such sadgurus as this.

Some do tapasya. Some acquire some stages in yoga but have desire for fame. There are many such sadgurus.

Some will do pranayama (control of breath), will sit always in Siddha Padmasana yoga posture and will claim themselves as having knowledge of past, present and future. Many pose such illusions.

Some will gather disciples comprising youths, young women, widows, etc. They just want their desires to be satisfied. But inside they are never pure.

Some will create temples, will call them the kingdom or world (loka) of a certain deity, will keep elephants, horses, palanquins–but are actually enjoying all that wealth personally. Nowadays there is a wave of such Babajis becoming gurus for personal gains. Therefore the path to spirituality is lost, or becomes difficult.

But even though this is true, those who yearn for spirituality, who are completely ascetic in discipline, who have conquered the inner enemies such as desire, can achieve real spirituality.

As pure drinking water is always filtered, similarly search for a peaceful, loving, unaspiring and compassionate guru. For such a guru as this, you will have to search. Whoever can show the true path to spiritual attainment, who opens the seekers' eyes to real spirituality, who can help them attain Self-realization while in this physical body itself–consider him as a sadguru. Then through his instructions and your diligent practice you will see the Self within and make it permanent by practice. The knowledgeable will understand.

The Self is very deep. The Self is very valuable. It can encompass the entire universe yet be beyond it. Yet all of it is also a form of the Self. There is nothing other than the Self. With true jnana this can be understood.

Visions can be seen, but with the practice of sadhana even that will disappear. This is the experience of diligent sadhakas. At first in their practice they may see visions, but because they are eager to reach the Goal such things cease and they enjoy the bliss of the Self in meditation. Such is the true Raja Yoga method which gives complete bliss. It cannot be explained in words. There the mind does not exist, it is unwavering, that is where happiness knows no bounds.

CHAPTER THREE

SPIRITUAL EXPERIENCES OF VARIOUS DISCIPLES

Experiences of Mr. Sadashiv Khanderao Garude, of Parel, Mumbai.

Myself and my aunt's son, the late Mr. Moreshwar Ramachandra Mathure, were staying at Lower Parel. Sri Gajanana Maharaj used to come to see Mr. Mathure. I came in contact with him on one such occasion. Looking at his costly dress no one could have any idea that he was a Maharaj or saint, but we came to know that he was so later on.

One day he asked my wife for wine as prasad. I came to know about it in the evening when I returned from my office. Owing to this, I began to lose my feeling of respect for him. Although I had money to spare for buying wine, still I could not get any one to go to the shop to bring it. [Devout Hindus will literally not even touch a bottle of wine, as it is considered supremely defiling. *Editor's note.*] I never visited such shops myself, and now I think that I was purposely put to this hard test.

My wife secured a little brandy from a neighbor on the pretext that my young daughter was suffering from stomach ache, and having poured it into a bottle kept the bottle before the deities in our shrine. I thought that a drunkard, although he may be a Maharaj, was hardly the person who would ever be able to lead me to the right path. I did not get any sleep that night. Also I did not go the next morning as usual for his darshan to Mr. Mathure's room.

But at about 9:30 a.m. he came inquiring about me, supporting himself on a cane and repeating a line of a Hindi song to the effect, "Be always on the watch, keeping always an eye on the workings of your mind."

122

I was then about to sit for my meal, having completed my worship of the deities. He began to eat the papad (a crisp, pungent and salty kind of cake baked on fire) in my dish. [This is considered very unclean by observant Hindus. The only time two people eat from the same dish is to show that they consider each other the closest in relation. I have only seen it once, by a man and his brother-in-law. This was done by Gajanana Maharaj both as a test and as a sign of the closeness he felt for Mr. Garude. *Editor's note.*]

My wife told me to give the wine as prasad to him, but Maharaj offered it to me. I was at a loss what to do as it was almost next to impossible that I should drink that kind of prasad at the time of going to the office. But he said that I must drink it and, having poured the wine from the bottle into a small pot in our presence, placed his hand over it and asked my wife and myself to drink it. To our wonder we found that it had turned into fresh milk. We both of us then took it, and since then I quit making any criticisms about him.

On one Mahashivratri day my elder brother, Mr. Ramachandra Khanderao Garude, my aunt's son Mr. Moreshwar Mathure, myself and some other persons went for the darshan of Maharaj to the house of Mr. Narayanrao Samartha. The lamps had just been lighted there, as it was nightfall. Maharaj told me to look at the lamp which was near me. As I did so, I saw that around every person and every thing there was a shining big orb like the sun. This vision continued for about half an hour, then Maharaj placed his hand upon my head and the experience stopped and I began to see things in their ordinary form. Some time later we all returned home.

Maharaj had once been to my brother's place at Worli. At that time he jokingly asked my mother to take him on her hip [as babies are carried by their mother]. As Maharaj is very thin and light, my mother could easily lift him up, but he again asked her to do so, and she found it impossible as he had then grown very heavy. [The ability to be very light or very heavy at will is a well-known yoga power. Krishna himself did the same as a child. *Editor's note.*] He performs such miracles whenever he likes to do so. But he becomes annoyed if any one asks him to perform them.

One can never get tired of Maharaj's company. Whatever may be the state of mind of a person, if he comes near Maharaj he always enjoys a feeling of quiet and happiness and becomes oblivious of the passing of time. My friend Mr. Balkrishna Ganesh Dixit and myself took him several times in a carriage to some saints, and these saints all paid him respect.

Whenever Maharaj stayed with me or with Mr. Dixit, he never took anything except tea and on rare occasions chivda [a light rice snack that tastes like popcorn]. We thus know that he never eats any ordinary meals.

Experiences of Mr. Bhabani Charan Sidhanta, a resident of Calcutta

I am a resident of Calcutta in Bengal where I was employed in the Judicial Department. I have a wife and three children. I am a devotee of Kali and used the name of the Goddess for my meditation and japa.

In Calcutta there are a number of cults or missions named after their founders: great yogis or bhaktas of Kali. In these missions the heads are generally sannyasis, but I found them not of very good moral principles. I visited these missions and approached the heads with a view to obtain the knowledge of the way to the realization of the Almighty, but I am sorry to say that I failed. Not only that, but I found them no better than ordinary grihasthas.

During the last five years I was very much keen on having guru upadesh (instruction from a guru) for spiritual realization. One day while I was lying down on my bed half awake, I observed a ray of light between the eye-brows. It remained for about ten minutes and then disappeared. This ray of light encouraged me to leave my employment and home and go forth in quest of God.

I wandered forth to various holy places, and while in Brindaban (the birthplace of Krishna) for the second time, after six months I heard a voice telling me to go to Nashik. I had no money as all my finances had by this time been exhausted. So I walked from Brindaban to Nashik [over seven hundred miles], and stayed there with the Mahanta (Head) of the Chatus Sampradaya Akhada [association of sannyasis]. I enquired of the Mahanta whether there was any yogi in Nashik. One of his disciples knew about Sri Gajanana Maharaj and took me to him. On my appearing before him my first impression was that I was sitting before Sri Ramakrishna Paramahansa and I felt that was the place where I would find my guru.

On the 15th of October, 1938, which was a Saturday, I went to Sri Gajanana Maharaj at about nine a.m. He took compassion on me, gave me the mantra of Soham, and placed his hand on my head. As soon as he did so, there was a loud sound of Soham, my mind became concentrated and void of ideas, and a wave of extraordinary joy arose in my heart. This feeling of joy lasted till the next day, which was Sunday. On that day I again went to Maharaj at nine a.m., and sat before him in meditation. The sound of Soham which was loud became more and more soft, until I could see the Sahasrara lotus (the thousand-petalled lotus of the brain) in a dim light.

That evening I again went to Maharaj to take his permission to go home. He asked me to begin my worldly life again, and said that I would experience real joy even while carrying on worldly life. That night when I was sitting in meditation at the place where I was staying at Nashik, I found that a flood of joy poured itself upon me and I could see before me the form of my sadguru Sri Gajanana Maharaj.

On Monday the 17th of October 1938, at 10 a.m. I went for Maharaj's darshana and after taking his permission left Nashik.

Experiences of Mr. D. D. Bhave

On December 10, 1937, Sri Gajanana Maharaj conferred his grace upon me by giving me the mantra Soham.

One day when I had been to Maharaj in the evening as usual for his darshan, Maharaj said that one must worship Shakti. Then one gets all the siddhis (powers) of the yoga path. Only care must be taken to not utilize those powers for oneself. There must not be a single thing in the Yoga path which one does not understand.

Next day when I sat for meditation early in the morning, the goddess having six arms, whom I had once seen before, stood before me and told me to do japa of the stotra beginning *Namo Devyai, Mahadevyai....*" [This is a hymn to the goddess, part of the Sri Durga Saptasati, also known as the Chandi. *Editor's note.*] She said that by that japa one can acquire the whole power of the universe in oneself, saying which she disappeared.

After I had repeated the japa for about a week or fortnight the goddess again appeared before me and said, "I have not got six arms; I have only two. But I showed six arms to you as I had to put down your six enemies (the six passions), and for that purpose I had equipped myself with six arms. But now there is no necessity for me to put down your six enemies as they are being slowly conquered by you without effort by the japa of the mantra Soham. I have originally only two arms and one should meditate upon me in that form because my form of two arms represent dwaita (duality); and through this dwaita you have to go into adwaita (non-duality; oneness)."

[In Hindu theology, the Six Passions, Arishadvarga, are the six enemies of the mind, which are: kama (lust), krodha (anger), lobha (greed), moha (delusive, often emotional, attachment or temptation), mada (pride), and matsarya (jealousy): the negative characteristics of which prevent man from attaining moksha or salvation. In this experience of Mr. Bhave, the two syllables of Soham are the two "arms" of the devi (goddess) which take the sadhaka from duality to non-duality. *Editor's note.*]

I narrated this incident to Sri Gajanana Maharaj. He said "Through the grace of my guru you have acquired so much power that the goddess has of her own accord given you her grace although you had not asked or begged for it. Among all these different stages of the powers of Shakti, the power of Soham is the most exalted."

Experiences of Mr. Vishnupant Chaphekar, Nashik

I am a Brahmin, a follower of the Vedic tradition and devoted to the path of action (rituals, etc.). Like other people of the world I, too, used to attend kirtans, recitations of puranas and also discussions on the Vedanta philosophy. My mind, however, attained no peace. I was for about twenty-five years repeating the japa of Gayatri and also the japa of the twelve-lettered mantra of Vasudeva [Krishna]. Still I obtained no peace of mind. But I thought that if I would meet with a real saint I would get peace of mind, and my life in this world would then have fulfilled its object.

When I was at Sinnar I happened to meet Amritanath, alias Baba Maharaj Kopargaonkar of Kopargaon. He gave me advice regarding spiritual matters and encouraged me to follow my usual practice. But even though twelve years passed after that, the restlessness of mind did not stop, no peace was attained and no spiritual experience was gained. On one occasion I prayed to him that although I was following his advice for the last so many years I had not got any spiritual experience and he should, therefore, confer his grace upon me. He listened attentively to what I said and replied, "The ground of your mind has been now prepared, and you will very soon meet with a saint of Self-realization, and your life's purpose will be fulfilled. You will get a guru of real atmic experience. Do not ruin yourself by looking merely at his external conduct. Even if people blame you for accepting initiation from him, do not feel sorry for it. Whatever he will tell you, follow it accordingly." After this I always remained longing to meet this sadguru and continued my former practice.

Four years passed after that, and I was transferred to Nashik. There I heard that a dhyana yogi, Gajanana Maharaj, had come to Nashik. I made an attempt four or five times to have his darshan but he sent me away with harsh words. From the appearance of his face, I thought he was in a superconscious state akin to madness. I felt that this must be the saint hinted at by Amritanath Kopargaonkar.

Then on the Dattajayanti day in December of 1933, I went to him and caught hold of his feet and prayed, "I am now in the last years of my life and I have come to you with a sincere desire that my life should have its real fulfillment. Save me or not, as you like."

As soon as I said this, he raised me up with great affection and spoke words of consolation to me. Then I began to go to him daily and listen to his words of advice for about an hour or two. Fifteen days later, he told me that I should sit at night in darkness and try to make my mind peaceful. When I did this for four or five days, my mind got peace through his grace. Seven or eight days later, when I had been to him in the morning, he made me sit near him, whispered the mantra Soham in my ear, removed my cap and placed his hand on my head. He had me sit for an hour and repeat that mantra internally without pronouncing the words with the mouth. When I began to repeat the mantra, my eyes shut of themselves and before my internal sight there appeared a brilliant light. I mentioned this fact to Maharaj when I later on recovered full consciousness. He thereupon said, "Continue your Brahmakarma (duties of a Brahmin) as you have been doing for so long. Only after all your ritual is over, repeat without break the mantra Soham internally."

After he said this, I bowed to his feet and started to go away, but Maharaj again asked me to sit down. As soon as I sat down, my mind became concentrated, a brilliant light began to shine and I felt that someone from inside was telling me not to fear. A short time after that I regained consciousness and then experienced a feeling of great joy and all my restlessness disappeared.

After I obtained the grace of Maharaj, I found that the japa of Soham naturally of its own accord began to be repeated internally. A year after I was admitted into Maharaj's grace, Kopargaonkar Maharaj came to visit me. As soon as I saw him, I felt overflowing joy. I placed my head upon his feet and narrated to him the whole account regarding my meeting with my sadguru which I had through his (Kopargaonkar's) grace. He was very glad to hear it and he asked me to take him to Gajanana

Maharaj. I did accordingly. Both the Maharajas embraced each other closely. Words fail me in describing that meeting of the two saints. Kopargaonkar Maharaj said to Gajanana Maharaj, "I have entrusted this child," meaning me, "to you." To which Gajanana Maharaj replied, "If you give me the power, what will I not be able to do? I want only your grace. I am only a servant of your feet." All people who were then sitting there were quite wonderstruck at seeing the meeting and hearing this talk.

One day in the evening instead of going to the Godavari for my sandhya-adoration, I went to Maharaj. He asked me why I was there instead of giving arghya (oblations of water) to the sun and performing my sandhya. I replied that I had come there through his (Maharaj's) inspiration. He then told me not to have any misgivings, but to go home and quietly perform my sandhya. Accordingly I went home, performed my sandhya, and after having taken my evening meal, I as usual sat for meditation. Then I saw the sun just as by day. I narrated this next day to Maharaj, who said that as the sun of knowledge had arisen in my heart, I could very easily see at any time the moon, the sun and the stars.

On another occasion I was sitting by the Godavari river entirely absorbed in meditating upon the joyful countenance and the clothing of Sri Gajanana Maharaj, and in worshipping him mentally. At that time I was sitting near the river whose waters were rising, and my dhoti became wet, but I was unconscious of all this, and it was only when people round about raised cries that I regained consciousness. [Near the coast of India, when the sea tide rises, so does the water of the rivers that flow into it.]

I then got up quickly and went in haste to Gajanana Maharaj and told him what had happened. I was greatly wonderstruck to see the same clothing hanging on a peg there which I had seen Maharaj wearing in my meditation. I asked him why it was so, to which he replied that he had only put me to a test.

The net result is that my attention is less and less directed to worldly matters and cares, and my mind is always at peace. What is really wanted is this absolute cessation of pain and pleasure.

[*Editor's note*. The following incident regarding Mr. Chaphekar was told by a fellow disciple.] Once Mr. Chaphekar was meditating by a huge lake called Bageshree. Many carnivorous wild animals, snakes, insects, etc., were there in abundance. A tiger came to drink water and passed by close to him. Seeing this some cattle-herders immediately came and started telling him that a tiger had come and gone. "Why are you sitting here? What are you doing here? There was a scorpion sitting in your lap. What if he had stung you? Then you would have experienced great pain. Don't sit in such places. When you might be in danger, nobody can tell." Listening to this Vishnupant only said, "Guru-mother is protecting me."

Experiences of Madhukar Damodar Chitnis, a student in St. George's School, Nashik.

I was born in Nashik. My father has long been acquainted with Mr. Bhise, with whom Sri Gajanana Maharaj stays. I am now telling things which happened when Sri Gajanana Maharaj probably came for the first time to Nashik. I was about six or seven years old then. My father used to go occasionally to Mr. Bhise's house and saw Gajanana Maharaj there. He at that time had no faith that he was a yogi or a Maharaj, because there were no signs or characteristics in his conduct showing that he was a saint or a yogi. His dress was like that of an ordinary gentleman, his conversation was quite ordinary and full of wit, humor and jokes. Sometimes he used to speak harsh words also. Women in my family also had no faith in him. Besides, Maharaj also did not ask anyone to sit near him, nor did he himself go to anybody's house.

A few days later, however, my father had a dream in the early morning in which someone said to him in a clear voice that Maharaj was a great saint, and that my father should go to him and get initiated by him and fulfill the great object of human life. My father was greatly delighted at this dream, and told it to me and all the members of my family. He then took us all to Sri Gajanana Maharaj. He was then lying on a cot. We all bowed down to him. He shouted out, "I am not a Maharaj or a saint. I am also not a pseudo-saint cheating people. I am an ordinary man like you. Hence I do not like these foolish acts of yours." He then asked us to go back home, which we did.

My father once more went to him and prayed to him. Then he said, "You come on Thursday, then I shall do as I may be inspired by my sadguru." On the very next Thursday myself and my father went to him with a cocoanut, a garland of flowers and one rupee as dakshina, and my father got himself initiated. Maharaj returned the rupee and materials of worship to my father, and told him to offer the things to our household deities as he had not as yet arrived at a stage of being worshipped.

He further said, "I am neither a saint nor a Maharaj, but owing to you being acquainted with me, I am giving you the Soham mantra given to me by my guru. In this I am simply doing my duty. That mantra has great powers as it has come out of the mouth of a saint of great Self-realization, and owing to its powers a man is sure to have the goal of human life fulfilled. Meditate and repeat this mantra Soham in your mind." We returned home with the worship materials returned by Maharaj.

After that my father had many experiences on the path of yoga, during which a fragrant smell pervaded our whole house.

When I became about sixteen or seventeen years old, I used to wonder at the experiences told me by my father. I however was unable to put any faith in them. I used to say that there are many gurus regarding whom such things are told. I used to ridicule these experiences of my father, and to find fault with and censure Sri Gajanana Maharaj. My father was later on transferred to various places, but I continued to stay at Nashik for my education. I however never visited Maharaj. On the contrary, whenever I heard his name mentioned anywhere, I used to speak in terms of disparagement.

Over the years I read the works of Ramatirtha, Ramakrishna Paramahansa and Vivekananda, practiced pranayama, had various inner experiences, and felt a tremendous attraction towards the spiritual path. I told all this to my maternal uncle, Mr. Raje, who in his turn told them to Sri Gajanana Maharaj. He thereupon remarked that Madhu (*i.e.* myself) had not seen him for the last six or seven years.

My maternal uncle was in a short time after this transferred to Deolali. I took a letter of introduction from him and went to see Sri Gajanana Maharaj. He listened to all the details of my experiences, and then with very great solicitude explained this subject to me. He said that I was a yogi in my former birth, hence I could see these visions in my early life. I then had firm faith in those experiences implanted in me. I then prayed to him that he might kindly lead me to the proper path. He replied that he would do so.

Two or three days later I went to see Sri Gajanana Maharaj. At that time a book entitled, *Shatchakra Bhedan* (*Passing Through the Six Chakras*), written by Dr. Vaidya, was lying there. I took it up and began to read it. I suddenly got into a trance, my prana went up, and the book dropped down from my hand. At the time Sri Gajanana Maharaj had gone into the inner apartment of his house. He came out and finding me insensible, shook me for a long time and brought me back to consciousness. I told him how I had gone up. He ordered me not to practice pranayama at all and rebuked me sternly. But his face showed that inwardly he was extremely pleased. This was the first time that I went into the state of samadhi in his presence.

He then immediately initiated me and told me to repeat the mantra Soham internally. I did it sitting in front of him. I found that the japa began to be repeated in the Sahasradala (the thousand petalled lotus of the brain). Then I found that the whole current of my thought was full of Soham, and all the pain and troubles that I had undergone owing to pranayama stopped altogether. Not only this, but my meditation decidedly got a different turn owing to the japa of Soham, which was made internally, being brought to its fruition.

On one occasion when I was sitting near Sri Gajanana Maharaj in meditation, I thought I was going through a deep valley. There was partly light and partly darkness there, and when I went almost to the bottom, I heard the sound of "Soham" coming from above, and the sound of "Koham" coming from below. When I asked Maharaj what it meant, he said, "'Koham' means 'Who am I?' to which the answer is 'Soham, I am He'–God."

In this manner Sadguru Gajanana Maharaj has brought me to the right path. At present I feel no trouble and I remain in this peculiar state surrounded by light, and I enjoy great happiness and peace.

Experiences of Raosaheb Gupte, L. C. E., retired Engineer, Nashik

I had the good fortune of getting the darshana of Sri Gajanana Maharaj for the first time at Dhulia in the year 1926. He had then been on a visit to Mr. Raje. My friend Mr. D. M. Saswadkar, obtained information regarding him, his practice and progress in the path of yoga, and his high standing in that path, and then communicated the information to me. Since the time I arrived at maturity of understanding, I had faith in the existence of God, which had increased owing to the various experiences and difficulties in life.

When I used to go for a walk with Mr. Saswadkar in the evening, I would have discussions with him regarding spiritual matters. I also heard the talk of Maharaj with some people visiting him about yoga, and also saw miracles which appeared to take place at his hands easily and naturally. All these things produced a great impression upon me and I decided to get myself initiated by Maharaj, with the sole object that I might enjoy peace of mind in the remaining part of my life after I retired.

On the first Monday in Shravana of that year, I managed to take Maharaj to my place in the morning. I worshipped him with great reverence, and having placed a garland of flowers round his neck and bowed to his feet, I humbly prayed him to lead me to the path of the Lord. Maharaj told me to repeat the japa of Soham. It is still going on.

I have realized how the ajapa japa is going on and the mind also loses itself in it.

I asked Maharaj about visions, to which he replied that visions are only guides taking a sadhaka towards the bliss of the Self. The visions themselves are not the real thing. These visions later on disappear and the sadhaka then experiences the bliss of the Self. That is the goal of human life.

I am gradually getting experience of this bliss and I pray at his feet that through his grace the state of Self-realization may more and more be developed.

My wife also has been favored by Maharaj, and even in her old age (68 years) she sits for two hours at a stretch.

I have seen miracles which appeared to take place easily and naturally.

Once when Maharaj was sitting in the house of Mr. Pradhan at Dhulia, and near him Messrs. Pradhan, Raje and Saswadkar were sitting, I saw a shower of bukka (black scented powder) falling from above for some minutes. I kept a quantity of that bukka with me for several years.

I saw with my own eyes at Dhulia that Maharaj turned wine into milk.

Once when he was suffering from fever, in order to keep his strength up people near him, including myself, decided to give him a boiled egg. When the boiled egg was broken, the internal part of it had been turned into potato. All persons present there observed this.

From the time I went to Sri Gajanana Maharaj, there was a good effect on my health, also. While I was in Dhulia, I had hernia on the right side. I began to use a belt as advised by the doctors, and at the time I used to practice Dhyana Yoga according to the instructions of Maharaj. The swelling on my right side slowly began to subside and in about two years it disappeared altogether. For the last three years I have stopped using the belt also. I regard this as a result of my sadguru's grace.

I came to Nashik in November of 1927. About two years after that my wife had an attack of paralysis on her right side and she was under medical treatment. One evening Maharaj came to my place and told my wife to stand in front of him and to go walking to the back door and to come back. She did so without any support. After this was repeated for four or five times, he gave her the blessing that she would thenceforward feel all right. More than five years have now passed since then. She is now feeling no effects of the paralysis at all. She is also experiencing the good effects of Sri Gajanana Maharaj's grace. This shows Maharaj's power of curing diseases.

Experiences of Mr. P. L. Inamdar, Nashik

Since the time I was a school boy, I was always thinking on spiritual topics. The sight of a dead body carried along a road, bodily ailments of a person in old age, condition of the blind and the lame, and the different natures of different individuals and their different circumstances gave me food for thought which ultimately resulted in restlessness of mind. Except the time actually passed in the school, the whole of my other time was passed in thinking over these problems in secret, and I could not do anything else sincerely. I had an aversion to read anything not dealing with spiritual matters.

A sort of fear was generated in me by pondering over these problems of life, suffering and death, and I began to feel that it was the primary duty of a person to try to acquire a state of fearlessness. Seven or eight years passed in this state. I got the idea that I was someone different from the body, that I was not the body. I suffered great tribulations in the attempt to satisfy my mind about the truth of this idea.

I used to sit looking at my own reflection in a mirror for a long time and then direct my gaze to the various parts of my body. I then got the idea in my mind that all the actions of the human body and of the whole world depended entirely on the existence of some invisible power. In order to strengthen this idea, I used to ponder over the problem for hours together. I was convinced that if the life-principle be removed from the body, the body would not be able to do anything. Hence the body was a sort of machine which works according to the will of the moving power inside. I thought and thought over these matters and was anxious to get a satisfactory explanation—of course satisfactory so far as my poor reason was concerned.

I have given above a brief outline of the trend of my thoughts in those days. It is not possible to give a detailed description of all the thoughts and the conclusions arrived at. Then I was convinced that I would not get any further conclusion by mere thinking. I arrived at this stage owing to the following ideas.

Once while I was engaged in thinking, I suddenly got an idea that the happenings in the actual physical world, the joys and sorrows, the results of good and bad actions, resembled exactly incidents seen in the dream-world. While we are in a dream, we feel the incidents to be equally real. Just as our physical body is quite detached from the pains and pleasures which we experience in a dream, similarly we are really detached from the pains and pleasures which we experience in this big dream of human life, which dream is the result of our ignorance of the real truth. Just as when we become awake, all the sensations in the dream are seen to be unreal and unsubstantial, similarly when we shall awake from this big dream, we shall see the unsubstantiality of all pains and pleasures, and we shall reach the state of fearlessness. Hence the only thing that must be done is to get a knowledge of one's real Self, which means awakening from this big dream of ignorance.

When I reached this stage in my thought, I stopped all thinking about these matters and became extremely eager to obtain a knowledge of the path which would lead to this realization. I then felt that unless I met a sadguru and obtained his grace, there was no other way of getting knowledge of the right path. Only God himself in the form of a sadguru could show it.

In March 1939 I came to know of Sri Gajanana Maharaj from Mr. Baba Satpurkar. I went for his darshan and told him the whole history of the process of my thought. He said, "I will see if my sadguru extends his grace to you." After a few minutes he told me not to be anxious as

I would get the object of my desire. I then began to visit him daily and sit with him for about an hour, praying to him to extend his grace to me soon.

Soon after this Sri Gajanana Maharaj went to Mumbai for about a month. During this period I had a dream as follows. I saw that I was sitting in front of Sri Gajanana Maharaj. We both looked at each other for a short time. A dim fog-like light appeared between him and me and I got into a trance-like state, then the appearance vanished.

After his return from Mumbai, on the afternoon of April 6, 1939, he initiated me by giving me the mantra Soham. Since that time I began to repeat the japa. I do not see any visions while sitting in meditation. There is generally darkness and only sometimes a dim light is seen. My mind, however, becomes concentrated, the repeater of the mantra, the listener, and the heard become one, the body becomes motionless and there is a feeling of deep joy. I feel that the japa of Soham is going on in various parts of the body: in the head, in the heart and in the pupils of the eyes.

Occasionally the concentration is almost complete and for some time I have no remembrance of my body. Throughout the day at present the mind is under the influence of joy and meditation. In short, although I see no visions at the time of meditation my mind becomes concentrated and I enjoy a feeling of joy and peace through the grace of my sadguru.

One day while I was asleep I got a great shock inside the spine which turned me sideways. (Originally I was lying on my back). I suddenly became awake and found that the japa of Soham was going on of itself.

After that experience, when I sit for meditation through the grace of guru my mind becomes concentrated without any great effort and all other thoughts disappear. In the beginning there appears darkness which is soon succeeded by a mild light which slowly becomes more lustrous. My attention then withdraws itself from the light and fixes itself on the mantra Soham. I feel a desire to reach the source whence this mantra proceeds. The japa goes deeper and deeper. Some time later while I am listening to the sound of my inner repetitions Soham, the vibrations go deeper and deeper and then the sensation of those vibrations also stops. This state, however, lasts for a very short time. A sense of great joy is felt in that state and I feel that that is my real Self.

On July 6, 1939, in the evening I took my meal after having as usual finished my meditation of Soham. Some time later the japa commenced of itself internally with great force, owing to which I had to keep sitting down in that state for some time. Then I wrote my daily accounts and went to bed. As soon as I lay down on the bed the japa again automatically began with great force and my attention was perforce attracted towards the japa and the feeling of sleep passed away. Three or four hours passed in this manner. During this period of time, thrice I experienced such joy that it cannot be described in words. To attempt to do so would be as ridiculous as to try to describe the sweetness of sugar in words. After that I could not get sleep owing to this excessive joy. I was lying on my bed and a feeling of a great and pure love for my sadguru overpowered me. I felt that just as a mother always looks after the child and the child is therefore fearless, similarly the sadguru is always near us, guarding and protecting us. This feeling of love for the sadguru produced fearlessness. I have tried to describe the feeling of the great joy which I experienced on that night, but the real joy which I experienced was a myriad times greater.

At about 4 a.m. on that night I fell asleep and had the following dream: I was sitting on a carpet in the outer hall of a big house. Maharaj was also sitting there talking with some persons. Maharaj then went inside the house. I too followed him inside, wishing to ask him to come outside. I saw him standing there (he was not lame in the dream), and people coming one after another, taking his darshan and going away. He was, however, looking here and there and sometimes looking at me. I also placed my head on his feet, when he caught hold of me with both hands, sat down and brought his mouth near my ear. Instead of, however, hearing any words, I felt that he sent through the aperture of my ear a wave of that extreme joy which I had previously experienced in my waking state, which wave spread through the whole of my body.

For the last eight or ten days, as soon as I sit for meditation I begin to see a dim light, but immediately afterwards I see clear white light and the japa continues automatically in the mind and no effort is required. I become almost absorbed in the light. The delight and concentration experienced at the time cannot be adequately described in words. While in a state of meditation a sound of snoring is occasionally heard at intervals. Persons round me might think that I am then sleeping soundly but internally I am enjoying the bliss of complete quietude of mind and am seeing the light. (November 11, 1939)

Two or three days ago I got the following experience at the time of meditation. I saw light on all sides of me and felt that all thoughts are merely moving in this light like waves on water. If I made any sound myself, I heard it and also its echo. Suppose we go to a temple and are sitting there alone. If we make a sound, we hear it as well as its echo. Here the producer of the sound and its hearer are one and the same; similarly I feel that everything is produced from the One Being and it is also experienced by that Being. To remain without giving rise to any sound or thought produces a sensation of great delight. As long as one remembers this One Being as truly the cause of every action, its stay and support and its ultimate goal, there is no delusion. But when one becomes completely engrossed in the action and forgets the Self, then all trouble arises and delusion holds its sway. While doing actions, when we forget that we are merely observers of the actions and identify ourselves with the actions, we are carried away from our firm position and become victims of delusion and trouble. This is what is known as egotism.

When this fact has been clearly experienced in the light seen during meditation, remaining quiet there without any disturbing factor is what is known as sakshitwa: looking upon oneself as merely the observer. If by practice one becomes absorbed in such a state, I am sure that one would go into nirvikalpa samadhi, where there is neither knowledge nor absence of knowledge.

Experiences of Mr. Vaman Keshav Mahegaonkar

Being hard pressed by domestic difficulties, I became disgusted with this worldly life which is so full of misery and my mind became full of penitence. I felt that I had made no good use of my life as a human being. I had neither achieved success in the worldly life nor had I gotten any insight into the spiritual side of life. I then thought of devoting at least the remaining part of my life to spiritual matters, and since then began to hanker after spiritual life and to try to find out a path leading to it.

Through good fortune–or in other words through efforts made in past births having come to fruition–I got introduced to Sri Guru Gajanana Maharaj Gupte through my good friend, Mr. Vishwanath Gopal Vaidya. After having his darshan I told him the whole history of my life and expressed my longing for the spiritual path.

Seeing my intense desire and also knowing what was passing in the innermost part of my mind, he gave me assurances. And he never misled me. On the contrary he said, "I am neither a saint nor a Maharaj. As ordered by my guru, Sri Narayana Saraswati, I tell the mantra Soham given to me by him to any one who comes to me. I do this in the manner of a friend. In the words of Ramdas, 'One should teach others what one knows and make all people around one wiser than before.' My master has allotted this work to me. Whoever comes to me with a sincere desire, I tell him this mantra, through the power of my master.

"I look upon all human beings as being equal. All living creatures bear the Divine Spirit and hence every human being is fitted to follow the spiritual path. I do not look upon any one as wicked or unfit to follow the spiritual path. Whoever comes to me, I tell him what I know. But it is not my custom to accept any worship, service, dakshina or arati as a guru first and then to instruct that person. Nor do I mislead women."

He then told me the Soham mantra and conferred his grace upon me and asked me to repeat the japa with firm faith. Not only this, but he for about two and a half to three months, used to have me sit near him to practice meditation. Hallowed be the name of my Master! I am very glad to say that this conferring of his grace changed the whole course of my life.

For the last twenty or twenty five years there was not the slightest change in my mental tendencies. But after being instructed by Sri Guru Gajanana Maharaj and having come into contact with several of his disciples, I was deeply impressed with the wonderful individuality of Sri Gajanana Maharaj and I do not believe that this impression will ever be wiped from my heart.

This great saint will never mislead even an ordinary person, much less a real aspirant. Whatever may be a man's religion or whatever may be the duties devolving upon him he does not ask him to leave them. He only urges that man to repeat the mantra Soham with firm faith. He further gives the following advice in the spirit of a friend:

"My sadguru had me drink the nectar of Nama (Name of God) and I tell you the same Nama, being ordered by my sadguru to do so. I am approaching the stage of perfection. If you also wish to come with me, you should repeat that Nama, Soham, in your heart with firm faith. Your deep-rooted mental tendencies will vanish and the dirt of desire accumulated in previous births and in this birth will be washed away and your individual Self will be merged into the Universal Self and you will always remain in your real, original state and thus attain everlasting peace.

"The advice that I give to others is not given in the capacity of a guru, but in that of a friend. I give this advice through the inspiration of my guru Sri Narayana Saraswati, and almost in his words. I, too, am still a student and I am sure that in some birth, either this or future, I shall attain the state of perfect union with Brahman (the Supreme Self)."

In this manner Sri Gajanana Maharaj had several conversations with me regarding knowledge and humility, and then he blessed me with his grace and had me practice meditation. During my practice of meditation my mind became calmer and calmer. I also began to experience joy and the current of thoughts began to grow less and less.

Once in meditation I saw Sri Dattatreya, who asked me whether I had understood the meaning of Soham. According to my understanding I replied, "'So' means 'He'–that is, God–and 'Ham' means 'I am.' Hence Soham means that God is my Self." Hearing this reply Sri Dattatreya nodded His head in approval, but asked me again whether I knew any other meaning of that mantra. I, however, could not answer this question. Then Sri Dattatreya told me with His own lips that "So" meant taking in of the breath and "Ham" meant letting out of the breath. Hence, he said, Soham meant Taking In and Letting Out. What is to be taken in and what is to be let out? The answer to that is that bad qualities, passions, egotism etc., are to be let out and then good qualities–that is, good morals, faith in truth and devotion to God–are to be taken in. First of all bad qualities are to be let out and then good qualities are to be taken in. Soham can be interpreted in this manner also.

Experiences of Mr. Vasanta Narayan Nirokhekar

My uncle, Mr. D. L. Nirokhekar, was often going to Sri Gajanana Maharaj since the Diwali of 1938. I accompanied him to the house of Maharaj on March 15, 1939, and had the darshana of Maharaj for the first time. I had a desire that Maharaj should have compassion on me and shower his grace upon me.

On April 13, 1939, Maharaj told me to do the japa and meditation of Soham, and said that by daily practice within a period of about six months I would get peace, happiness and joy. I began to meditate for about two hours daily. After a little less than a month my mind became more concentrated and I began to feel that the japa was going deeper and deeper inside. I got these experiences during the space of only a month and a half. I pray that my progress in this path may continue and that I may enjoy real bliss always.

Experiences of Mr. Bhargava Vaman Parchure, Nashik

I came to Nashik and for twenty-one years worked in the police department, retiring in 1935. Some months before my retirement I came to know that one Gajanana Maharaj lived there. But when I actually saw him, my common sense could not let me think that he was a saint or a Maharaj.

Mr. Appasaheb Walawalkar, who was living in a house near the one where I was staying, used often to talk about Sri Gajanana Maharaj to me. So when I retired, I requested Mr. Walawalkar to take me to Gajanana Maharaj and introduce me to him.

After my introduction I began going for his darshan daily in the morning and in the evening. Seven or eight days passed, and on one Thursday he conferred his grace upon me by instructing me in the mantra Soham. Accordingly I commenced the japa and meditation of Soham, and experienced a great calmness of mind and began to repeat the mantra with great earnestness.

Only a few days after I was favored with the grace of my master, I began to experience the smell of fragrant flowers, owing to which the mind always felt refreshed. So also, whenever I bring before my mind Sri Gajanana Maharaj, whether he be in Nashik or not, I experience the smell of incense and I feel as if I had gotten his darshan in that form.

On one occasion I committed some mistake while repeating the japa. Maharaj appeared before me and gave a forcible slap on my thigh and brought me to the right path. Even when I came back to ordinary consciousness, I felt the aching sensation on my thigh. From this experience I am led to think that our sadguru is always near us when we are repeating the japa, discharging his responsibilities regarding us.

At present I am not perturbed by worldly difficulties. I have a feeling that I have to discharge certain duties through this mortal body and my peace of mind is never in the least disturbed.

Experiences of Mr. Dattatraya Shankar Sakrikar, Nandgaon, District Nashik

I first saw Sri Gajanana Maharaj at Nandgaon in 1928. In that year he might have come there after that once or twice, but I had no talk with him. I used simply to sit as an observer or spectator. I had a fixed idea in my mind that I would only acknowledge that person as my sadguru who would recognize me and mention the path which I had been following up to that time. On the third or the fourth visit, when I was alone with Maharaj he began to talk with me, and then he described the path I was following, and also the degree of my progress.

One day Maharaj was sitting quietly without talking. Suddenly all his clothes became wet. One or two days after this incident a letter was received from somewhere containing the information that some person while about to be drowned in the sea had been saved by meditating upon Maharaj.

Experiences of Mr. Shankar Malhar Sant, Nashik

I suffered many troubles in this worldly life and my mind became absolutely restless. I then visited many saints and mahatmas and received their blessings. The result was that I began to entertain a keen longing for spiritual knowledge and a firm faith in its efficacy. While I was in this state of mind somebody told me that Sri Gajanana Maharaj was coming to Nashik in a day or two, and that I should take his darshan and receive initiation from him. I was greatly delighted at this and I passed the two days in anxious eagerness. When he arrived I went for his darshan with my mind full of eager longing. He asked me several questions and conversed with me for some time.

At that time, Messrs. Bhave, Vaidya, Mahegaonkar and others were sitting near Maharaj. The conversation is briefly given below.

Myself: Please initiate me and make me blessed.

Maharaj: Who told you that I am a Maharaj?

Myself: I came to know about you about six or seven days ago. I became anxious to see you, and hence I have come now.

144

Maharaj: What works have you read?

Myself: I have read Jnaneshwari and a part of Dasabodh.

Maharaj: How long have you been staying at Nashik?

Myself: I have been staying here for the last seventeen or eighteen years.

Maharaj: Have you been initiated by any saint?

Myself: I received initiation from N., about thirty or thirty-five years ago. I have not as yet attained peace of mind. I am at present about eighty years old. I have no worldly ambition; still for maintaining myself and family I am even now writing petitions in the court.

Maharaj: Baba, I am like your son. I am not worthy to bless you. I might mislead you. I am myself a student still, and not an adept.

Mr. Bhave then said to me, "Baba, Sri Gajanana Maharaj is a Kayastha by caste. Have you thought about this?"

I laughed at this and said that a Brahmanishtha (one who has become one with Brahman, the Supreme Self) has really no caste.

Maharaj: How do you know that I am a Brahmanishtha?

Myself: As soon as I bowed down at your feet I felt a great calmness, and felt as if I was meeting a long-lost acquaintance. I therefore firmly believe that you can benefit me.

Maharaj: I am not a saint who has realized the Self. I have got certain experiences by the practice of meditation and japa. I shall give you certain directions through my guru's grace, which you should follow and see what happens. If you are not benefited, you may leave them aside.

Maharaj then asked me to come to him on a Thursday. I went there and placed a garland of flowers on the portrait of Maharaj's guru and distributed sweetmeats as prasad. Maharaj then had me sit down, placed his hand on my head, and told me to repeat the japa of Soham. I immediately went into a trancelike state in which the japa of Soham was going on. For forty minutes I did not return to ordinary consciousness and experienced a great joy. Maharaj told me to carry on the practice. I have been doing it since then.

145

Experiences of Mr. S. T. Saygaonkar, Nashik

I reside opposite the house in which Maharaj resides and I have been seeing him for the last so many years. But up to this time I had not understood that there was anything special in him, nor had I made any effort to understand it. A person generally forms an estimate of the personality of others in this world by placing reliance upon his own intellectual capacity. But the powers of our intellect are very limited, and in the search for truth, when the cloud of ignorance rolls away from one's intellect, the light of real truth shines forth. I understood the truth of the above when I came into contact with him only for a few days, and I got certain experiences which are narrated below.

About a year before this time I had begun to take a very keen interest in spiritual things. I had tried to acquire knowledge of the subject from various books, and had made various self-directed efforts to get realization in actual experience by trying to put into practice the knowledge gained from books. But having no idea whether my efforts were in the right direction or not, my mind was often full of doubts and uneasy. From this bookish knowledge, I could not be sure on what particular step on the spiritual path I was standing.

About a month and a half ago, while my mind was in a very uneasy state owing to worldly troubles, Sri Gajanana Maharaj sent someone to call me to see him in connection with some photo work. I went to him, saluted him and sat near him. He handed over to me the negative of a photo and asked me to supply him with some copies of the same. Then he began a casual talk with me in his usual witty manner. I too, made some funny remarks and diverted the current of the conversation to spiritual topics which had become dear to me.

Once while I was sitting in meditation I heard words to the effect that a Bengali saint would call me to his house and meet me there. This happened about ten or twelve days before I got this seemingly accidental call from Sri Gajanana Maharaj.

As the conversation turned on spiritual topics, Maharaj while sitting on his bedstead asked me to read out to him some papers. They contained an account of the spiritual experience of a Bengali and of his having attained the everlasting bliss of nirvikalpa samadhi by coming in contact with Sri Gajanana Maharaj.

The message which I had received in meditation, and the practical realization of it in my being called by Maharaj and given his darshan, made me think that there was something wonderful in this individual about whom I had no conception before. And with the idea that I should get some spiritual experience as a mumukshu, and that thus my life should be made worth living, I made an humble supplication at the feet of Maharaj and he, too, understanding my keen desire, gave me an assurance that he would confer his grace upon me and asked me to meet him again. Maharaj then went to Mumbai. Eight days later I was again called in connection with the photo, and again I proffered my urgent request.

For about two or three days after that, I daily went to him and passed about fifteen to twenty minutes near him. At that time he was suffering from fever and was lying down. However, in our conversation on spiritual topics he told me that he would confer his grace upon me after he would be cured of his illness. I then began to visit him daily for making inquiries regarding his health. I used to sit near him, and the conversation was sometimes light and witty, and at other times on spiritual topics. I sometimes used to read out to him portions from newspapers, throwing light on these topics. I was also minutely marking everything, and realized that some inscrutable divine power was repeatedly bringing before me thoughts, words or deeds in consonance with the workings of my heart.

Some days later he wrote with his own hand some portions of the work of Swami Vivekananda, *Karma Yoga*, which work I was reading every day, and asked me to read them. The wonder of it was that these were the very portions which I had read the previous night before going to sleep. Later on I felt that during his conversation he had, as it were, described with his own mouth my daily actions. My faith in him began to increase day by day, and later on I got very unusual experiences owing to which my faith in him got firmly fixed.

One day in the morning at about nine a.m., Maharaj and myself were sitting together after having drunk tea. I smelled a delightful fragrance pervading the atmosphere. It struck me as if it proceeded from a place where someone was performing worship. I was about to ask about it, but dropped the idea, thinking that somebody must be performing worship in the house. While these ideas were passing in my mind, I thought that Maharaj was closely looking at something with concentrated attention. He told me that I should bring a garland of flowers the next day, and that he would communicate to me something more according to the order of his sadguru.

The next day was the first day of the month of Margashirsha. I bathed in the morning and having taken with me a garland of flowers, went for Maharaj's darshan. As directed, I placed the garland on the photo of Sri Narayana Saraswati and took my seat in front of Maharaj. He was sitting in front of me and was describing the experiences of his previous disciples. The same fragrant smell which I had experienced on the day before occurred, and the whole atmosphere in the room became full of it and felt purified.

I began to feel a sensation resembling a trance stealing upon me. Maharaj continued talking, and when he found that my attention in listening had become less, he told me to repeat the mantra Soham in my mind and fixed his gaze on my eyes. My mind was becoming calmer and calmer, and I felt that it was being submerged under the waves of extreme joy. I felt that I was going down and down somewhere, and a sense of complete forgetfulness of the external world was increasing. There appeared to be dense darkness everywhere, only the beating of my heart continued. In this state I felt some power moving up towards the brain through the spinal cord at the back, and a sensation like that of heat from inside was experienced at the center between the eye-brows.

Something seemed to fall down in a line from the center of the brain upon the heart, and the former darkness then gave place to a faint light and I had the darshan of my favorite deity. Slowly the face of the deity began to change and assume the features of my master sitting in front of me. All my doubts dissolved away, my mind became assured, and my heart became full of joy.

I was then about to place my head on the feet of my master when he lightly touched my head and told me to come back to my original state. I opened my eyes and found Maharaj looking fixedly at me. His face appeared to be changing till it looked like his original face. This being a novel experience in my life, I found that it gave me extreme delight. I cannot say how long I was in this state.

Maharaj, who was still sitting in front of me, was describing the experiences of some of his disciples, but I could hear only in a sort of indistinct and hazy manner. An extremely good fragrance was pervading everywhere, and some vague and indistinct forms of deities appeared to pass before my sight.

Later on when I used daily to repeat the japa of Soham, my mind got into a state of absorption and I was convinced that the only true and eternal thing, which I had been seeking so long, was extremely close to me, and that I had been groping in darkness for it owing to ignorance. When my heart was enlightened by the light of knowledge through the grace of my master, many things which had appeared mysterious became completely clear. I got the experience of nirvikalpa samadhi and the darshan of the deity of my heart's desire and of the place of that deity, which was familiar to me. All my misgivings and doubts disappeared in this manner.

Soham.

Experiences of Mr. Vishwanath Gopal Vaidya of Nashik

For the last five years since the darshan of my master, Sri Gaja-nana Maharaj, and the bestowal of his grace upon me, I am becoming engrossed in meditation and am almost swimming continuously in an ocean of joy.

On Dattatreya Jayanti day, Sunday the 15th of December 1929, I had the following dream: I saw that I was in the house of my son-in-law, Mr. Narayan Gangadhar Sahasrabuddhe. While I was sitting in the front hall, a lame and decrepit person carried on the back of another came there with ten or twelve other persons, got down and went crawling into the inner hall of the house and took his seat there. All persons then bowed to this person. Observing this I also went there and bowed to him. I thought that he might be a saint. Then I returned to the front hall. Some time later the lame person (saint) came from the inner hall to the front hall near me and asked me, "When did you come from Nashik?" I replied that I came on the day before. He said, "Come to my house, we shall talk there." He then went away with some persons, being carried on the back of another person. Some persons remained behind to accompany me, with whom I went to the saint's house, which was situated on a hill beyond the Saraswati river. I went and sat down in a room. Then the lame saint came there and asked me about all the events at Nashik. I told him that a sacrifice [yajna] was being performed at Nashik and many shastris had assembled there. The saint then took a piece of paper, wrote upon it Rupees Seven and gave the paper to me. I saw what was written upon it, then looked into my pocket but saw that I had not got seven rupees. The saint said that it did not matter, but that I should not forget to give that amount when the time would come. I then started from that place after having bowed to him again. Here the dream ended. After I awoke I wrote down the dream in my diary.

Four years later I found the dream realized. How this happened will be described in its proper place and sequence.

In February of 1933, a Mr. Saswadkar started one day by the railway train to go to Pune. Mr. Jayarambhau Karmarkar, proprietor of the Samartha Press of Nashik, who is residing in my house, also started by the same train to go to Sajjangad, the place where there is the samadhi of the great saint Ramdas. The two gentlemen happened to meet in the train. During their conversation Mr. Saswadkar casually remarked that a great saint was staying in Nashik for the last eight or ten years, and that it was a wonder that the people of Nashik did not know him, nor had they any idea of his greatness. Mr. Karmarkar asked him about the saint's name, original place of residence and his present address. But Mr. Saswadkar instead of giving the information merely remarked that everything would be known in the near future.

Mr. Karmarkar, who is a friend of mine and who is my neighbor, narrated this talk to me when he returned to Nashik. I then made inquiries in Nashik but I could not trace the whereabouts of the saint. I then intended to go to Niphad and see Mr. Saswadkar, but owing to some unavoidable reasons I had to postpone my plan till the month of May.

I then went to Niphad on Sunday, May 2, 1933, and introduced myself to Mr. Saswadkar and asked him information about the saint at Nashik. Mr. Saswadkar was only too glad to give me the information. Not only this, but he also showed me some letters written to this saint by some of his disciples containing a description of their spiritual experiences after they had received initiation from this saint, Sri Gajanana Maharaj. I was simply wonderstruck after reading the experiences described in those letters.

After returning from Niphad on Wednesday, May 3, 1933, I went on May 4 to Sri Gajanana Maharaj, and having given him information regarding myself had a frank talk with him for some time and then I returned home. Even in the short time that I was in his company, I could see his child-like innocence, his absolute want of egotism, his even-mindedness and his extremely keen desire to uplift other human souls. I found that he was as if absolutely unconscious of ego, and I was greatly delighted to see this. Then I every day used to go to him for darshan.

Six or seven days later, when I had come for his darshan he lighted a cigarette and began to smoke it. All along it was burning in a flame, which is generally not the case. It also emitted a fragrant smell like that of an attar. I was greatly surprised at this. Maharaj then said, "I shall show you the unextinguishable flame of the Self, just as I have shown this flame to you. Come to me tomorrow in the morning."

Accordingly on the next day in the morning I went to him. He told me the mantra Soham and asked me to repeat it and also explained to me how to practice. I accordingly started practicing for half an hour in the morning and in the evening. Two days later Maharaj remarked to me that I was committing mistakes in my practice. He explained to me my mistakes. Within a week after that I got the following experience.

In my meditation I saw a flame which began to enlarge and in the flame I saw the extremely shining form of Sri Krishna. When I mentioned this fact to Maharaj, he appeared to be glad and asked me to continue the practice. Then every day at the time of meditation I saw the flame and in the flame the shining forms of various deities. When this had continued for some time, Maharaj stopped it.

Some days later Maharaj went to Niphad to visit Mr. Saswadkar, and I followed him there two or three days afterwards. One night when all the other people were asleep, Maharaj said to me that he would take me into the nirguna state (where there are no forms and attributes), and placed his hand on my head. Instantaneously I began to hear the sound of Soham loudly in my ears. Then he asked me to repeat the japa of Soham while lying down. I did so and in the state of half consciousness and half sleep I began to hear the loud sound of Soham. I described this in the morning to Maharaj. He said, "You will get the darshan of the Supreme Self by going into the Brahmarandhra (the center of the brain)."

A few days before Maharaj went to Niphad he asked me for money. I had with me a five rupee note, which I handed over to him. Upon this he said, "Now only two rupees are due from you." At that time I did not understand the meaning and context of what he said.

On the next Guru Purnima day, although Maharaj was not at Nashik I went to his house, garlanded his photo and put two rupees as dakshina before it. A few days later while I was reclining on a chair and had shut my eyes, I suddenly remembered the dream which I had in the December of 1929. The saint whom I saw in the dream was lame just as Maharaj is lame. The saint had written Seven Rupees on a piece of paper. When Maharaj asked for money and I gave five rupees, he had remarked that two rupees had remained. Then I had put two rupees before his photo on the Guru Purnima day. All these things tallied with the dream which I had been favored with four years before, foretelling that I would meet Sri Gajanana Maharaj. I looked upon it as nothing less than the grace of Sri Dattatreya, and was greatly delighted. I was also greatly amused to see this divine arrangement of things. When I went to Maharaj in the afternoon, I told him the whole thing regarding the dream and how the account of seven rupees tallied. He merely smiled at this.

On August 14, 1934, when I had gone to Maharaj in the morning, he said, "What sort of trouble is going on at Bombay [Mumbai]?" People in his house told me that he was talking like this since the previous night. I asked Maharaj whether any letter, etc., had been received, to which he replied, "Where is the necessity of a letter? Can we not see ourselves?" While he was saying this, a telegram from Mr. Nanasaheb Samartha was received from Bombay to the effect that his nephew Shankar was lying seriously ill, and requesting the immediate presence of Maharaj there. Maharaj proceeded immediately to Bombay and found that Mr. Samartha's nephew Shankar was seriously ill, suffering from meningitis and doctors had given up all hope. This nephew recovered from the illness through the grace of Maharaj. This incident shows that yogis can see what is going on in different places.

According to the orders of Maharaj, I practiced meditation for two years, half an hour in the morning and half an hour in the evening. Owing to this, now as soon as I shut my eyes I can see light at any time and at any place. My mind becomes so engrossed that I become unconscious regarding my surroundings and I forget all mundane matters. If a person has to leave his mortal coil while he is in this state, he again becomes a yogi in the next birth, as the Gita says.

Experiences of Mr. Balkrishna Mahadeo Gadkari

I first got the darshan of Sri Gajanana Maharaj in the month of May, 1929. After I had the good fortune of being in his company for four or five days, he had me sit near him and placed the right palm of his hand on my head. He told me to shut my eyes and fix my mind inside on the movements of breath, and he favored me with the japa of Soham. When I had repeated the japa of Soham for five minutes, he in his great mercy manifested to me a strong light and said, "This is the light of your own Self. By means of the Soham japa you will be able to see it constantly."

Experiences of Mr. K. K. Pradhan

I had been living at Nashik for five years or so, but it was not till February of 1937 that I heard about Mr. Gajanan Murlidhar Gupte, alias Sri Gajanana Maharaj of Nawa Darwaja, Nashik.

It was in the course of some talk with some visitors to my place. Our conversation drifted from everyday casual talk towards the intricacy of adhyatma (the Self). Finding me interested in the subject, especially in acquiring some insight into the spiritual world, one of the visitors just by way of information referred to the name of Gajanana Murlidhar Gupte. His words about him were very cautiously worded, with the utmost care to eliminate exaggeration either way. The description was enough to arouse curiosity in any heart. I immediately made an appointment with my visitor friend to come to me at a particular hour on a particular day and take me to the so-called saint.

After the visitor left, my mind had quite a riot of thoughts, ideas, and imagination. I thought to myself "If he is really a saint as said, how is it that for the last five years that I am here in Nashik I did not hear anything about him? Again I have never heard of a real saint belonging to Kayastha Prabhu Community except Sri Rama Maruti Maharaj of

Kalyan whose fame to the effect is far and wide. His friends and disciples have published a book about his life. How is it that not even a single writing about this man ever came to my notice? Who can say the report is not an exaggeration of the man's qualities?" However my heart within me was almost jumping with curiosity to meet the saint at the appointed hour.

My mental inclinations from my early boyhood were towards implicitly believing in Divinity, construed by my imagination in whatever phenomena or deity. I read about various spiritual luminaries at a very young age and my passion for attaining some spiritual experience grew so strong that, when I was in the first year in college, I actually used to go to the Fergusson Hills at Pune and practice meditation. However, I felt that I was standing at the edge of two worlds, the outer and the inner, and it became imperative to bring about an adjustment between these two views. Anyway I could not do it, and I felt many times quite unable to attend to ordinary daily routine duties as efficiently as I should, nor could I concentrate properly on my studies. My friends had occasions to remark about my absent-mindedness. My career was about to suffer, and I left the pursuit of the divine knowledge halfway. A curtain was dropped by me on that aspect of the inner faculties as if with a vehemence and I became quite stolid and a practical everyday man.

I very well remember the day and the hour we went to meet the saint. Our way lay through lanes and by-lanes of Nashik City and we ultimately came to a low-roofed humble house at the corner of one of them, near the temple of Rama popularly known as Bayancha Rama. It had a small open area in front with an old-type well in the middle. The way to the saint's room was through a narrow corridor in the interior. I was half embarrassed, half afraid within myself. I took off my shoes at the door and went in to find a very emaciated and lean man with high cheek-bones and an intelligent expression on his face welcoming us there with folded hands and a winning smile. He was not old as I had assumed him to be, but rather a middle-aged man. The room was a spacious one with a bedstead in one corner covered by a bedspread and a mosquito curtain on its frame with red sewn borders. Some photos of unknown saints adorned the whitewashed walls. There was a gramophone machine on a stand in another corner. A few chairs and an humble but clean carpet spread on the ground were the only additional contents of the room.

He started his talk with humor. There was a tin of cigarettes near the man, who enjoyed a few from them during our talk which was about several everyday matters. We had tea there and returned homewards, I having found nothing unusual in the person. I said to myself, "Is this man a saint? As for me I do not find any saintliness about him. I can say, he is a loving and good man—good to have as a friend." I very carefully hid my opinion about the man from my visitor friend so as not to wound any feeling of reverence fostered by him about the person. To his queries I replied only half-heartedly and returned home with a feeling of having wasted time and trouble. I almost forgot the incident of my visit by the time I was in my house.

But somewhere deep within my subconscious mind remained the memory of the man. I felt, God knows how, an inclination to practice a little meditation after my return. I sat for dhyana almost without my will and lo! intense joy was suddenly felt within my heart. I felt I was as if peeping into a temple to view the steady flame of the oil lamp before the deity. Who caused this all? How is it that I did not get the joy before, and who is HE, the great one, that caused it to arise in me this evening? The reply to all these queries...?

From that day I feel I have launched my boat on a steady course; steadily but surely I feel I am advancing on the path of spirituality and a master hand is guiding my spiritual destiny. Whenever I find leisure I hasten to my master, sit in his aura, get the divine thrills and come home. Can I now say my acquaintance with him has ripened? With such a really great soul, I now find acquaintance is too poor a word to use. No, it is not intimacy, not friendship. It is a merging into experience of him in his fullness.

He who holds that spiritual beauty within must have its expression in polished outward actions and behavior. He many times says, "Oh, we Haridasis [Servants of God] stand at the confluence of three rivers: Beauty, Truth and Joy. I actually feel within like that. Nay, I have caught hold of the origin of these three aspects of the all-pervading One. Oh, I have become that One."

And the nectar-like words from his lips have a divine effect upon those around who understand him. His manners are naturally very sweet, so nobody who visits him can expect to meet with discourtesy; rather he will be very hospitably received with scrupulous care to make him feel that he is enjoying an extraordinary happy company.

The secret of this saint's greatness appears to be in carefully hiding his inner towering greatness. His humility surpasses all his other virtues and has given him a childlike temperament. He listens with rapt attention equally to learned discourses on adhyatma and the everyday gabble about the minor details of living. He calls himself a student in spiritual matters, while those who call themselves masters cannot with his tremendously quick flash actually arouse the inner adhyatmic energy of their visitors as this humble-looking individual does. Verily God on earth is here represented by his humble messenger Sri Gajanana Maharaj of Nashik, the unrivalled yogi.

Experiences of Mr. Kurdukar, Vaidya

In April, 1940 the following conversation took place when I went for the darshana of Maharaj.

Maharaj: What is your name and why have you come to see me?

Myself: My name is Krishnarao and my surname is Kurdukar. I am a Vaidya [Ayurvedic physician] and for the last seven or eight years I have been practicing as a Vaidya from altruistic as well as interested motives.

Maharaj: Who told you that I am a Maharaj?

Myself: Mr. Pundit first gave me information regarding you. I wanted to come to you for darshana but somehow or other I could not do so up to this time. I then met Madhukar Chitnis who also gave me information about you. I knew that Madhukar Chitnis was practicing yoga, and so I was greatly delighted at the information given by him. I thought that perhaps I, too, might be graced by you. With this idea I have come to you.

Maharaj: I am a poor cripple. You have practiced yoga for a long time and have made great progress. I, therefore, consider myself as lucky in having obtained your darshana. Well, how long are you going to stay at Nashik?

Myself: I am here for two days more. I shall then go to Sangamner. I have private dispensaries at Nashik and Sangamner. I visit Nashik every fortnight or so. I shall give you in writing a brief account of my life from my childhood.

Maharaj then asked me to give him a short sketch of my previous practice of yoga. I told him what practices in Hatha Yoga had been done by me, and how later on after practice for three years I had to quit it owing to a feeling of fear which was generated at the time of practice, and how I had gone to various saints with the hope that they would guide me further and how ultimately I opened dispensaries at Nashik and Sangamner. I then bowed to the feet of Maharaj and left his house.

On the third day after that I had been to see some people staying in the locality near Maharaj's house and after the visits were over I had gone a pretty long distance on the side opposite to Maharaj's house. At that time I had no idea of going to Maharaj or of asking him about yoga, but somehow or other my feet began as it were to be drawn back, and for two or three minutes I went backwards. Then an idea struck me that I should go for Maharaj's darshana. It was about 9:30 in the morning. I fell at his feet. He asked me, "Why have you come?" I replied that I had gone there for his darshana.

Maharaj: All right. I suppose you have no particular object in seeing me.

Myself: Yes. I have a particular object in coming here. Since you have as it were forcibly dragged me here, there must be some purpose in it. Kindly fulfill that purpose.

Maharaj: I am neither a Baba nor a hatha-yogi. I have no power of knowing what is in your mind. I consider myself as fortunate in having your darshana. Please do not think that I am indulging in a bit of exaggeration.

Myself: I have tried various things and I am now absolutely tired. The restlessness of my mind, however, has not abated. I have left off the practice of yoga for the last so many years. It is in your hands to guide me further on the right path.

Maharaj: All right. I shall tell you through the grace of my guru.

Maharaj then asked me to sit in a particular posture. I sat in the siddha-padmasana posture. Maharaj then told me to repeat Soham. As soon as I did so, my mind instantaneously turned inwards and became absolutely calm. All the bad effects of my old practices of hatha yoga disappeared. [In the past, for three years Mr. Kurdukar engaged in very drastic hatha yoga disciplines until he weighed only 48 pounds and was living on nothing but one pint of water a day. *Editor's note.*] The breath which had been going astray, straightway entered the sushumna and reached the brahmarandhra. Since then I feel no trouble and am enjoying great joy.

Mr. Upadhye

Mr. Vithal Pandurang Upadhye, an attorney of Nashik, has been on terms of friendship with Maharaj for the last several years. Mr. Upadhye is a man of very peaceful temperament and is very social. He has a knack of explaining the principles of Vedanta in a simple and easy manner. He is also very fond of reading. About two or three years ago on the second day of Diwali in the evening, there were many persons sitting chit-chatting in the hall in the house of Mr. Saswadkar, who was then staying at Nashik. Maharaj was also there.

Mr. Upadhye said to Maharaj, "Maharaj, you make many people sit in meditation near you almost daily. Here is Mr. Baba Satpurkar who has a great desire to sit in meditation. Why do not you ask him to do so? He has been waiting for a long time hoping that you would grant this favor to him."

Maharaj thereupon said, "Vakil [Lawyer] Saheb, you also have made great progress in your previous birth, and even now you must be practicing yoga to some extent, because you have received grace from your guru. Notwithstanding all these facts, and although you have been in my company for so many days, have I ever asked you even casually to sit in meditation? I have never done so up to this time. But it appears that the opportunity has come today. Instead of asking me to make others sit in meditation, why do not you yourself sit before me?"

As soon as Maharaj said this, Mr. Upadhye suddenly got up and sat before Maharaj, and the wonderful thing was that he became completely absorbed in meditation with his eyes open. For nearly an hour and a half he had no consciousness of his body. People called out his name, then shook him and tried various other means of bringing him back to consciousness, but they were of no avail. His whole body had become stiff like a piece of wood. He regained consciousness after about an hour and a half. Immediately he drank two lotas of water, and lay down, reclining completely. He was still in a trancelike, dreamy state of joy. He did not speak for about twenty minutes. Maharaj also called out to him several times but he could not utter any words. He only made signs with his hand, asking Maharaj to stop for some time. After about fifteen minutes he got up. At that time Maharaj was sleeping.

People asked Mr. Upadhye regarding his experience and he gladly gave the following description: "In the beginning the tip of my tongue turned inwards and pressed itself on the uvula in the throat and there was a slight checking of the breath and my eyesight became drawn upward internally. I saw the Sudarshana chakra at the center between the eye-brows. It was whirling around and a light similar to that of fire-works or of electric lamps appeared. Then I saw flames near the navel region and felt that the whole of my body was burning. I tried to come upwards, but it was no use and I again went downwards. Then I began to feel very cool and then hot. I then came upwards, and as I proceeded upwards I began to feel cooler and cooler until I felt I was drinking nectar dropping down in drops from the uvula in the throat. Its taste was so sweet that I cannot describe it in words. It cannot be compared with any other taste. It has been written in works on Yoga Shastra that some yogis can drink this nectar. I got actual experience of this and hence I am extremely delighted."

While Mr. Upadhye was describing his experience, Maharaj had been sleeping. He got up and said to Mr. Upadhye, "Oh Vithal! Oh Pandurang! Let me also know what you saw, so that I, too, may share in the joy. One does not tell such experiences to others. Everyone has got this in himself and he can experience it in himself. Owing to merit acquired in previous births, if a disciple carries on the practice as instructed by his guru with firm faith and disinterestedness, he becomes fit for treading the path leading to the highest goal, although he may be leading a worldly life. He becomes submerged in joy within himself."

Then Mr. Upadhye again described his experience to Maharaj, and said, "Maharaj, if you had not slept, I would not have been able to regain consciousness soon." All the people then got up and went to the river Godavari for a walk.

The next day when Mr. Upadhye came to Maharaj, he said, "Maharaj, yesterday I reached home with great difficulty because waves of that joy were again and again overwhelming me and I was afraid that I might fall down." He then again described his experience of the previous day to some other people who were then sitting near Maharaj at the time. As Mr. Upadhye has read various works on Vedanta and has also thought a good deal over spiritual matters, he could describe his experiences graphically and in an understandable and easy manner.

Experiences of some other disciples

Shankar Keshav Fansalkar was a spiritual and moral person with a strong attraction to the path of devotion (bhakti). He was given a mantra by a yogi, but whenever he repeated the mantra he felt great fear, even terror. Therefore he went to Nashik and searched for Sri Gajanana Maharaj, to whom he revealed his dilemma. For some days Maharaj had him visit him and then gave him the Soham Mantra, explaining how to do japa and meditation with the mantra. All his fear left him. At first he saw some visions, but they stopped and after some months his mind became always engrossed and joy-filled in japa and meditation. He would tell people, "Sadguru Gajanana is compassion personified. He has shown me the right path."

Narayan Lakshman Samarth believed in spiritual attainment through karma yoga. He and his wife often went to have darshan of Maharaj in whom they had full trust and whom they loved as one of their own family. Mr. Samarth used to become engrossed in meditation, forgetting his physical state in the vastness of infinity.

CHAPTER FOUR

ATMA PRABHA
(LIGHT OF THE SELF)

Inspired Thoughts of Sri Gajanana Maharaj of Nashik, collected,
arranged and translated
by D. L. Nirokhekar, B.A., LL.B., M.B.E.

Edited by Swami Nirmalananda Giri for this Printing.

Preface

In the month of November 1943, Sri Gajanana Maharaj received a
letter from the secretary of the Sri Ramana Maharshi Jayanti Utsav
Committee of Matunga, Mumbai, inviting him to grace the occasion
by his presence or to send a message in case he could not be present
personally. Accordingly, a message was sent which was printed in the
pamphlet published by the Committee of the Utsav Celebrations. In
continuation of the thoughts contained in the message, Sri Gajanana
Maharaj expressed later on from time to time certain thoughts connected
with the subjects touched in the message. These thoughts were jotted
down at the time and later were collected, arranged and translated by
me into English. They are incorporated in Part One of this book.

In November 1945, a similar invitation was received by Sri Gajanana
Maharaj and at that time also a message was sent which was similarly
published in the pamphlet issued by the committee. In continuation
of the topics treated in the message, Sri Gajanana Maharaj gave expression to various thoughts regarding spiritual matters from time to time.

These thoughts were also jotted down at the time and later on collected, arranged and translated into English by me. This second series of thoughts forms the subject matter of Part Two of this book.

From his life it appears that Sri Gajanana Maharaj is a born Siddha. He has had no school or university education in the modern sense of the term. And yet he has a fund of intuitive knowledge which even the modern scholars in philosophy and religion rarely possess. Not being a man of science, it is not expressed in scientific language. It could not be. Nevertheless truth remains truth, even though it is expressed in ordinary language; and we are only concerned with truth, reality and the Spirit-Self–not its trappings.

The Maharaj speaks from his own experiences. He got those experiences through the grace of his guru, Sri Narayana Saraswati, who had told him to meditate on the Soham mantra. And as there can be no higher authority than Self-experience, his thoughts must command due respect.

The book is not a systematically written thesis. The Maharaj had expressed certain thoughts on different occasions, and they are collected in this book. Hence, the reader finds some repetitions. The Maharaj urges upon all his disciples the importance of following the method of meditation which he has practiced, and asks them to wait for the results which, he says, are sure to follow as day follows the night.

The quintessence of his teaching is the japa of the Soham mantra. The charm of the Soham mantra lies in its ease, simplicity, and naturalness, and hence his preference for it. Besides, it reminds the follower of the universal truth Aham Brahmasmi [I am Brahman] or Tattwamasi [Thou Art That], as Soham means "I am He."

It is very difficult for a rational man to believe that mere repetition of a mantra leads to Self-realization. But in spiritual matters reason sometimes does not help us much. There we have to depend upon other and higher faculties such as intuition, inspiration or insight. Science cannot account for the knowledge gained through them, and yet that knowledge is as exact and precise as scientific knowledge can be, if not more. Hence we must realize that there are some higher faculties in spiritually gifted men which can lead us into spiritual realms undreamt of by science. Some, at least, can peer into these higher regions and can guide others qualified to enter there.

These gifted men experience some things which ordinary mortals cannot even imagine. They read the past, the present and the future as an open book. If such extraordinary men can be found amongst us, how can we possibly deny their Self-experiences? And what better authority can be found beyond Self-experience which is not tainted by any possible error? Moreover, if such gifted men are absolutely disinterested and are working for the good of others, what possible motives can there be for them to lead their admirers astray? We are therefore compelled to rely upon their word of honor and trust them fully in what they say and do for us.

The Maharaj has proved his bonafides in this field beyond any shadow of doubt, and therefore his words based upon his own experiences must be relied on till the contrary is proved. The Maharaj says that he is always open to correction. He simply wishes that his simple method may be given a trial. There is absolutely no harm in it. His follower is not asked to renounce the world. His simple advice is, "Concentrate upon the mantra and the result will inevitably follow." What can be simpler than this method?

"The proof of the pudding lies in its eating," so says the proverb. Some of the Maharaja's followers have tasted this pudding by eating it. They confirm what he has said. I pray, therefore: let others try this for their benefit.

I myself found these thoughts very stimulating and useful. The general topic, of course, is the contemplation and japa of Soham, which mantra Sri Gajanana Maharaj gives to all his disciples. But these thoughts also explain how to overcome various difficulties which beset an aspirant on the spiritual path and also solve many doubts which assail the minds of sadhakas and also those of ordinary people who are desirous of getting

a knowledge of spiritual matters. Very deep and searching light has been thrown on various doubts and the answers given will be found to clear the fog surrounding spiritual matters and carry conviction to the hearts of at least believing persons. Non-believers also will find something useful in these thoughts, which will at least make them think.

With this hope and trust I have ventured to offer them in an English garb to all persons who are interested in spiritual topics.

D. L. Nirokhekar
Nashik City: 23rd May, 1945.

Since Then...

Sri Gajanana Maharaja left the mortal coil of his physical body and entered into mahasamadhi at Nashik on the 28th of September, 1946. An attempt was made to get this book printed and published during Sri Gajanana Maharaja's life-time, but owing to various difficulties of obtaining paper, etc., the attempt was not successful. His disciples and admirers keenly felt that his inspired and invaluable thoughts regarding the power and efficacy of the Soham mantra which he gave to all who came to him for initiation, should be published and made known to all aspirants of the spiritual path. This book, therefore, has been published now for the benefit of all souls who have a desire to be liberated from the troubles and tribulations of worldly existence and of entering into the everlasting peace of the Supreme Lord of the Universe.

D. L. Nirokhekar
Mumbai, 23rd October, 1948

THE DIVINE MESSAGE
OF
SRI GAJANANA MAHARAJ OF NASHIK

Part One

Soham

O my mind, be always repeating the japa of Soham.

Through faith in Soham external worship has been left behind.
The soul has been realized in the form of Soham. Through the
sound of Soham the guru has been beheld—that guru who saves
people by the principle of Soham.

Mad Broom

Sri Ramdas has said, "Oh mind, you yourself have accumulated sin
and merit in previous lives, and hence you have to endure the result-
ing good and evil in this life." Every creature has to endure the effects
of his sins and good actions done in previous lives, and there is no
escaping them.

Although I am continuously suffering from bodily ailments I enjoy
bliss in the contemplation of the Self [Atman]. The joy that I then experience is beyond description in words. The nature of every experience
is such. If you want to realize the sweetness of sugar or the bitterness of
quinine, you must taste it yourself. Any amount of description in words
will never make you realize it. Self-realization is similarly a matter of
experience, and firm faith alone will enable one to get that experience.

168

I am merely a broom in the durbar [court] of my sadguru. [This is why Sri Gajanana Maharaj called himself "Mad Broom."] To speak the truth, I am neither a learned man nor a man of philosophical knowledge. But owing to some merit acquired in previous lives I have been enveloped with the shawl of his grace by my sadguru, and I firmly believe that the thoughts I give expression to are not my own but the self-inspired thoughts of my guru who is, as it were, making me his mouthpiece and giving expression to them.

Saints appear to be different but are all one

Although saints appear to be different, they are all one as they have all become merged in the one Paramatman. Remembering this principle, I consider that all saints are as worthy of reverence as my own guru. Wherever my mind goes, I find my guru's form there. Such has been my angle of vision since my childhood, and owing to this even the idea of knowing "Who am I?" never arises in my mind.

My guru showered his grace upon me and gave me the ajapa japa mantra of Soham. This grace has deeply entered the innermost recesses of my heart. Most of my time is spent in the company of my friends and companions. I can only say that I am enjoying complete rest in the shade of my guru's grace.

I have above described in short the state of supreme peace that I have been enjoying. Naturally, all my actions are directed in creating as many sharers in this my state as possible. A description of my experiences is merely a part of these activities, and I try to see that others also get similar experiences. It would not, therefore, be out of place if I describe some of my experiences and other matters incidentally connected with them.

Every human being is ceaselessly trying to acquire happiness

Every human being is ceaselessly trying to acquire happiness or to increase his share in it and to avoid pain, or at least to lessen it as much as possible. But the experience is just the contrary. He is ever feeling the lack of something and is always plunged in misery. Things which are pleasant in the beginning end in sorrow, and misery is always on the increase and gets the upper hand. As man does not really understand wherein lies his happiness, he passes his days in the vain hope of securing happiness some time or other. Death catches him in its grip while his search for happiness is still going on. People do not profit by the example of their companions and fellow-beings, and so continue the same search and follow the same path. They, however, do not stop to think wherein lies real and lasting happiness. A man, if he thinks deeply about this, will come to know that all things in this world which appear pleasant are perishable and false like a mirage. They either cause pain or increase the pain which is already there. No one, however, acquires this insight. On the contrary, everyone is entangled more and more in this snare of misery and finds it difficult to see a way out of the maze.

It is therefore necessary that some royal road should be pointed out so that people going by that path might root out this unending sorrow and pain and reach the destination where there is everlasting peace and happiness. I am putting before the world my experiences in order that people might find an easy, short and sure way of reaching this goal of everlasting happiness. When you get experience for yourself, you will be sure that you are on the right path. You will yourself enjoy full, complete and everlasting happiness and also lead other forlorn and miserable fellow-beings to the same path. It is the grace of my guru that prompts me to show this easy and royal road to the people who are engaged in worldly pursuits.

A simple and royal road to real happiness and bliss

There is a simple and royal road to obtain real happiness and bliss, a road which does not require the abandoning of worldly life and of our usual worldly activities. This path is known as Dhyana Yoga or Raja Yoga or Karma Marga.

If you follow this path you are sure to reach the goal. The series of difficulties which a person has to undergo in this worldly life in due course awakens a desire in him to find out this path leading to unchanging and everlasting happiness. He then tries his utmost to discover this path, but he is almost always groping in the dark. The main object in writing this is to shed light in this darkness, and to illumine the path for the sake of these struggling human souls.

The goal of human life and steps to attain it

To thoroughly understand the "I," to seek for It and to catch hold of It, is the goal of this path. For a human being, whether man or woman, this is not an easy task. A keen desire to find out this "I," a firm determination to carry on the search for It and great perseverance in sticking to this pursuit: these are the steps which an aspirant has to ascend if he wants to reach the goal. Once you reach the high pinnacle you can sit and cast a glance on the panorama of worldly existence spreading out below you. A person who feels this urge to find out the "I" and thus to enjoy this unrivalled empire of complete and unchanging bliss, is known as a mumukshu [a seeker after liberation–moksha]. To complete this search and to be in the enjoyment of this everlasting happiness is known as obtaining moksha. The path which leads to this moksha is known as yoga. This yoga is merely a means leading to the end. There are different paths leading to moksha which are the different yogas and are known by different names. But the paths other than the one described here are difficult to follow.

Things necessary to find out the "I"

To find out the "I," the following things are necessary. First, a person must obtain the grace of a sadguru. Without giving the least scope to doubts and misgivings he must have firm, unswerving faith. Then he will be able to see clearly the path before him. This is known as Anugraha. When this Anugraha is obtained, he must carry on the japa of the mantra. This mantra is Soham, which is the answer to the question "Who am I?" The meaning of the mantra is: "I am He," "I am God." The sadhaka must carry on the japa with firm faith.

The continuous repetition and meditation of this mantra, Soham, is known as abhyasa (practice). This japa will not interfere with any of your worldly duties. As the contemplation proceeds, the broom of Soham will sweep off the dirt of the innumerable desires entertained through the course of previous lives from the heart, and the heart will then become pure. Owing to this, a sense of detachment will grow and the mind will be entirely free from desires. As soon as you reach this stage, you will be immersed in the bliss of the Self. Then you will reach the summit and attain your goal.

Supposing all these things happen: you try to keep your mind pure and by continuous contemplation a feeling of detachment grows up in your mind. Still the question remains whether you, the sadhaka, can be said to have progressed. You can get a very satisfactory answer to this question.

To understand this clearly, let us take the very familiar instance of university and other examinations. There is a fixed curriculum and the question paper is the same for all candidates. We find thousands of students appearing for these examinations. All these students have completed their studies and have answered the question papers. Then why should there be the necessity of looking to the results of these examinations? All the candidates do not pass. Not only that, but several of them have to appear again and again and continue the same studies till their efforts are crowned with success. This is a matter of common experience. We see that the various candidates get marks according to their preparation and that many get failed and have to appear again. The same analogy holds good in the case of spiritual matters. Every aspirant must, with perseverance and firm faith, carry on the abhyasa (practice) until he becomes fit to be the recipient of the final experience. His progress will depend upon his practice in this life. But it goes without saying that he is sure to attain the goal sooner or later.

The next question is, "How far has the sadhaka progressed and has his aptitude for getting the ultimate experience increased or not?" There is a very easy method to find out the answer to this question. Just look back retrospectively. Consider what was the tendency of your thoughts before you began your practice, what were your defects and what were your merits then, and observe the tendency of your thoughts now. See whether your good qualities have increased and your defects have become less. If you observe these things minutely you will get an answer to the above question.

The following are some of the characteristics that accompany the stage of the realization of the final experience. Desire, aversion, attachment and fondness for sensual enjoyments are conspicuously absent. A feeling of complete detachment reigns. The mind is, as it were, nullified. All disturbing waves of thought subside and the deep calm ocean of peace pervades everywhere. The real object of getting this human life is fulfilled. The real nature of "I" is thoroughly understood. The continuous practice of dhyana and japa leads to this stage. In that stage, the dhyata, dhyana and the dhyeya—the contemplator, contemplation and the object of contemplation—become one, and thereby the real object of devotion is fulfilled.

As the sadhaka progresses, he gets certain powers (siddhis) in the natural course. He, however, must not be attracted towards those powers, but must carry on the practice with firmness. If he allows himself to be attracted by them, he becomes their prey and various obstacles then arise in the path of his progress, which sometimes is altogether stopped.

Now there is another question: Whether there is any use of carrying on the japa of Soham if we have no faith in its efficacy.

Is there any use in carrying on the japa of Soham without faith in its efficacy?

The answer to that is that the repetition of the japa will always be useful, even though done without faith. It will never do you any harm. No doubt all the shastras and saints lay stress on faith, and hence the above statement will appear contrary to their teachings. However, if you go deep into the matter and observe minutely, you will easily be able to reconcile the two statements. Without having faith–although it may be in the subconscious mind–no one will be induced to practice the japa. As soon as a person begins to repeat the japa, faith is there accompanying the japa like its shadow. If we carefully follow this argument the seeming contradiction will cease to trouble us. A real mumukshu or devotee will never be deceived by the seeming contradiction, and will never allow his mind to be disturbed and turned away from the path.

Comparing Dhyana Yoga with other yogas

As an illustration of comparing Dhyana Yoga with other yogas, let us take the case of the nine-fold path of Bhakti (Devotion). In this all the organs [jnanendriyas and karmendriyas] have to be utilized in the service of God. In the repetition of mantra or the contemplation of God, however, only the mind is utilized. It is not necessary to make a comparison with all the other yogas. This illustration will convince anyone why Dhyana Yoga is by far the easiest. In the Yoga Sutras we find: "Its japa and fixing one's attention on its meaning." Patanjali makes clear the method to be followed. Once you get accustomed to the continuous repetition of the Soham mantra, ajapa japa will necessarily follow. This japa of the mantra is the sadhana (means) and ajapa japa is the goal to be reached.

The aim of all yogas is the realization of the Godhead. The state is known by various names such as Sayujyata, Soham, Aham Brahmasmi, or Sakshatkar. To reach this goal, persevering effort, complete devotedness, concentration and a capacity to persevere are necessary. If a sadhaka carries on practice in the manner mentioned above, he is sure to reach the goal of Self-realization sooner or later, according to the merit acquired by him in previous lives. If a sadhaka does not carry on the practice for a sufficiently long time with firm faith, but leaves it in the middle, being tired of waiting, he will never attain Self-realization.

The sadhaka alone, who has gained this aptitude for spiritual knowledge in his previous life, will develop a liking for this practice leading to oneness with Brahman, and he alone will ultimately enjoy everlasting bliss. All dross is sure to be swept away from the heart of such a sadhaka by the constant japa of Soham. If the seed of Soham is sown in such a field, it is sure to sprout into a beautiful tree which will be laden with the fruit of the bliss of Self-realization. Such sadhakas will be enjoying unchanging bliss and will very easily cross the river of worldly existence. When a sadhaka reaches this stage he can very easily control his mind, intellect and ahamkar. The power generated by the constant repetition of the Soham mantra is sure to lead to the complete deliverance of the sadhaka.

Why should not the method of scientific experiments be followed?

Modern rationalists say, "The present is the age of experiments. We shall put our faith only in those things which will be proved by experiments. In schools and colleges at present every day experiments are made by teachers and professors, and students are also coached in making them. The age of blind faith is gone. There is a method in making these scientific experiments. Why should not the same method be followed in the spiritual field?"

The following reply may be given to this sort of reasoning.

There were saints in the past, there are saints at present and there will be saints in the future. No saint in the past made such experiments. No saint at present makes them and no saint in the future will make them. There is a world of difference between material sciences and spiritual matters. The region of spiritual matters lies beyond mind, intellect and ahamkar (egoism). Owing to this, no saint can demonstrate by actual experiments matters pertaining to the spirit as modern scientists do in the case of matter. Similarly, saints do not get these experiments performed by others.

There has been no instance in history of such experiments being performed by any saint. Cast a glance at past history. Take the case of great saints like Sri Jnaneshwar, Tukaram, Ekanath, Janardhan Swami,

Matsyendranath and others. They had many disciples. But the select few who were found to have a special aptitude alone reached perfection and became famous in the world and carried on the tradition in their turn by making disciples of their own. Why should these great saints do so? Why did they not establish universities for conferring the Degree of "Saint" and open coaching classes in which experiments were performed and ocular demonstrations were made? Answers to all such questions can be had from illustrations with which we are all familiar.

At present many examinations are held every year. We also read about the results of these examinations. Many candidates appear for these examinations. The results show that some of them have passed while others have failed and have to prepare themselves again. Only one or two of those that have passed get scholarships or prizes. All candidates who have passed did not get an equal number of marks. Their marks differ and they get their rank according to the number of marks secured by them. This shows that scholarships or prizes are not given to all, but only to the select few. That is because they alone are found deserving.

When we clearly see such examples in the world, to raise such questions on the strength of argumentative powers is nothing but a waste of time and energy. It only shows that these people who do so are not really desirous to ascertain the truth, but only want to carry on discussions and to indulge in intellectual subtleties. If these rationalists would only think sincerely on the matter, they would easily get answers to such questions. I am neither a shastri nor a pandit, nor a modern educated man with university degrees. I have given answers to such questions in my humble way. I leave it to those rationalists to see whether they fit in or not.

My own experiments

My guru has ordered me to describe my own experiences in these matters in order that various doubts which assail the minds of people may be dispelled and the secret of these matters be easily grasped by them. I shall therefore describe how I pray to God, how I was favored by the grace of my guru and the actual experiences which I have got through his grace. Please ponder upon them sincerely, and with an open and independent mind choose things of which you approve, bring them into practice, obtain the knowledge of the real nature of the Self, become immersed in the bliss of the Self and be favorites of fortune.

I think that I must have made preparations in my previous life and that I must have been favored with the grace of the guru. I must also have carried on the practice of yoga. To these things the little practice that I did in this life was added. In this life I put firm faith in the words of my guru and considered that my guru's words were more valuable than all the shastras put together. By constant practice this firm faith reached its climax.

I firmly believe that I never did anything with my will power. I did all actions as naturally as a child. Owing to this attitude of my mind, my guru became pleased with me and showered his grace upon me. He blessed me by giving me the mantra of Soham. This mantra is the inner, subtle sound produced by the incoming and outgoing breaths. Everyone is breathing and producing this sound, but no one is conscious of it. Hence no one practices this japa. But if anyone carries on the practice by fixing his attention upon this japa, he will be sure to obtain its fruit. After being graced by my guru I carried on the japa with perseverance and firm faith, and later this practice became my nature. Ordinarily I pass most of my time in the company of my friends, enjoying it as innocently and joyously as a child.

Sometimes my friends say to me, "Maharaj, you are now more than fifty years old; why do you act as a child? Have some gravity and serious-ness." At this I do nothing but laugh. When I look to this lila (sportive working) of God, I am impelled to say, "Oh God, you are not seen by my physical eye. I cannot even conceive about you in my mind." Although such is the real case, some people say: "Gajanana Maharaj is a great yogi. He has great will power. He is a saint, he is an adept. He mixes with all. He becomes small in the company of the small and great in the company of the great, poor in the company of the poor and rich in the company of the rich. In fact he considers himself as one with all. Notwithstanding all this, he has no feeling of caste or relationship and no sense of honor or dishonor."

Some people with devotion in their hearts come to me and persist in asking me to be their guru and favor them with my grace. They later on tell me that they had sakshatkar (realization). I listen to all these things and also observe them. Oh God, all these things come to pass through your grace alone. There is not the slightest doubt about this. You yourself gave me the mantra of Soham. I give them the same mantra. Through the power of this mantra you shower your grace upon them and bless them with real knowledge. I am only sorry that you have all along kept me an ignoramus. I, however, have determined to serve my guru to the end of my life, having fixed my firm faith in him. If you wish, keep me the same sort of ignoramus in all my future lives also. But I only pray to you to save all those who put their faith in the mantra of Soham, each according to his aptitude. According to your will the cycle of worldly existence will be carried on. Only let me never be separated from your feet.

My brothers and sisters, if you also carry on the practice with firm faith and assiduity, you too will get experience in a greater or lesser degree. From amongst all who thus try, only those whose practice reaches perfection will get Self-realization. Faith, perseverance and continuous effort lead to success and realization of the Self. If your efforts are weak, or if you abandon the practice in the middle and ask why you do not get experiences which others get, it will be a senseless question not deserving any answer. "There is no firm conviction and the mind is wandering everywhere." If such is the state, abhyasa (practice) will be useless and will be of no avail. Hence you must have firm faith and realize your oneness with Brahman through the power of the mantra.

Different kinds of "I," their extent and mutual relation

Let us now consider the different kinds of "I," their extent and their mutual relation. The word "I" is used in two senses. The first is "mind," and the second is that principle or element inside our bodies which is very subtle, which is all-pervading and which is the seer and knower of all things. This means that in worldly parlance it is used in the sense of the vital principle of Brahman. That ever-present witness inside who knows both these kinds of minds and who himself is beyond all sense perception, is the real "I."

As described above, the "I" is of two kinds. That "I" which is devoid of ahamkar feels that it pervades everywhere. It knows no distinction between a learned man and a dunce. It is always immersed in joy. While doing worldly actions, although the actions are correctly and methodically done, it all along is enjoying atmic bliss. In order to attain this attitude it is necessary that the principle of Self-realization or renunciation must be firmly and thoroughly assimilated. This does not mean that actions are to be abandoned. Only the desire of obtaining the fruit of those actions is to be renounced. All actions must be done quite naturally.

A person should always try to read his mind and see how far this tendency of renunciation has developed. If he finds that while doing various actions his mind does not cast any glance towards the good or bad result of those actions, but actions are done solely from a sense of duty, he should be sure that he is progressing and rendering himself more and more fit. In the Gita the word tyaga (renunciation) has been used in this very sense. If the letters in the word Gita are reversed we get tagi, which is the same as tyagi.

A mumukshu is terribly afraid of this panorama of worldly existence and, not being able to know who he really is, becomes full of bewilderment and misery. Then Soham is shown to him. His bewilderment disappears, he begins to enjoy constant and everlasting peace and ultimately obtains moksha.

If a sadhaka has recourse to Vedanta or the other different kinds of yoga, he gets confused. The Dhyana Yoga of the Nath Pantha which has been handed down from Matsyendranath acts like a light which clearly shows the right path. I say this from my own experience. As the sadhaka has to repeat the japa and also to meditate, this path is known as Dhyana Yoga. With firm faith, having turned back the course of thoughts from the outward world to inside himself, a sadhaka has to carry on the japa and meditation for a long time. As he progresses, he gradually reaches perfection and realizes that his own soul has been his sadguru. This stage is known as oneness of jiva (the individual soul) and Shiva (the Supreme Soul). It is also called sakshatkara. A sadhaka then naturally enjoys the bliss of the Self and becomes devoid of desire for anything else. This path is also known as Dhyana Yoga or Karma Marga, because a sadhaka gets sakshatkar after progressing through many steps. He also attains complete knowledge, hence it is called Jnana Yoga. I therefore again and again say that people should have recourse to this simple path of self-deliverance.

How to act in worldly life to aid spiritual progress

Now let us see how a man should act in worldly life so that he may progress spiritually while leading a life of the world. It must be admitted that it is very difficult for an ordinary person to leave the worldly life. He thinks that there is a great responsibility upon him in this world. He is always putting forward excuses such as that he has a large family and that he alone is its supporter; he has, therefore, no time for the present to devote to spiritual matters; he will see about them later on when his responsibilities become less. To him I will say, "My good friend, do not leave your family. Continue to do your worldly duties as you are doing now. Only begin the practice of Dhyana Yoga and carry it on and stick to it with perseverance. You can thus kill two birds with one stone. You will be able to lead a worthy worldly life and also to progress spiritually. Try it and you will be convinced of the truth of what is said above from your own experience."

Now let us see how this can be accomplished. No human being can ever escape from the necessity of doing actions. There are, however, two different ways of doing these actions. In the one, we do all actions with the desire of achieving some object as a consequence of those actions. If our object is fulfilled, we become happy and full of joy. If, on the contrary, we fail in achieving our object and are unsuccessful, we are cast down and we become full of sorrow. Thus we see that the real cause of our happiness or sorrow is not the actions themselves, but the object or motive behind them. If we then abandon the object and do not pay any attention at all to the consequences of our actions, but do them from a sense of duty only, we shall never fall into the clutches of sorrow and our peace of mind will never be disturbed. Actions done with the desire of achieving some object are known as sakama and those done merely from a sense of duty without any object in view are known as nishkama.

Now if we cast a glance at the worldly experiences of our own and of others, what do we see? Do we find that all our actions are successful and that our desires are in every case fulfilled? Do the actual results of our actions correspond to the expectations entertained in our mind regarding them? No. On the contrary, we find that in the majority of cases we are unsuccessful and have to swallow the bitter pill of disappointment. There are various obstacles which intervene and frustrate our desires. We sometimes overcome some expected obstacles and triumph over the difficulties. But almost always we succumb before unexpected obstacles and difficulties. In such circumstances we get confounded, and getting submerged in the slough of despondency are completely at a loss to know what do. We are sometimes quite tired with our life and wish that it were ended. Why is it so? It is because when we do actions with some object in view, all our attention is directed towards the object, and once that is frustrated the equanimity of the mind is entirely disturbed and we become a prey to sorrow and despondency.

If on the other hand we do actions merely from a sense of duty without paying any attention to the result, and taste the fruit of those actions quite naturally as it comes, we shall not be affected either by joy or sorrow and our peace of mind will never be disturbed. This is because vasana (desire) which is the root cause of all sorrow is nullified.

To do actions in this manner is known as Nishkama Karma Yoga. If a person follows this method while leading his life in the world he will surely attain Self-realization. Such a person need not renounce the world. Only he must follow this method with great perseverance and firm determination. He must only have the will to do so, and his efforts will surely be crowned with success. Let us take a few illustrations to make the above points clear.

Suppose I am a big official. I can misuse my power and give great trouble to others and humiliate them. I can also through the exercise of the same power reach the summit of material prosperity by benefiting myself in various ways. There cannot be two opinions regarding the reprehensible nature of my conduct. All people will condemn it. I can also make good use of my power and be of good service to many people. Suppose I take the opportunity afforded by the power vested in me and try to be useful to other people as far as I can, quite naturally and without any ulterior object of any benefit to myself. I therefore pay no heed to what people say about me, whether they praise me or censure me. I do these things from a sense of duty; I am not overjoyed if people praise me. I simply taste the natural fruit of my actions and my peace of mind is not disturbed. I might perhaps get involved in great troubles like Saint Damaji [who risked his life for the sake of others by distributing grain from the royal granaries to the people in the time of famine *Editor's note*]. In that case, I shall not allow my peace of mind to be disturbed, but bow to the will of God with due reverence and submission and calmly endure the result of my action.

Take another illustration. Suppose I am a merchant. In trade we cannot definitely say when and how much profit we shall get. Suppose fortune favors me and I get a huge profit which was not even dreamt of by me and I am, at a single bound, raised to the status of a millionaire from the position of a poor man. I could spend all this unexpected money in various items of luxury, licentiousness and dancing and music parties. But I, however, spend the money in opening hospitals, building dharmashalas, feeding the poor, improving agriculture and founding educational institutions. I thus am greatly useful to society. Yet suppose no one praises me. I am not garlanded in public meetings, my name does not appear in the newspapers and celebrated as that of a great generous donor. No one ever acknowledges his obligations to me. Still I do not feel sorry or get disappointed with the ingratitude of men. I feel that I unexpectedly got the huge profit and naturally spent it in doing these useful deeds. All this happened quite naturally at my hands. If such are my feelings, I can be said to follow the method of Nishkama Karma Yoga.

Take a third illustration. Suppose I am devoted to the study of medical science. I make various experiments and discover remedies for various diseases. I give my advice and treatment to patients free of charge and many ailments are cured and suffering humanity is greatly benefitted. The number of my patients is vastly increasing and my name is in everybody's mouth. The ruler of a great state honors me and offers me the present of a big sum of money. I never resorted to all these activities with the object of getting money or fame. I simply wanted to be useful to my fellow-beings to the best of my abilities. In these circumstances, if I get fame or a big sum of money as mentioned above, I cannot deserve blame in any way because when I did those actions my mind was absolutely disinterested. The fame and the money naturally came to me. This is also Nishkama Karma on my part.

All actions, therefore, which are done by us without any desire of obtaining the fruit, and simply from a sense of duty, are nishkama. Such a person is known as a Nishkama Karma Yogi. He easily achieves success in spiritual matters, and in course of time attains the bliss of the Self.

While practicing Nishkama Karma Yoga or Raja Yoga, many a time various miracles take place at our hands. This stage is known as the stage of siddhis (powers). There is a danger at this time of our becoming either afraid or triumphant or proud. Very great care must be taken at this time. Otherwise we shall become as blank as we were at the beginning of our spiritual career. If we make use of these powers for obtaining fame or wealth, our spiritual progress will be entirely stopped and we shall stray away far from our goal of acquiring the knowledge and realization of the Self. If we however consistently maintain the attitude that we are not the authors of these miracles, we are not responsible for them and they happened naturally, these siddhis will not operate as obstacles on our path and we shall easily attain our goal and gain complete peace and happiness.

I therefore humbly request you all: Think of all things with an independent and unbiased mind, through practice root out all likes and dislikes and acquire a sense of complete detachment. With Nishkama Karma Yoga carry on your worldly duties and through meditation and practice become one with the universe and enjoy everlasting bliss.

A special characteristic of Dhyana Yoga

I shall conclude by dealing with a special characteristic of Dhyana Yoga as compared with other yogas. In all yogas there are experiences culminating in samadhi. In the state of samadhi or a state resembling it, visions of various deities and great saints are seen and conversations held with them. So these things are common. But sadhakas following the path of Dhyana Yoga say they have experiences of the kind mentioned below. We shall later on see what inference is to be drawn from such experiences.

A sadhaka is sitting in meditation. A person not at all acquainted with the sadhaka is living at a distance of many miles from the sadhaka. The sadhaka sees that person's house in his vision. That house was never seen by the sadhaka before. He sees a storeroom in the house and in that room a box in which he sees some volumes of Yoga Vashishtha. This sadhaka is of a curious disposition. He mentions the things seen by him in the vision to a few of his acquaintances who have no faith in yoga and other spiritual topics. The sadhaka, accompanied by these acquaintances, goes to that person's house in order to test whether the vision corresponds to actual facts or was merely a dream. To the wonder of these acquaintances and of the sadhaka himself (although to a slightly less degree), the house corresponded with that seen in the vision. They tell the owner of the house their object in visiting him. He says that there is a box in the storeroom but it does not contain any volumes of Yoga Vashishtha. But he does not like to send away these persons with a feeling that they had come on a fool's errand. He therefore takes the trouble of opening the box in their presence and begins to take out of it one thing after another, and lo! the volumes of Yoga Vashishta are found in the box. The sadhaka then begins to think that the things seen in meditation are not merely creatures of imagination, but are actually true. He begins to ask himself why and how this could be so. While he is engrossed in pondering the answer to his question, Sri Jnaneshwar's following line suddenly flashes before him and gives a complete answer to this question. The line runs thus: "If we look to this (Brahman or Atmarama) carefully, it is neither outside nor inside. It alone is sporting everywhere." This completely satisfies him. [This actually happened to one of Gajanana Maharaj's disciples. *Editor's note.*]

The process of reasoning which thus solves his doubts and silences his questions may be briefly summarized as follows: We say that we are the body and also mean it. The mover inside the body, who undoubtedly exists, cannot be actually seen nor can anyone demonstrate his existence by actual experiments, nor can anyone say what are his attributes. This element inside is known as the Ego or Chaitanya or by some other name. The same element is pervading all things outside our body. It cannot be seen by the physical eye. Those who have studied modern science know that in the atmosphere surrounding us there are various gases whose existence is not perceived easily. Similarly, heat and electricity cannot actually be seen. After performing experiments we come to know about the nature of these elements. Then we become sure about their existence.

Similarly, there is one element which is inside our body and outside it, pervading everywhere. We have to infer its existence. We find space around us and say that it is empty. But it is not so. It is filled with the atmosphere which is full of air and its component gases. The air inside a bottle and in the atmosphere outside the bottle is of the same kind. Similarly, the Chaitanya which dwells in the body is the same as the

Chaitanya which pervades everywhere outside. Even in the things which we call inanimate, there is Chaitanya. Only its existence can be experienced under certain circumstances.

While trees and grain are being dried in the light of the sun, they store up the heat of the sun within themselves. This store of heat lies dormant in food, vegetables, fuel, coal and other things. By friction or by the application of heat, by burning a piece of paper, a piece of cloth or oil, this store of heat is liberated and then these things throw out all the heat accumulated by them within themselves. Similarly, the existence of the Chaitanya is felt or experienced when the eye of knowledge is opened by means of yoga.

The vital force or energy in nature is one and the same. We can never create it nor can we destroy it. Only we convert one kind of energy into another. This law of the conservation of energy has been accepted by all, and all have faith in it. Similarly, Chaitanya cannot be increased or decreased. It assumes different forms of material things, and its existence is then perceived.

If we consider these laws of material science and apply their principles to the understanding of the all-pervading Chaitanya, we shall be intellectually convinced of its existence and we can get its actual experience by means of yoga. If we follow this process of reasoning, the idea that Brahman is a vague and nebulous conception of speculative philosophers will, I think, entirely disappear.

If a sadhaka again and again gets such experiences and if he follows the process of reasoning indicated above, he will be convinced that one and the same Self is sporting everywhere, inside him as well as outside him. By deep and constant pondering upon this principle, he will clearly realize the all-pervading nature of the Self. This, I think, should be called Atma-Sakshatkara.

Part Two

"Through faith in Soham external worship has been left behind. The soul has been realized in the form of Soham. The guru has been clearly manifested through the sound of Soham—that guru who saves all the poor, troubled souls by the truth of Soham."

The Mad Broom

"Such is the nature of pure love that it loves without any motive of self-interest."

Saint Tukaram

My dear brothers and sisters,

I am deeply thankful to you for the kind and affectionate invitation you sent to me for the Jayanti Utsav of Sri Ramana Maharshi. You have also asked me to send a message if I am unable to attend personally. I cannot personally be present amongst you although I would have very much liked to be there. But your pure affection has prompted some thoughts in my mind, which I herewith send to you.

Saguna is the Manifestation of the Unmanifested

Let us take the subject of the Unmanifested (Avyakta). We have to designate all things by some word. This necessity of using some word to designate things is felt by all, whether saints, learned persons or ignorant people. When a child is born, it does not say that it should be called by a particular name such as Govinda or Gopal; but people give it some name. The same is the case with the Unmanifested. A child was born from the Unmanifested and the saints called it Maya. From time immemorial saints have come out of the Unmanifested, assuming a saguna form and having bodies–embodiments of light–in order to teach human beings and to spread spiritual knowledge in the world.

Every human being is sent into this world for the purpose of enjoying the bliss of the Self while doing worldly actions in a detached spirit, and of realizing the Godhead.

We must not get entangled in the nets of sex and money [lust and greed: materialism]. Thus, our ahamkar will be sattwic and not tamasic. It is the tamasic ahamkar that makes the world so full of misery. If we want to make our whole worldly life full of bliss, we must meditate on the Self through the mantra of Soham.

Such has been my own experience and I feel that this body is not mine. I have reached this stage entirely through the grace of my sadguru and through meditating on Soham. I cannot say that I have attained this stage through my own efforts. This Soham which has come out of the Avyakta (the Unmanifested) has brought the shakti (power) of the Avyakta with it, and owing to this shakti everything of mine has become Krishnarpana (one with the Godhead). Hence, Maya does not trouble me. I have become one with Soham and I have realized my Self by meditating on it. I am enjoying unchanging bliss.

The mantra Soham is the sole savior

Every religion has got its own saints and prophets. If a person of whatever religion has firm faith and meditates on the Self, he is sure to go beyond pleasure and pain and to attain everlasting bliss. The mantra Soham is the sole savior. I am absolutely sure of this, not merely intellectually but through experience of the Self. This does not mean that I have become a saint or that I deserve to take my seat along with the great saints. I only say that all saints have resorted to this very mantra, and when their thoughts become entirely merged in the Supreme Self they become one with Brahman and shine forth in this world. I have not reached that stage as yet, but I am sure that through their grace and through meditation on Soham I am enjoying the same bliss which they enjoy. I have not as yet arrived at the stage of such great saints as Jnaneshwar, Tukaram or Ramdas. But I am following in their footsteps and taking draughts of the supreme bliss. These saints have boldly declared in their imperishable words that they have been saved by Soham, and that others will also be saved by the same mantra. Future saints also will preach the same principle.

Any act (karma) which happens automatically is really nishkama although it may appear to be sakama. This is what my Self-experience tells me. In saying this I am not in any way criticizing other saints. It is they who handed over to me the mantra Soham which was hidden in the Avyakta in the deep recesses of my own soul. This treasure was with me but I had forgotten the place where it was hidden. The saints pointed out to me that place, and from that time I have been continuously contemplating on the Self. This Soham which has come out of the Avyakta is ever present in the hearts of men. Saints become one with this Soham which is in their own hearts and then the Soham merges itself again into the Avyakta.

I therefore think that Soham is the real Karma [action leading to liberation], it is the "I" and the saints have made me realize this "I." This Soham is the real secret. It is God, it is Karma, that makes us realize this through their grace. Through continuous practice and meditation on the Self a person attains a stage in which actions become automatic. Such actions may be called sakama or nishkama. Just as saguna and nirguna are one, similarly in that stage sakama and nishkama are one. He does not look to the result and is indifferent whether the actions result in loss or gain. He is ready to endure both. He is sure that the body, this earthly tenement, is not his own. Hence he does not not care whether pleasure or pain is the result of that action.

Pure love is the real "I"

Pure love is the real "I." It is the real sadguru. When a person becomes an embodiment of this pure love, he has really conquered the whole world. The same thought is expressed by Sri Tukaram when he says, "He who humbles himself before all creatures holds the unlimited (God) within himself." If you have unqualified pure love in your hearts you will really be blessed with grace. This love should be absolutely pure without the least malice towards anyone. A typical example of this love in worldly life is a mother's love. If that love which a mother feels for her child is felt by us towards all creatures, then God will surely come to dwell in our hearts. This love is awakened in our hearts by the words of saints and by coming in contact with them. It is this idea which Tukaram has expressed in the following words: "The nature of pure love is such that it loves without any motive of self-interest."

The mother sometimes reprimands the child and disciplines it in order that the child might acquire wisdom. We see the mother disciplining the child, but know that her heart is full of love for the child. Similarly, saints sometimes verbally chastise their disciples or even other people and use seemingly harsh words to them. But their heart is full of love and their object is that all egotism should disappear from the hearts of their disciples and that they should enjoy eternal bliss. In this stage kama, krodha, etc. (desire, anger, etc.) are not destroyed altogether, but their force is spent and they become immersed in bliss. Their kama and krodha can be compared to those of a child. A child if irritated sometimes gives a slap to the face of its mother. The mother, however, does not take it ill. The child's anger is quite momentary and not deep-rooted. The next moment it laughs and embraces its mother. The anger rises in a flash and is soon extinguished.

The love of saints is akin to the love of a mother

I shall now tell you a true and simple story. It will illustrate how the love of saints is akin to the love of a mother. Pundalik in the beginning gave great trouble to his parents. Later on, he met with a guru who was a saint and who had realized his Self. He said to Pundalik, "My boy, a mother's love is really nishkama although you think it to be self-interested. Hence, instead of serving me, serve your mother. You will thereby attain real bliss. Nay, you will be bliss incarnate. You will see God." When Pundalik followed his advice, God Vithoba (Vishnu) appeared before him. And Pundalik, as he was then busy serving his parents with pure love [and saw Vithoba standing in mud], made Vithoba stand on a brick which he tossed towards Him. All sadgurus similarly arouse this pure love in our hearts. When once this love arises in our hearts, we experience the bliss of Brahman although we may be leading our lives in this mayic world.

Brahman is nothing but Atmic bliss

Maya was born from the Avyakta and the world was born from Maya. You may also say if you like that the world was born first and then Maya was born. It is just the same. Saints have said in their imperishable words that Maya is Brahman and Brahman is Maya. A sadhaka has to get an understanding of this principle. When he does this, his whole samsara (worldly life) becomes full of bliss. Whatever actions he then does, his mind is always steeped in bliss. That action may be sakama or nishkama. He becomes absolutely detached. In that stage the thoughts expressed by him are of great benefit to all, whether they are ignorant or learned. If people listen to these thoughts and act to bring them into practice, they become full of love for their "guru." Then, their egotism, kama (desire; lust), krodha (anger) and lobha (greed; avarice) become as if dead. Their kama, krodha, etc., produce no reaction in others or in themselves.

This is the true path of progress for a mumukshu. A mumukshu must carry on this practice with great devotion and selfless love for at least twelve years. He will then be able to reach Self-realization. The faithful sadhaka then reaches the stage of vijnana (supreme knowledge). He reaches the stage when his own Atman (Self) becomes his guru. This love was born from the Avyakta; saints were born from love. Maya was born from the saints and the world was born from Maya. In order to reach the Avyakta we have to go back by the reverse process. God is enshrined in the hearts of saints who are full of love. It is the saints alone who teach how to look upon samsara as Brahman, and Brahman is nothing but Atmic bliss.

To trouble a saint regarding our worldly affairs is detrimental to our spiritual progress

To trouble a saints regarding our worldly affairs is detrimental to our spiritual progress, because this shows that we attach undue importance to them. And when our worldly desires are not fulfilled, our faith in the saint becomes shaky. Some persons come to me and ask me to remove their worldly troubles. "I have incurred a debt of four thousand rupees. This makes my mind uneasy. Kindly shower your grace upon me and make me free from care." Such are some of the complaints which are often brought to me by people. They desire that I should ward off their difficulties and troubles.

It is quite true that adversity is good for a man as it often leads to his spiritual advancement. A person who is extremely troubled by adverse circumstances and has lost his peace of mind many a time goes to a saint. If the merit acquired by him in his previous life is of a high order, and he comes in contact with a real saint who has attained Self-realization, the emotional state of his mind then is such that he naturally puts his faith in what the saint tells him and accepts it with full reverence and submission. He then carries on the practice of the japa of the mantra given to him and is greatly befitted. It however does not follow that the saint will remove that person's worldly difficulties and troubles. A real saint will never do this.

Therefore when people come to me for the redress of their worldly troubles I plainly tell them that every person must patiently bear the troubles sent to him by his fate (karma), and that the best way of solving worldly difficulties is to follow worldly and practical methods. They however argue as follows: "A saint is like a mother to his disciples and other people who come to him for shelter. A child is full of frolic and joy and is engaged in various games and playthings. But when it becomes hungry, it comes crying to its mother. Does not the mother then see to its wants and pacify its hunger? Similarly, we are leading our lives pleasantly in this world as long as our circumstances are good. Our mind is then at ease. When, however, troubles arise and our peace of mind is lost, if we go and fall at the feet of a saint, should not that saint shower his grace upon us and ward off our difficulties like a good mother?"

My answer to such sort of arguments is this. There are some persons who come to me solely with the object of achieving their worldly objects. They have nothing to ask in spiritual matters. To such I say, "This is not my business. You should go to those saints who happen to possess such powers."

It is the mission of real saints to point out the path which leads to sure and everlasting peace and happiness to persons who, being extremely harassed by worldly troubles, are in urgent need of finding out a way which will take them out of all troubles and establish them in everlasting peace. Real saints have this power of granting boundless happiness and complete peace of mind. My sadguru has put this very responsibility upon me. He, through me, shows this path with ardent love to spiritual aspirants. He takes into consideration all the obstacles and difficulties that beset this path, and removes them. If the removing of a worldly difficulty or the fulfilling of a worldly desire is necessary for the further spiritual progress of the disciple, and positively helpful to him, he will fulfill that desire also. But it must be remembered that in such cases there is no opposition between the fulfillment of that desire and the decree of fate or karma—in other words the will of God. This means such a fulfillment is in consonance with the law of karma.

I therefore say that people should pay careful attention to what I have said above and keep firm faith in their guru and in the mantra given by him. This faith should be such as the child has in its mother. Just as the child never has any doubt that she is its mother and that she will fulfill all its desires, similarly they should have firm faith in their sadguru who is none other than Soham, and have not the least doubt that this mother Soham will deliver them from all troubles and difficulties.

My dear brothers and sisters, devote all your energies to acquire this love which is pervading the whole world but of which we are not conscious. By the japa of Soham you will establish this love in your hearts and become blessed. This Soham japa is like an ocean which is full of unlimited bliss.

The repetition of Soham may be sakama, or nishkama

The repetition of Soham may be sakama, or nishkama. As Soham is based on the workings of nature, its japa, though it may be carried on with the object of fulfilling earthly desires, will ultimately be united with the real Soham which is enshrined in the innermost core of our being, and thus bring into awakening the power of the Paramatman. Objects of earthly desires are not permanent. The joy which is felt in their attainment is evanescent. But the effect of even the sakama japa is not altogether lost. It retains its force and awakens the power of the Self.

The japa of Soham should be repeated in as natural a manner as possible. There is no necessity of assuming any particular posture (asana). It should be carried on even while doing worldly actions. No misgiving should be entertained regarding its effect even though there may be absence of concentration. Such doubts are groundless. Even when we feel that our mind is concentrated, that state of concentration is only apparently so. The mind is in its very nature extremely fickle, and we cannot be sure when it will dart away and throw us into a whirlpool of thoughts. Everyone knows that this state of concentration is generally momentary. It is no doubt true that in the state of samadhi the mind is concentrated for a longer duration, but that state of samadhi also is not permanent; it lasts only for some time. After that the person again descends into consciousness of surrounding worldly objects, the play of good and bad desires generating pleasure or pain is resumed, and the body carries on its usual activities.

The state of samadhi or concentration can be compared to that of sleep. In the state of sleep there is real concentration. When we get up we say that we had very good sleep, that we were entirely unconscious of the world and that our mind was completely merged in the Self. Our Self alone was present as the Seer. Still we often see that sometimes even in sleep we dream and find ourselves taking part in the dream world. That is to say, we leave the state of concentration and again enter into the world of thoughts. If this is so even in the state of sleep, then how much more difficult would it be to go into a state of concentration in our waking state? Hence it would not be proper to abandon the japa on the ground that one cannot concentrate upon it.

Some people think that if they carry on the japa they may get into a state of continual indrawn or abstract concentration, and then it will be difficult for them to carry on their worldly duties easily. This idea also is false. Soham is our real nature. If we become one with it we will, on the contrary, be able to carry on our usual worldly duties more efficiently.

"Who am I?"

An atheist might say, "I cannot understand all this. God and the Paramatman are all ideas and guesses. What have I to do with them?" Let us for the sake of argument admit that what he says is true, that these are all ideas. Now let him answer the following question: "You know that these are all ideas. Who is it that knows about these ideas and is conscious of their being mere ideas?" A person sometimes says, "I am ignorant." Let him consider who is the knower of his ignorance. A person sometimes says, "I do not want this, I do not want that." Even though he might say that he does not want anything, still the "I" will always remain. This "I" is Soham, and eternal peace is its nature. A person might say that he does not want all this bother about God, dhyana, devotion, faith and concentration. All right; but let him say whether he wants peace, calmness and happiness or not. Even if he thinks that these ideas about God, etc., are false and

196

illusory, still he must admit that there is somebody inside him who thinks them false and illusory. This knower inside us is the "I" and that "I" is Soham.

As long as the breath goes on, life goes on, and the activities of the body go on. The saints have explained the meaning of the incoming and outgoing breath, and Soham is the sound which is produced by the incoming and outgoing breath. This Soham sound is ceaselessly being repeated in our body whether we are conscious of it or not. If we become conscious of this internal Soham, we shall experience peace of mind. If we fully understand this Soham, we shall attain complete bliss, which is the real nature of Soham, and become one with it.

The difference between meditation and concentration

Some persons do not understand the difference between meditation (dhyana), and concentration (ekagrata). Suppose a sadguru asks a person to sit before him and repeat the Soham mantra mentally. A few minutes later the guru asks him, "How did you feel? Had you any thoughts? Was the flow of thoughts going on as usual, or was there any difference? How was the japa going on?" When such questions are asked the aspirant appears to be a little confused, and is usually found to answer in the following manner: "Maharaj, my mind was quite calm. Not a single idea arose in my mind. The japa was going on in an undisturbed manner. I was enjoying peace. But, Maharaj, my mind was not concentrated. I could hear the sounds and movements taking place around me."

It is a common idea with ordinary aspirants that as soon as they hear the mantra Soham pronounced by the sadguru their mind should become concentrated and they should enter into the state of samadhi. It is a laudable wish, no doubt, but it is out of place at the time. Because when the sadguru tells the aspirant to meditate upon Soham, he does not tell him to get concentrated at once. He tells him to repeat the japa of Soham in order that he may be able to meditate properly. The main idea in meditation is that while the japa is going on there should not be the flow of other thoughts disturbing the repetition of the mantra. Our mind is naturally fickle. It is very difficult for it to concentrate itself upon one idea. The guru tries to bring the aspirant to experience a state in which, although he is not consciously repeating the mantra, the mantra appears to be going on while his mind is entirely at repose. At such a time the guru through his own power gets this done, even though the disciple by himself has not been accustomed to it and is not in a position to keep his mind absolutely calm. The experience is, of course, only temporary.

In the case of some aspirants, however, owing to some practice done in the previous life they get concentrated as soon as they begin meditation according to the instructions of the guru. They also see some visions. But this only shows that they must have practiced to some extent in their previous life. They therefore get all those experiences almost at once. But this does not mean that they have, owing to this, got everything which is to be obtained from a sadguru. They, too, must not stop there, but carry on further practice until they reach the final goal of human life.

"All possible troubles beset the worldly life." Keeping this truth firmly in mind, it is necessary to get deliverance from samsara (worldly exis- tence) by the internal repetition of Soham. The seeing of many visions is not a sure sign of progress. Real progress lies in the continuous meditation on the sound of the inner Soham japa going on without a break after the visions have stopped. If a person carries on the continuous practice of the Soham japa, his mind will in course of time get concentrated upon it, and he will then experience the state of samadhi.

Attaining the state of samadhi is not the final goal of our life

In the state of samadhi there is no consciousness of the external world, and there is experience of bliss. But this state lasts only for a short time. As soon as the normal consciousness is gained, the world makes its pres- ence felt as before and the old play of desires, full of pleasure and pain, commences. Thus it will be seen that it is a mistake to suppose that we have reached our final goal when we reach the state of samadhi. What is necessary in this stage is that even while we are conscious of worldly objects our meditation on Soham must be ceaselessly going on, and the worldly objects and events should produce no reaction on our mind, making it unsteady. Hence it is necessary to carry on the meditation of Soham ceaselessly. When this practice is carried on continuously, a state is reached when the presence of Pandurang (the Paramatman) is felt in all the three states: the waking, the dreaming and the sleeping. Then we get the experience described by Kabir: "Rama does my japa. I am sitting at ease." Thus, the stage of ajapa-japa is reached, and when this is reached we experience the state of samadhi even while we are doing worldly activities. The mind itself becomes one with Soham and the truth of the following words is realized: "The mind has become fixed and motionless in one place. Atmic bliss has, therefore, been realized to the full. Nothing remains lacking."

Many aspirants go to a guru taking their stand on Sri Tukaram's lines, "The sadguru makes his disciple like himself at once. No time is required for him to do this." They however, should also remember the words of the same saint to the following effect: "Tuka says that haste is of no use. Unless the proper time of acquisition has arrived, nothing can be achieved." They will thus not be deceived in their expectations.

The object of the above-mentioned discussion is not to make aspirants despondent and abandon the practice through a sense of frustration if they find that their efforts are not crowned with success in a short time. They are sure to realize the real power of Soham after some days if they carry on the practice continuously, with great intensity. There is absolutely no doubt about this. I say this from my own experience. The aspirant should have the firm determination that he will carry on the practice of Soham intensely in the future, although he might have failed to do so in the past. He should always remember that his sadguru is always there to back his efforts.

Continuous meditation on the sound of the inner Soham japa at the time of death leads one to sadagati (high status after death)

If an aspirant carries on the continuous meditation on the sound of the inner Soham japa, he will become one with Soham. If he happens to die in this stage he can be sure of attaining sadagati (high status) after his death. It is very difficult to bring our mind to bear upon the contemplation of God at the time of our death. The force of desires is very great at that time, a person becomes a prey to them, and owing to this has to go through the cycle of various lives. If, however, he gets himself accustomed to the continuous intense contemplation of the sound of the inner Soham japa, his mind at the time of death will not be entangled in the meshes of worldly desires, but will be merged in Soham and hence he will be sure to go to a higher state after his death. I therefore say to you all: commence the japa of Soham and carry it on ceaselessly.

What is necessary is that we must devote our attention to this Soham. The more your attention is directed towards Soham the greater will be the change in your mind and thoughts. Your kama and krodha will not altogether be destroyed or obliterated. They may be there, but the sting of hatred will be entirely absent. When someone does us an evil turn we keep it in our mind and feed the grudge and when an opportunity arises we try to return the evil, perhaps tenfold. This attitude of mind is what is known as hatred. This hatred will be entirely obliterated. The flow of thoughts will be full of love.

Soham is the real nature of the "I" in the body, and this Soham is ceaselessly going on: the "I," the Soham inside. The speaker, doer, the action itself and in fact everything will be one with Soham. I am at present experiencing to some extent the bliss of such a state, and anyone else who will do as I have done will attain similar bliss. As long as the "I" dwells in this body, we must get into the habit of repeating Soham. Ceaseless repetition will make the trend of all thoughts full of Soham.

One should not give any thought as to when the japa will lead to the final attainment of the goal

This "I" inside the body may be called by any name. It may be called God or Nature or any other name. The knowledge of this "I" leads to peace and happiness. Is there anyone who does not want this peace and happiness? Our mind is like a mirror. Various thoughts are always arising and having their play in the mind. According to the different thoughts, the mind is plunged in sorrow or in joy. We should think about the "I" inside, who is the witness of all these thoughts. That is Soham.

If we sit quiet and at ease divesting the mind of all disturbing thoughts, we shall get a glimpse of this witness inside. The mirror of our mind has been covered over with the dirt of innumerable impressions left by bad thoughts entertained through the course of innumerable previous lives. The dark soot of kama and krodha is lying in thick layers on the surface of this mirror. It is our duty to try to wash away all this dirt and soot by means of good desires, and by increasing the flow of good thoughts.

Various doubts and misgivings assail the mind. This is the natural result of evil impressions left on our mind by bad thoughts in previous lives. But there is no reason why we should feel discouraged. Our present duty is to get ourselves accustomed to the entertaining of good thoughts.

Every mumukshu should ceaselessly put up strong efforts to meditate upon Soham. It does not matter even if the japa is sakama. He should not give any thought as to when the japa will lead to the final attainment of the goal. His efforts should be directed towards trying to keep his attention fixed on the sound of the inner Soham japa. He should try to fix his attention on Soham even while doing worldly actions. This Soham will in course of time remove the dirt of bad thoughts and make the mirror of the mind clean. As soon as the mirror becomes clean, the blissful nature of Soham will be realized. Hence we should direct all our efforts towards keeping our attention fixed on Soham without any break. If we do so we shall surely attain complete peace and happiness and life will be full of bliss.

Sri Tukaram says, "Wherever I go you are always with me to bear me company." The companion here referred to is none other than Soham. Wherever you may be, in whatever condition you may be, this Soham, this witness, this Paramatman, is always your companion. You have never been or will ever be separated from Him because you and He are one. Only you are not conscious of His nearness and presence. You must first become fully conscious of His nearness and presence and then lose the sense of this consciousness also by becoming one with Him. Then you will be bliss incarnate, everlasting, unchanging bliss.

I am telling all this from my own experience. If you put forth strong efforts in the direction I have mentioned above, you are sure to attain success.

The mind must be internally immersed in Soham and become full of bliss. If my mind is absolutely clean and full of the bliss of Soham, entirely devoid of egotism and concentrated in the internal sound of the inner Soham japa even when outwardly doing worldly actions, I shall consider myself as extremely fortunate. Through the grace of my sadguru, my practice is going on in the direction of obtaining this eternal bliss and I can say from experience that I feel that I have ascended some steps on the steep path leading to the temple where eternal peace and happiness have been enshrined.

Soham is always present as a witness in everybody's mind

About a fortnight ago a learned shastri came to visit me. He had read some of the letters sent by me to my friends, and also the messages which I had given to some religious institutions, and owing to it a sort of respect had been created in his mind for me. He said to me, "Maharaj, the thoughts expressed by you are of a very high order. They receive much support from the Upanishads and treatises on Vedanta."

I replied, "Punditji, you have considered the thoughts expressed by me from the shastric points of view and called them sound. This does not give me any very great pleasure. The reason is that I do not attach any importance to the delight obtained from high and beautiful thoughts of others. If you had expressed your agreement with at least one of these thoughts, having felt the truth of it from your own experience of the state mentioned in it, I would have felt highly delighted.

"If a person comes to me and tells me his own thoughts, the truth of which has been tested by his own experience, I will pay more respect to him than to a person who repeats like a parrot the thoughts, however high they may be, of great men like Sri Shankaracharya, Jnaneshwar or Tukaram. It does not matter whether the thoughts of the first-mentioned person are highly developed or not.

"I understand the minds of the various persons who come to me and ask me questions, because I have gone through those various stages and hence can identify myself with the stage of the questioner. I therefore never get irritated with any person for asking questions, however absurd they may be. The only thing required is that he must be thoroughly honest and sincere. I then answer his questions according to what my inner Soham suggests to me. The answer given by me will, I am sure, necessarily remove the doubts of the questioner, and he will see the clear path of truth before him."

When that shastri heard this reply given by me, he was overcome with emotion and requested me to explain how Soham is always present as a witness in everybody's mind. An ordinary man of the world is not conscious of this "I" which is always awake. As soon as a man gains consciousness of the ever-existing presence of this "I" he attains the goal of human life. This stage is known as sakshiavastha (the state where the "I" is consciously felt to be the ever-present witness). This Soham is ever present in every being in the form of his own Self. This Soham is continuously going on, it never stops. This Soham which is seen in all animate and inanimate things is my Jani Janardan (God present in all human beings), and wherever I use the words "Jani Janardan," I mean by it this Soham, present in all.

I therefore tell you with all the emphasis I can command that you should at once begin to repeat the japa of Soham with firm faith. It does not matter if you place no faith in me. Have firm faith in Soham and you will attain the same bliss that I am enjoying.

Pure and simple words of advice

I shall now give you an illustration from everybody's experience. When we sleep, we sometimes dream and after that go into complete unconsciousness. In that state nothing is felt, we go into the Avyakta. When we awake, if somebody asks us, "How did you sleep?" we reply, "I got very good sleep and was full of bliss." Thus, when a person is born, he begins to speak about his experience in words. That is, when he comes out of the Avyakta he begins to describe his experiences in words. Every person, be he learned or ignorant, saint or an ordinary person, is required to have recourse to words in order to express his ideas.

Saints like Sri Ramakrishna Paramahansa have given the illustration of a doll made of salt. They say if a salt doll enters water it is turned into water. Can it then describe its experience of water? If it wants to describe the experience, it must keep one foot in water and the other on land. Hence, saints who have been one with the Avyakta come out of the Avyakta by assuming bodies full of light, and are born into this world for the deliverance of other human beings. By their own acts and advice they teach the world how to make this Maya full of bliss, how to go beyond pleasure and pain and how to obtain eternal peace and happiness. They say to the people in the world, "Your treasure (of bliss) is with you; only you have forgotten the place where it is hidden." The saints neither give anything to the world nor do they take anything from the world. They carry out their mission and remain aloof and at peace with themselves.

If the mumukshus follow implicitly the advice of the saints without entertaining the least doubt, with full faith and real love, by continued practice they will succeed in curbing all evil tendencies and in resisting all temptations of lust and greed. They will then get realization of the bliss of the Self, and attain the stage which was attained by such immortal saints as Sri Jnaneshwar or Sri Tukaram. There is not the least doubt about this.

I have given expression to these ideas which have arisen in my innermost heart, and as such they are not my words but the words of the Paramatman dwelling in my heart. Whether they are true or false, I leave it to the world to judge. Those who have some Self-experience will understand that these words are not mine, but my guru's. If anything appears to be false, consider it to be mine. You know that I am absolutely uneducated and ignorant. I have no learning. My presumption in undertaking to write to people like you is like that of a crow trying to emulate an eagle on the ground, that the crow, too, can soar high in the sky. Although I am the abode of all possible bad qualities, still my attempts to fly into the sky like an eagle are not altogether condemnable.

Brothers and sisters, I have told you what I had to say in as simple a manner as possible by taking illustrations from everyday life. Still I would like to say a few words more in conclusion before closing the subject.

Jivatma, Shivatma and Paramatma

Those who have read some religious books and those who have listened to religious discourses must have often heard the words: Jivatma, Shivatma, and Paramatman. Jivatma is the individual soul who experiences pleasure and pain in this worldly life. Shivatma is the Paramatman who is the root cause of all the activities in the Universe. The absolute Being who pervades all things and is also beyond them is the Paramatman, otherwise known as Brahman. One and the same Being has been given these different names according to the different aspects in which he has been looked at.

Thus there is one absolute principle on which the ideas of Jivatma, Shivatma, and Paramatman have been superimposed. We get superficial, wordy knowledge of these terms from religious books and discourses, and our mind is confused. Now, where is he located who gives these different names and utters these words? He is located in this body, in the heart. This "I" located in the heart of all human beings, conceives these different aspects and gives utterance to these different names. If you search for this "I," you will come to know it is an absolute principle having no form, no attributes and which cannot be described in words. If it is without attributes and without form, can it ever be perceived by the eye? No.

Then if you ask about the nature of this principle, for an answer you should see what all saints have said about it. They say that the real nature of this "I" is unchangeable bliss. The everlasting bliss residing in our heart is the sign by which the absolute truth can be traced. Every human being is ceaselessly trying to get happiness. Nobody is needed to tell him to do so. The reason why every human being ceaselessly tries to find happiness is because unchanging bliss is the real nature of the "I" inside him. When a person realizes the nature of this bliss, he has nothing more to do. All his activities stop.

When the "I" has been seen by the "I"—that is, the real "I" has been realized by the egoistic "I"—the duality between the seer and the seen disappears and now nothing further remains to be seen. When this stage is reached one realizes that the "I" pervades everywhere, and that nothing has existence except this all-pervading Self. In this stage the phenomenal world has no existence. Referring to this stage, Sri Ramdas has said, "Why are you asking about the cause, etc., of this world which, in fact, has no existence and was never born?" This state is indescribable in words. All words, therefore, are meaningless, and silence is the only eloquence regarding it.

The practice is the most important means of controlling the mind

In order to attain this natural stage, saints have prescribed a certain practice. The Soham which is in the hearts of all saints who have obtained Self-realization has manifested itself, and helps the saints to realize the blissful nature of the Self. In this connection Sri Tukaram has said that the body is the real Pandharpur and the soul is the real Vithal.

I, too, told myself, my mind, to contemplate ceaselessly on Soham. The mind is pliable and turns towards that to which it is made to turn. When the mind, therefore, was made accustomed to the japa of Soham, the mind became one with Soham, and thus became merged in the Paramatman. Through the ceaseless contemplation of Soham, the mind became one with the Paramatman, and began to enjoy the everlasting and unchanging bliss which is the nature of the Self.

All actions that one does in this stage naturally become dedicated to God (Krishnarpana), and therefore are nishkama. There being absolutely no egotism, the idea that "I am doing the actions" is altogether absent, and therefore the karma becomes nishkama, and the apparent doer is all the while immersed in his natural bliss, and is thus absolutely detached, although leading a worldly life. I have therefore to request you all to carry on the practice of japa continuously.

Do not care to see whether your actions are sakama or nishkama; only take care to see that your attention is continuously directed to the japa. It does not in the least matter if you do not have recourse to any other sadhana. You are sure to be successful in the end.

Lord Krishna has said in the Gita that the mind, which by nature is fickle and hence difficult to be controlled, can be brought under control by constant practice (abhyasa). Thus, practice is the most important means of controlling the mind.

If we carry on the japa with firm faith, we clearly realize after some time the power of the mantra. If we train our mind to entertain only good thoughts, not only are we ourselves benefitted, but our conduct produces good effects upon others also. This light of Soham inside us, sheds its luster on our whole life and makes it full of happiness. Its beneficial influence is also felt by the whole external atmosphere around us. The first thing required is firm faith without any doubts and misgivings, and the second is the continuous practice of the mantra japa.

If therefore you continue the practice steadily, the tendency of the mind towards good thoughts and actions will be more and more increased, and owing to the ceaseless contemplation of Soham there will gradually be the realization of your own inherent blissful nature, and the mind will be enjoying complete peace and happiness.

Brothers and sisters, if you carry on the practice of japa with full faith, and ultimately realize your oneness with Soham you, too, will become full of bliss like myself. Be assured that the blessings of my sadguru will accompany you all along in your practice.

Signs of spiritual progress

While carrying on the contemplation of Soham, an aspirant should always be carefully observing whether his worldly desires are gradually dropping off. The gradual dropping of worldly desires, and the capability to perform worldly actions solely from a sense of duty and not with a view to achieve some object, are sure signs of spiritual progress. If an aspirant makes it a point to see that his attention is continuously fixed on Soham, that his mind is growing more and more detached, and that he is continuously carrying on the practice with firm faith in the path prescribed to him, I am sure that he will certainly reach the goal. Whether a person is a mumukshu, a sadhaka, or a siddha, if all his desires have completely disappeared and he has attained a complete sense of detachment, then he attains a stage in which Pandharpur is always with him wherever he stays. There is no necessity for him to go anywhere.

As I am not educated, the words which I use may not be clear. They may express the meaning only indistinctly. But these words are the expressions of my internal intuition. The expressions used may not be polished and beautiful, but I humbly request that on that account people should not be indifferent to what I say. I have first practiced what I preach. Hence people should also translate these precepts into practice, and then see whether they are true or not. I therefore urge all people, whether ignorant or learned, mumukshus or sadhakas, to carry on the japa of Soham with their attention continuously directed towards it.

External conditions are almost the same in all Yugas

Some people say that the present age is the age of material happiness. The present Yuga is Kali Yuga. In this Yuga it is extremely difficult to attain the highest goal of Self-realization. Naturally, men in general will be always striving to obtain material happiness. I, however, think that it is not proper to be complaining about external conditions. A little consideration will, on the contrary, convince us that external conditions are almost the same in all Yugas. The change lies in the mind, the attitude it adopts. According to the attitude of your mind you will feel that the age is Satya Yuga or Kali Yuga. Everything thus depends on your mind. Hence I say that you should get your mind immersed in the ceaseless contemplation of Soham and then you will find that the difficulties created by troublesome external conditions will automatically disappear.

A few words of advice on abhyasa (practice)

Now, I shall say a few words regarding abhyasa (practice). Some persons carry on the japa for some time, but owing to want of intensity on their part, when they find that they are not making marked progress, or when they do not see any visions, they give up the practice, thinking that fate is against them. Or if they carry on the japa, they do it merely mechanically without any heart in the matter.

If our mind is unsteady, if it does not feel any joy in the contemplation of Soham, we should ask ourselves the question: Why do we not enjoy pleasure in doing the japa? The obvious answer is that it is our own lack of faith that comes in the way, and bars us from getting this joy. There is also another thing. Thousands of bad impressions have been accumulated in our mind through the course of previous births. How can all these impressions disappear at once?

In the case of those whose bad impressions have been cleared away to an appreciable extent, if they carry on the practice they will get some spiritual experiences sooner or later according to their merit. If any bad desires have beset their mind in this life, the continuous contemplation of Soham will gradually destroy all those desires in this very life. In the next life the remaining bad impressions and bad desires, and kama, krodha and lobha, generating them or generated by them, will surely disappear. You should have no doubt regarding this in your mind. You may have no faith in me, but you must have faith in Soham.

Soham is the real path of knowledge (Jnana Marga). Owing to this, egotism disappears. In the path of knowledge, the sadhaka's consciousness becomes more and more comprehensive, until it becomes all-pervading. But all this is nothing but the play of the "I," and Soham teaches this very principle.

Thus, in the path of knowledge one becomes all-pervading and one with the universal Being.

The real power lies in the mantra and this power is also centered in everyone

I therefore say again and again, that the real power lies in the mantra, Soham. This power is also centered in you. If you thoroughly realize this power, and become one with it, you will easily attain atmic bliss, even though you may be leading a worldly life. You will be thoroughly happy internally, as well as in your worldly life. Soham awakens the power in you which is lying dormant.

My brothers and sisters should remember that a liking for and devotion to God is the result of the accumulation of great merit in previous lives. If you have this liking, God in the form of Soham who has His dwelling in the outgoing and incoming breath of every human being will be realized by you. I say this from my own experience. You may have no faith in me but you should have faith in this Soham.

Do not allow your faith to be shaken although in the beginning you do not get any experiences. If you give this consideration to the matter of Soham, you will find that having faith in Soham is a matter solely depending upon your own mind. Even if owing to bad impressions of past lives doubts assail your mind, it lies with you to drive away these doubts with assiduous efforts, remembering that therein lies the successful fruition of your life. If persistent and continuous practice is carried on, the mind is concentrated and becomes one with the mantra, and all thoughts disappear. Only you must have a true and firm determination. We can be said to have a true and firm determination only when we are able to translate our ideas into action. Hence saints have said, "God grants the fulfillment of true and firm determination, and the desires entertained by the devotees are crowned with success" (Tukaram).

Hence, it is clearly your duty to have firm faith in the mantra. If you have this absolute faith, you will surely attain your goal. About that there is no doubt. There is no room for doubt in the case of real affection, which is absolutely free from any doubts and misgivings.

The real meaning of Paramartha (spiritual realization) and its means

The real "I" which dwells in the heart of everyone is the sole abode of this unchanging happiness and bliss. He who becomes one with this "I" gets hold of this sole source of happiness, and therefore feels no need of any pleasure which is derived from the enjoyment of external objects.

The path which leads to the true knowledge of this "I" and to the realization of oneness with it, is the path of spiritual progress. He who desires to go by this path must naturally practice self-restraint and keep himself detached from material pleasures. Abandoning of material pleasures outwardly, or abandoning them by merely forcibly curbing the mind, is of very little use. The renunciation must be mental: the mind must gradually develop a dislike for these material pleasures. If you will try to immerse your mind in the continuous contemplation of the sound of the inner Soham japa, this renunciation becomes easy. The mind becomes one with Soham, and then the ajapa japa begins. In this stage our whole worldly existence becomes full of happiness. The mind of a person who attains this stage goes beyond pleasure and pain. It becomes full of universal love, and he feels nothing but love in this material world which to others is full of pleasure and pain.

Only saints like Jnaneshwar and Tukaram obtained Paramartha. When this state of everlasting joy is reached, this world, the next world, heaven or hell–which to an ordinary person appears to be full of contrasts of pleasure and pain–becomes nothing but universal, all-pervading joy and bliss incarnate. This stage is what is known as Paramartha.

To obtain this Paramartha is the goal of human life, and you can obtain it by your own persistent and honest effort. Efforts are necessary to obtain any object in the world. Are we not required to put up strong efforts to obtain money or learning? And are our efforts always crowned with success? But do we on that account abandon efforts to obtain these things? Similarly, we must continually make strong efforts to obtain the realization of the real "I." The various difficulties and obstacles which arise in this path must be removed, just as we do in worldly matters.

The necessity of having strong sense and intelligence

Various qualities are necessary to carry on worldly transactions efficiently. But there is one thing which far surpasses all these qualities taken together, and that is strong good sense, which is natural and not acquired. By reading we can at the most obtain useful and varied information, but to make proper use of that information at the proper time requires natural good sense and intelligence. I here remember a saying: "God should be known through good sense and intelligence."

This is a simple statement, but it illustrates a very important principle. It shows that real intelligence is a very important qualification. If a person possesses this intelligence, he will not need to read various books. He will be able to solve all his difficulties by the exercise of his keen intelligence. Wisdom acquired from books is, after all, one-sided. This keen intelligence is useful in worldly as well as spiritual matters

When will a sadhaka reach the ultimate goal of human life?

My friends, such doubts are bound to assail the mind. To entertain various doubts and misgivings is quite natural to the mind. As long as a person is alive, his mind will always be full of thoughts, good or bad. Hence it is futile to wait till the mind abandons all mistaken thoughts and doubts. People who think that they will not be able to make any progress in spiritual matters until this inflow of thoughts is stopped should pay particular attention to the following illustration.

There are bound to be innumerable waves on the sea. If a person thinks that he will swim in the sea when all these waves are stopped, will he ever be able to swim in the sea? He will surely come to know that the waves will never stop and he will never be able to swim. Similarly, every person who wants to follow the spiritual path should not wait for the disappearance of all thoughts, but should start the contemplation of Soham and try to keep his mind fixed upon it. He should not allow his mind to be diverted from it by the waves of thoughts.

As long as a person identifies himself with this body these doubts and thoughts are sure to assail him and cause disturbance. A sure way to escape from the clutches of these thoughts is to develop a feeling that we are not the body. It is the nature of mind to carry on the continuous play of thoughts. The mind (manas), the intellect (buddhi), and the chitta (field of consciousness) are all inside us. Buddhi is the power which enables us to determine. The mind is always fickle and moving from one idea to another, and when the mind concentrates upon something it is called chitta. A sadhaka, therefore, should concentrate upon Soham and thus turn his mind into chitta. If he continues this practice for some time, his mind will gradually gain in calmness and ultimately will become one with Soham and with the inherent, everlasting bliss which is the real nature of Soham, and thus his chitta will become chit (consciousness). Once this stage is attained, that person will experience unlimited joy. Such a person is easily able to identify himself with all persons with whom he comes into contact, and with all circumstances in which he finds himself placed. His peace of mind is never disturbed, and he is always immersed in everlasting and unchanging bliss. He attains the goal, and the real purpose of human life is fulfilled.

The difference between the mind of an ordinary person and that of a person who is immersed in Soham

If the body falls in the gutter, it can be washed and cleaned by water, but if the mind is dirty, full of doubts and full of desires for many objects, how can it be washed and purged of its impurities? The only way of cleansing the mind is to immerse it in the contemplation of Soham. All the impurities are then washed away. Sri Tukaram has said, 'If your life is impure, what can soap do?" The mind is purified, and all the dirt from it is swept away by the broom of Soham.

He who has burnt away all avarice and destroyed the very roots of evil desires and thus completely purified and cleansed his mind by the continuous contemplation of Soham will never be attracted by the glitter of the worthless things of this world.

There is a great difference between an ordinary mind and a mind immersed in the contemplation of Soham. The most important principle is that he who wants to obtain spiritual knowledge must discard all material pleasures. It must be remembered that only when a person becomes entirely devoid of any desire of obtaining prosperity in this world or the next does he attains the goal of human life. He who wants to tread the path of spiritual progress must gradually acquire a sense of detachment.

The sphere of spiritual progress lies beyond reason and intellect. The question of pain or pleasure in this world or the next is absolutely irrelevant in this connection. By entertaining ideas of pleasure or pain, the mind gets entangled in the meshes of sankalpa or vikalpa (desire or doubts). Instead of wasting valuable time like this, you should utilize it in the contemplation of Soham.

My brothers and sisters: The current of love flowing in the form of Soham from my heart has gone on taking various turnings through various topics, and you have allowed it to flow on, having spent your valuable time in following it. This has filled me with unlimited joy and happiness.

The power of Soham

God has innumerable names, and people are calling out His various names according to their individual liking. Although it is so, still it must be remembered that Kabir says: "Rama Nama is repeated by almost all people–by thieves, by licentious people, and by rich people. But that Nama (Name) by which Dhruva and Prahlada [two children who attained spiritual perfection by calling on the Divine Name] were saved was something different." One must remember that the Siddha Name of Soham alone will be useful in easily crossing this ocean of worldly existence and ending the cycle of births and deaths. This Siddha Nama is a power; it is like a mother to the universe, and it is the entity that is calling itself "I" in the body. It is a flame of love.

The power of the Avyakta is such that it will more than suffice for solving all possible difficulties in your worldly life

If you repeat the Soham mantra in your mind, by continuous practice your mind gets concentrated upon it. The concentration may be called dhyana. If this force is uninterruptedly stored up in your heart, be sure that you have obtained the goal of human life.

Somebody might say, "We have carefully listened to what you have told us. But what would be the use of all this for solving the practical difficulties of our actual life in this world?" No doubt this question is very important.

If your difficulties remain as they are, all this effort of japa and concentration would be useless and good for nothing. But I say this with all emphasis, that once you get the experience of the Avyakta, in any way or by any method, the power of the Avyakta is such that it will more than suffice for solving all possible difficulties in your worldly life. There is no necessity of your trying anything else for that purpose. You should only try your best to obtain the experience of the Avyakta by any method you like. Once that is done, you will get such a power that it will either drive away all possible difficulties which beset you, or all difficulties will automatically disappear.

If you once fix your abode in Avyakta the distance between you and any other thing or person becomes nil. As the ideas of "mine" and "thine" are absolutely absent in the Avyakta, all the wealth in the world becomes your own. You will feel it to be so. You yourself may not be very learned or wise. But there must be someone in the world who is so. You will feel that you are one with him and that his learning and wisdom are your own.

True karma lies in remaining absolutely calm and undisturbed by fixing your abode in the all-pervading Chaitanya. I have said something about karma before. Here I put it in the shortest way and the fewest words: To remain indifferent to pleasure and pain, and to perform actions from a sense of duty supported by the basis of Self-knowledge, is the real karma. Lord Krishna describes himself as "Aham," that is, "Soham," which is the real power of Avyakta.

"Rama Nama is repeated by almost all people—by thieves, by licentious people, and by rich people. But that Nama by which Dhruva and Prahlada were saved was something different." I boldly tell you with firm assurance that the "different" Nama referred to by Kabir in these lines is none other than Soham. He who makes that Nama his own becomes one with the universal power. His words acquire the force of truth, and hence are full of power.

The ultimate responsibility of obtaining success in worldly or spiritual matters rests upon ourselves. It is through intense devotion and persistent efforts that we have to achieve success. As we progress, we shall ourselves come to know the stage we have acquired in our previous life. Through incessant practice, desires for sensual pleasures slowly become less and less and ultimately disappear, and the aspirant reaches the final goal of everlasting happiness. Only you must have the lighted torch of Soham with you, and must try to obtain peace in its light. I have said what I know from my own experience. Everybody should try to realize it by his own experience. Soham is the soul, and there is everlasting peace in the soul. That itself is the Avyakta, the Unmanifested, in which everything lives, moves and has its being. Obtain everlasting peace by the mantra of Soham. This simple method surely and certainly leads to the goal.

The world is like a big jail, and people are born into it to serve out their sentences. Have therefore a wholesome fear of this jail, and try to purge away your sins and evil desires by the japa and contemplation of Soham. You need not do anything else for the purpose of your deliverance. Keep firm control over your mind, and then you will easily get control over your prana (breath).

The Manifest (Vyakta) and the Unmanifest (Avyakta) are not really different from each other

Pleasure and pain come out of the Avyakta. That is, their source lies hidden in the Supreme Being, which has no form and which is beyond comprehension. To say that the Avyakta can be seen is meaningless. Then how can the experience of it be described in words?

Pay, therefore, no heed to the pains and pleasures which befall you, but carry on the practice of Soham with a heart full of faith and determination. The manifest (Vyakta) and the unmanifest (Avyakta) are not really different from each other. The manifest is nothing but the unmanifest assuming form, and has the unmanifest as its basis. Persons who have attained Self-realization will tell you that what we call karma is nothing but the manifestation of the unmanifest.

The real use of shastric treatises is to train and prepare the mind and the intellect in such a manner that they can grasp the ultimate truth. The discourses of pundits well-versed in shastras may be very interesting to hear, but they will be of no use in getting the real experience, and the everlasting peace which dwells in Soham. All sense of past, present and future is absolutely absent in that stage. That is the Avyakta. There is no past and present in it. It only exists. As to the Sun there is no night and day, similarly, there is no past and present in the Avyakta.

Karma is the manifestation of Avyakta. Along with the idea of karma, naturally comes the ideas of time and motion. These also are really unmanifest. Still, as we can conceive of them, they can also be considered as manifest or pratyaksha. They are, however, eternal and indivisible. Therefore how can we find in them the past, the present and the future, which are the creations of the mind? Similarly, in karma how can there be the distinction of akarma (lack of action), kukarma (bad action) and sukarma (good action) which are created by the mind of man? Similarly, the distinctions between holy and unholy, beautiful and ugly, also cannot be present there.

But how can people who have merely acquired learning, and thereby consider themselves as superior to others, ever experience the bliss of this sort of experience? In this experience shastras have no place, while these learned men base all their opinions on the shastras.

There cannot be karma without time and motion. These three together (karma, time and motion) are the manifestation of the Avyakta, and only in the stage of manifestation arises the necessity of being alert and careful.

This topic has taken a vast and comprehensive turn. But I had referred to the topics of Avyakta and karma before, and hence I have tried to elucidate them here. I had read of these things somewhere, and some ideas came of themselves into my mind regarding them. I have merely put them together here. Otherwise learned men would begin asking me questions about them. I would not be able to answer them to their satisfaction. I have got only the experience of Soham, and nothing else. I do not know anything about Vedanta or the shastras. My knowledge regarding them can be described by a big zero.

Hence I say that everyone should repeat Soham. It surely and certainly leads to the knowledge of the Self and the attainment of everlasting peace. One's actions then in the worldly life are automatically done, and one is absolutely detached from them, just as a lotus leaf is from water.

Three kinds of great men in the world

In my opinion, there are three kinds of great men in the world. I do not say that there are no real saints at present. Some perform miracles by making use of their siddhis. People take them to be great saints and bow before them. These saints obtain some powers by the practice of hatha yoga and perform miracles. As ordinary people in the world want the fulfillment of some desires or the averting of some calamities, they naturally go to such saints and become their followers. These great men, if they are at all great, are of the lowest order of the three kinds mentioned above. Just as in a village where all other people are illiterate, a person who has learnt to read and write is considered wise and learned, similarly these saints are respected by worldly people who themselves know nothing about real spiritual matters. The happiness obtained through such siddhis is transitory. These siddhis merely create a false show of happiness for a time, and then disappear leaving the saint completely bankrupt.

The second kind of great men are those who being filled with the desire to serve mankind, shine as great leaders of men and patriots. Their ambition is to make all their fellow beings or fellow-countrymen prosperous and happy. They sacrifice their personal comfort, and sometimes even their lives, in trying to achieve the good of their fellowmen. They try to weld all their countrymen into one homogenous whole, preach to the people the good which is derived from unity, arouse the consciousness of their rights as subjects, and make them worthy of putting up a fight for their rights and for the redress of their wrongs. Their lives serve as an ideal for ordinary people to follow, and they represent in their lives the sum total of the good qualities of the world. These great men at least do not mislead people by exhibiting miracles by means of siddhis. But these great men are of no use to a human soul striving to attain Self-realization. It does not lie in their power to grace human beings and to lead them to the path of realizing the highest bliss.

The great men who can do this are different. They are the great saints who take pity on all troubled souls who are floundering in the mire of worldly pains and pleasures, and who are at a loss to find a way out. They call such persons their own. They do not lead them to the search of worldly happiness which is illusory, but show them the path which will ultimately take them to the source of all happiness, the path which will clearly show to them the real nature of their Self and illumine their whole being with the all-pervading light of Self-knowledge. They say to the human soul: "The source of happiness is within you. The treasure is hidden within you. Only you have forgotten the place where it is hidden," and they point out that place, and show the way to reach it. Such great men are the real mahatmas, and they are the best of all great men. Sometimes miracles happen at the hands of such mahatmas also, but they happen naturally. They themselves are not conscious of having wrought them. They are always immersed in the atmic bliss, and whatever actions happen at their hands are natural and automatic.

Importance of spiritual visions and experiences

A few days ago, a gentleman from Pune came to see me. While talking on various topics, the following things were said.

The Gentleman: Maharaj, some years ago a Santa Parishada (Meeting of Saints) was held at Pune. Many maharajas, some having matted hair, some who had practiced tapasya and austerities, some sannyasins, some heads of maths, etc., had all assembled together at that meeting. From the name given to that meeting, "Santa Parishada," it was very natural to think that all these men were saints. Ordinary people think that saints are persons who, having realized the Self, are always immersed in the bliss of the Paramatman, and all of whom are directed towards leading other human beings to the path of everlasting happiness. A doubt, however, arose in my mind whether all these men were saints as understood in this sense.

At the present, meetings of "Nathas" often take place at Pune. Some say that they met Sri Matsyendranath, while some say they actually had the darshana of Sri Gorakshanath, and had received orders from him. It has been rumored that the famous Nine Nathas have been issuing orders through these various persons for spreading the doctrines of the Nath Pantha. If any one approaches any of these persons with the desire of knowing whom he should make his sadguru, he gets an order from these persons evidently inspired by one of the Nine Nathas, and he then exactly knows who is his destined sadguru. When I hear about these things, my mind gets confused and I ask myself: Are all these things true? Everywhere we hear about these Nathas and their messages.

In addition, we hear about various other saints. There are also different maths, temples, and different gods and goddesses. I am at a loss to know whether any of these things are true—or none are. My mind is absolutely confused. Hence, I request you to tell me in what I should believe, and how I should set my mind at rest?

Myself: You have asked a very good question. This question often troubles many thoughtful people, especially when they find saints and Nathas sprouting up like mushrooms on all sides.

Paramartha (spirituality) is a subject regarding which various misconceptions hold full sway in our present-day society. Sri Ramdas has said: "There is a bazaar of shastras, various gods and deities are crowding in it, and people are performing various religious ceremonies for securing the fulfillment of their desires. Various tenets and opinions clash with each other. Everybody thinks his own view to be correct, and anybody else's wrong. There is no agreement anywhere, and all are contradicting each other." Under these circumstances, how to find out the truth is a very difficult question. Sri Tukaram says: "There are so many gods. Where should I place my faith?"

No doubt this is all true. But it must be remembered that Paramartha is a thing which is to be achieved by one's own efforts. If anyone, therefore, has a sincere desire to obtain it, he should, instead of entering into discussion regarding it, and instead of visiting various places in search of reputed saints, approach a real saint who has attained Self-realization with due humility and reverence. Because only such a saint can lead others to the right path.

If, however, he finds it difficult to meet such a saint, or to distinguish between true and false saints, there is a very easy method which should be followed by him. He should remain quietly where he is, and at once begin the japa of Soham. He should repeat the japa with a pure mind, and should have firm faith that the Soham japa will fulfill all his wishes. Once he gets this firm faith, he will come to know who is his guru. The Soham mantra is the real savior. If it is repeated with intense faith, accompanied with a sense of detachment from all worldly objects, it will itself make him understand what is true and what is false. There will then be no occasion to find fault with the reputed saints, or to fall into the clutches of false saints. Our salvation really lies in our own hands. I therefore advise my mind to always get immersed in the contemplation of Soham, and thus to free itself from the snares of all such doubts.

The Gentleman: Maharaj, I wish to ask one more question. I have heard that on some occasions you turned wine into milk. Why should saints who have attained Self-realization perform such miracles? If we take up any book containing the life of a saint, it is sure to be full of descriptions of the miracles performed by that saint. I have also heard that on occasion the whole place about you becomes filled with powerful fragrant smells. Ordinary people like me are at a loss to know why saints like you should indulge in the exhibition of miracles such as turning wine into milk, etc. Instead of performing a miracle of spreading fragrant smells, would it not be much easier to enjoy the same kind of smell by purchasing scented sticks worth about six annas? Maharaj, kindly excuse me. I humbly request you to tell me whether all these my doubts are true or misplaced.

Myself: I would never be angry with you for having raised these doubts. I, myself, have gone through all these stages of the unripe mind. My mind can enter into the minds of others, and hence can take a comprehensive view and appreciate the reason behind these questions and doubts. Hence, I always try to solve such honest doubts to the best of my ability. Looked at from the worldly point of view, everybody knows that I am uneducated, and hence I say that I *try* to solve these doubts. It might be that my answers will not satisfy all persons.

You are wrong when you say that I work these miracles. When a person says that he works such miracles, he will be doing so on the strength of siddhis (powers). Such a person is not one who has attained Self-realization. In a man's life sometimes quite unexpected things happen. From that man's point of view, can they not be considered as miracles? We often see such unexpected things actually happening. Do we call them false? No. If, however, we would rely on such things happening, would we ever reach our goal? No. You should think similarly about these spiritual matters. If sometimes wine is turned into milk or some other miracles happen, these incidents should not be given any undue importance. The greatness of a real saint is not increased by such miracles. On the contrary, there is the danger of his being entangled in the clutches of egotism if he were to take the credit of these miracles to himself.

Some miracles naturally happened at my hands, even in my childhood. How can they be explained? The truth of the matter is that these miracles naturally happen through the power of the soul. It is not that such miracles happen at my hands only. Anyone who steadily pursues this path of Soham and perseveringly carries on the practice, will find such miracles taking place quite naturally.

Taking advantage of some old incidents, even now some ignorant critics raise objections as to why I should turn wine into milk instead of drinking milk directly. On the contrary, some jestingly remark and say: "Maharaj, you should turn the water of the Godavari into wine so that we shall immerse ourselves in it and drink to our heart's content." My answer to all such objections and remarks is that I myself do not know how to work miracles. They might happen or might not. If you want miracles, you should go to those saints who have acquired siddhis. In short, miracles are, after all, miracles. You cannot give reasons for them. But miracles which naturally occur clearly show what wonderful powers are centered in the soul.

The same reasoning applies to the seeing of lights of different colors and also to the production of fragrant smells. Just see. We can get smell from incense sticks purchased in the bazaar and we can see different kinds of colored lights in a chandelier. But do we attach any importance to these things? These results are achieved with the help of material objects which are easily had, and hence there is no wonder in them. But when any new discovery is made by a scientist, that scientist is applauded, and sometimes titles are showered upon him. Why should this be so? What has he done except finding out the properties of certain things which were not known before! Having closely studied the inherent properties of different elements, he achieves a certain result by a clever combination of certain things. When a discovery is newly-made we express our admiration for it for a time, and then the thing becomes common and ceases to excite any sense of wonder.

But the fragrant smells and the colored lights in question are not the results produced with the help of material objects. They are produced without the help of any external object, and therein lies their importance. To argue that these scents and lights are similar to those obtained from purchased scented sticks, or from a chandelier, shows sheer ignorance. This sort of argument would never appeal to a thoughtful person. The production of fragrant smells or colored lights without the help of any external objects—in short, the doing of these impossible things—makes the thoughtful mind to ponder, and it is but natural for such a mind to attach importance to these things.

These things are possible only through soul force [atmabala]. Everybody knows that the power of the mind is greater than the power of the body, and that the power of the will is greater than that of the mind. Then what can we say of the power of the soul, from which all power proceeds? When a person strenuously tries to find out the real power of the soul, these insignificant powers are easily and naturally obtained by him. These powers, although in themselves of not much importance, are very useful in proving the inexhaustible and all-comprehensive powers of the soul. A thoughtful mind will at once be convinced that these small powers are but an infinitesimal portion of the power centered in the soul.

While treading the path of Self-realization these powers are easily obtained by the sadhaka, but the sadhaka must not be lured by them and stop there, but go ahead, ignoring them, until he reaches the final goal of Soham: Self-realization. A real saint does not make use of these siddhis even for himself; then how would he say that he performed miracles, and take credit for them? All his efforts are directed towards going beyond the consciousness of doing anything, and thus to conquer his egotism, and get himself merged into the bliss of the Paramatman.

Just as a person who has fully acquired the art of swimming, if thrown in water will naturally swim, similarly, the natural powers acquired by a saint are sometimes manifested when a fitting occasion presents itself. How can you then blame him if miracles sometimes occur at his hands? When an aspirant obtains the grace of a sadguru, and carries on the practice, the production of fragrant smells, etc., and the visions of different kinds of light, follow in due course. These things are not creations of imagination or hallucinations. If things actually seen are to be considered as hallucinations, then these things may also be considered as hallucinations. If those who adversely criticize these visions are of the opinion that the whole panorama of the world is an illusion, then in that case we admit all these spiritual experiences also are illusory. But as long as the world is true, these experiences are also true.

During the practice of Dhyana Yoga, some sadhakas see these visions. As they actually see them, how can we call them illusions? To them at least they are true. If I actually see a thing, that thing is true to me, although it may not be true to others who have not had any experience. But others, who have not got that experience, are not justified in calling my experience false. Hence, to those who saw them, these visions are true. These visions cannot be characterized as mere hallucinations of their brains.

We find in this world many things which at one time were considered as impossible, but which are now not only possible, but of everyday occurrence. This is no fault of nature, but the fault lies in the human mind. If you look at anything superficially, you cannot really understand it. If you, however, go deep, and take a comprehensive view, you will be able to realize its truth. A really thoughtful man should try to acquire correct reasoning power by considering all these things carefully and minutely. I therefore again say that these experiences are true, and not mere illusions.

But even granting for the sake of argument that these subjective sensations of seeing visions are hallucinations, how can objective facts of turning wine into milk, and mutton into roses, which everybody can taste and smell, be called illusions? Such miracles are not subjective sensations only. They can be objectified, and hence beyond suspicion. They are actual facts and can be verified. And as Professor William James said, what are all our verifications, but experiences? I say that through these experiences a sadhaka comes to realize the power of the soul and ultimately to grasp that there is one everlasting and all-pervading Being which is present in everything, and which is the only thing that exists. He then becomes one with Soham. He obtains everything which is to be obtained, to him nothing remains unattained, all his doubts are solved, and he is immersed in everlasting bliss. He becomes one with Brahman, and never falls from this stage.

The Gentleman: Maharaj, I am thoroughly satisfied with your explanations. Really, we ignorant people never try to think over these things carefully and minutely for ourselves, but take for granted what others say, and hence our minds get confused.

Myself: Dear brother, I would like to stress further that one has to reach the goal of life by one's own efforts only.

What is Atmajnana?

Once another gentleman had a long conversation with me, in which the following was said.

The Gentleman: Maharaj, you have explained to me the meanings of avyakta, samadhi, dhyana, prarabdha, sanchita, and kriyamana. I have been enlightened on these subjects, and have clearly understood them. I know Sri Jnaneshwar has said that all skill and all arts are useless. There is only one thing: that is jnana (knowledge of the Self).

I have not clearly understood what is really meant by Atmajnana (knowledge of the Self), Atma Sakshatkara (realization of the Self), and spiritual progress. You generally explain by using homely illustrations, and hence I am able to follow your explanations very easily. I know that all things cannot be properly explained by mere words, or wordy explanations so as to carry conviction beyond doubt. Still, words seem to give at least an approximate idea of the thing, though they may fall short of carrying absolute conviction with them. Lord Sri Krishna has said, "Oh Arjuna, all actions are useless without the knowledge of the Self." Please explain the matter in a way that I can easily understand it."

Myself: You have put a very nice question. I like your questions. I shall try to explain the matter as best as I can. But why should I take the trouble for nothing?"

The Gentleman: If I understand the matter thoroughly, I shall consider you as my sadguru, and by continuous repetition of the Soham mantra I shall, with your grace, obtain the knowledge of the Self. Will this satisfy you?

Myself: All right. Just see. If a sadhaka thinks that seeing of divine visions is the ultimate goal, that it is Self-realization, that he has attained the highest stage, and nothing further remains to be done or achieved, it is sheer ignorance on his part. Because as long as there is duality, the flow of pain and pleasure continues unabated, and everlasting happiness is as far away as ever. If you think carefully, you will see that whatever is seen and heard is bound to disappear. But the knowledge of the Self is permanent and imperishable. This argument, I think, will appeal to all whether they are theists or atheists. Seeing of lights or visions and hearing of divine sounds do not indicate the achieving of Atma Sakshatkara. To realize that the One Eternal Being on which these visions and sounds play and move is none other than our own Self is the real Atma Sakshatkara. To be one with the everlasting Being is the real Sakshatkara.

When a person attains this oneness, his mind entirely becomes devoid of sankalpa (desire) and vikalpa (doubts), and it becomes absolutely indifferent. It goes beyond pleasure and pain. Actions are then automatically performed according to the prakriti dharma (promptings of nature). He becomes absolutely fearless, and is entirely devoid of egotism. When this state of mind is attained, then only can it be said that there is Atma Sakshatkara or Atmajnana. He is, as it were, merely sporting as a child while doing any actions. He is entirely detached from them. This is what is known as Sakshiavastha (the state of being merely a witness of one's actions). Progress means the gradual attainment of this state of mind. We can ourselves get a clear idea of our progress. There is no necessity to ask anyone else about it.

In that state, although passions may be there according to the previous character of the aspirant, still the passions come and go automatically, without taking effect in the form of wrong actions. Right actions are naturally and automatically done. This state is known as Atmajnana. When this stage is reached, never-ending bliss and peace are attained. This is what is known as the sahaja state. This is merely another word expressing the same idea as Atmajnana. Merely defining Atmajnana, Brahmajnana, bliss, or samadhi is of very little use.

Characteristics of an Atmajnani

In short, I wish to emphasize that he who has no attachment for worldly objects, who is perfect, has completely controlled his senses, and whose mind is entirely devoid of any desire for sensual pleasures, who remains in the world but is, as it were, out of it–because of his entire detachment–he alone obtains the sovereign kingdom of everlasting atmic bliss. He becomes one with Soham, and obtains the real grace of his sadguru. His mind is pure like the water of the Ganges, which moves in its course purifying all who come in contact with it. All bad thoughts entirely disappear, and his actions are quite naturally done. He is externally, as well as internally, quite calm and at peace.

In this stage, it is difficult to distinguish him from other ordinary persons. In this stage, he naturally attains the power of knowing the past, present and future. He becomes a Trikalajnani. With all that, he never tells others of what is to happen, nor does he make use of this knowledge for his own benefit. It may happen that his words may at times be prophetic, but this takes place automatically. Never, never does the Atma Sakshatkari (one who has realized his Self) tell others of their past or future on his own initiative. In this stage he sees Brahman in all things; in other words, he is entirely immersed in the experience that everywhere there is nothing but all-pervading joy and bliss. His joy and peace are not dependent upon anything else, and hence they are everlasting. They are not disturbed under any circumstances, however adverse. His experience tells him that he himself has taken the form of the biggest as well as the minutest things. This is the real meaning of Soham. This is the real Atmajnana. Without this Atmajnana, all actions are useless. This is the meaning of Sri Krishna's words.

I do not know whence these words come out of my mouth. You have kindly listened to them with favorable attention. I am thereby filled with extreme joy. There might have been mistakes committed by me through ignorance, or there might have been unpleasant expressions used by me inadvertently. You should kindly pardon me for them.

"My vani (speech) advises me in this manner, and it also tells the same thing to other people" (Tukaram). You should understand and appreciate the underlying meaning of the above lines of Sri Tukaram. With these words I stop and enter into the deep and changeless love and joy of the ajapa japa of Soham.

OM PEACE: OM PEACE: OM PEACE
SOHAM

There is a whole book on the subject of Soham Yoga entitled: Soham Yoga: The Yoga of the Self, *which we recommend you read.*

SOHAM MEDITATION: AN INTRODUCTION

by Abbot George Burke (Swami Nirmalananda Giri)

Some history

Yoga is an eternal science intended to reveal and manifest the Eternal. Although the identity of the Supreme Self (Paramatma) and the individual Self (jivatma) with Soham is indicated in the Isha Upanishad (16) and the Brihadaranyaka Upanishad (1.4.1) respectively, no one knows exactly when it was that the knowledge of Soham Yoga was revealed in the world, but the following we do know.

A young man was wandering in the mountains somewhere in India—most likely in the Western Himalayas. He had seen no one else for a very long time, but one day he heard the faint sound of a human voice. Following it, he saw from a distance some people seated together near a river. Slipping into the water, he began swimming toward them. All along the river on that side thick reeds were growing so he was not seen as he stealthily made his way closer.

Soon he began to understand what was being said. Fascinated by the speaker's words he came as close as he dared and for a long time remained absorbed in the amazing things being spoken. For the science of yoga was being expounded by a master to his disciples. Then he heard the master say: "There is a 'fish' in the reeds over there, listening to everything I am saying. Why doesn't he come out and join us?" He did as suggested and became a resident of the master's ashram and learned both philosophy and Soham Yoga.

After diligent practice of meditation for quite some time, the master asked him to return to the plains and teach that yoga to whomever would listen. He was given a new name, Matsyendranath. (Matsyendra means Indra Among Fish and Nath means Master. Indra is king of the gods.) We have no knowledge of what the master's name was. Matsyendranath and his disciples only referred to him as Adi Nath–Original/First Master. Some believe Adi Nath was Shiva himself manifested to teach yoga, or perhaps the primeval master Bhagavan Sanatkumara about whom the Brihadaranyaka Upanishad says: "To such a one who has his stains wiped away, Bhagavan Sanatkumara shows the further shore of darkness" (7.26.2).

Matsyendra wandered throughout India, teaching those who were awakened enough to desire and comprehend the yogic path. One day in his wanderings he came to a house where the owner's wife gave him something eat and a request: that he would bless her to have a child. In response he blessed her and gave her some ashes from a sacred fire, telling her to swallow them. Then he left. The woman followed his instructions and soon conceived and gave birth to a male child. Several years later Matsyendra came there again and saw the little boy outside the house. He told him to bring his mother, and when she came he asked if she remembered him, which she did. Pointing to the boy, he said: "That is my child. I have come for him." The woman agreed and Matsyendra left with the boy whom he named Gorakhsha, Protector/Guardian of Light.

Goraksha in time became Gorakshanath (usually called Gorakhnath), the greatest yogi in India's recorded history. In every part of India there are stories told of his living in those areas. He also lived in Nepal, Tibet, Ladakh, and Bhutan. There are shrines and temples to him in all those countries, both Hindu and Buddhist. His major temple is in Gorakhpur, the birthplace of Paramhansa Yogananda whose younger brother, Sananda, was originally named Goraksha. Considering all the lore about him, Gorakhnath must have lived at least two or three hundred years, and there are many who claim that he has never left his body but is living right now in the Himalayas.

Gorakhnath had many disciples, a large number of them attaining enlightenment. They were the first members of the Nath Yogi Sampradaya, which in time numbered in its ranks the great sage Patanjali, founder of the Yoga Philosophy (Yoga Darshan) and author of the Yoga Sutras, and Jesus of Nazareth (Sri Ishanath). For many centuries the majority of monks in India were Nath Yogis, but in the nineteenth century there was a sharp decline in their numbers, which continues today. However, there are several groups of "Nath Panthis" that follow the philosophy and yoga of Matsyendranath and Gorakhnath, and therefore are involved with Soham as the heart of their sadhana.

Soham

Soham means: I Am That. It is the natural vibration of the Self, which occurs spontaneously with each incoming and outgoing breath. By becoming aware of it on the conscious level by mentally repeating it in time with the breath (*So* when inhaling and *Ham* when exhaling), a yogi experiences the identity between his individual Self and the Supreme Self.

According to the Nath Yogis (see my book *Soham Yoga*) Soham has existed within the depths of God from eternity; and the same is true of every sentient being. Soham, then, will reveal our inner being. By meditating on Soham we discover our Self within which Soham has existed forever. The simple intonation of Soham in time with the breath will do everything in the unfolding of the yogi's spiritual consciousness.

The practice is very simple, and the results very profound. Truly wondrous is the fact that Soham Yoga can go on all the time, not just during meditation, if we apply ourselves to it. The whole life can become a continuous stream of liberating sadhana. "By the mantra 'Soham' separate the jivatma from the Paramatma and locate the jivatma in the heart" (Devi Bhagavatam 11.8.15).

The important thing about Soham Yoga is that it really works. It only takes perseverance.

The two oldest Upanishads on Soham

The Isha and the Brihadaranyaka are the oldest of the Upanishads, giving us the earliest record of Soham that we know.

The Isha Upanishad concludes with four mantras that are to be recited by a dying person to ensure his ascension to the solar world upon leaving his body. (These mantras are also recited by those who attend the cremation of the body.) The sixteenth mantra says: "O Pushan, the sole seer, O Controller, O Sun, offspring of Prajapati, spread forth your rays and gather up your radiant light that I may behold you of loveliest form. I am that Purusha [Spirit-Self]: I am Soham" (16). (The Sanskrit text is: *Yo sav asau purushah; soham asmi.*) At the core of every sentient being Soham exists as the Self—*is* the Self. *Soham asmi* literally means "I Am That I Am," which is exactly what God told Moses was his Name (Exodus 3:14).

The Brihadaranyaka Upanishad (5.15.2) repeats the identical words. It earlier says: "In the beginning this (world) was only the Self [Atman], in the shape of a person. Looking around he saw nothing else than the Self. He first said, 'I am Soham [*Soham asmi*]'" (1.4.1) Thus Soham is the "first speaking" of the Absolute Itself: the expression of the knowledge and knowing of the Self. Soham is the Name (Embodiment) of the Primeval Being, the Self of the Universe and the Self of our Selfs. Soham is the Consciousness of Brahman and of the Self of each one of us. We, too, are Soham.

The ancient yogis of India discovered that the root impulse of inhalation makes the subtle sound of *So*, and the root impulse of exhalation makes the subtle sound of *Hum* (written as *Ham* in Sanskrit). Since all creation is the thought or ideation of God, meaning is inherent in everything, including the breath: "That [*So*] I am [*Ham*]." In this way every living being is perpetually intoning Soham (Sohum) at the core of their being, saying: I AM THAT: the spirit-Self which is a divine part of the Divine Infinite.

No matter how many ages we wander in forgetfulness of our divine origin and nature, we are always affirming "I am That" without ceasing at each breath. But we have lost the awareness of that sacred thread of inmost knowledge and are now wandering without direction or discernment. But by mentally intoning Soham in time with the breath–*So* when inhaling and *Ham* when exhaling–we consciously take hold of the thread and begin moving in the right direction.

Repeating Soham in a constant flow with the breath turns the mind inward and produces spiritual awareness in an ever-increasing degree. So whenever we intone Soham in time with the breath, we align and link our consciousness with its origin: both our spirit and Divine Spirit.

For the repetition of Soham to produce its effect it must be pronounced correctly. Soham is pronounced like our English words *So* and *Hum*. (The short a in Sanskrit is pronounced like the u in *up* or *hunt*, so we say "hum" even though we write it as "ham.")

It is most important to pronounce the *O* correctly. It should be pronounced like the long *o* in the Italian or common American manner–as in home and lone. In England, Canada, and parts of the American South, the long *o* is sometimes pronounced as a diphthong, like two vowels jammed together: either like "*ay*-oh" or "*eh*-oh." This is not the correct manner of pronouncing the *O*, which should be a single, pure vowel sound.

The same is true of the *U* in *ham* (hum). It is pronounced like the u in *up* or *hunt*–not like the u in *truth* or *push*, as is done in parts of Great Britain.

A mantra is most effective if it is mentally intoned–that is, mentally "sung"–on a single note. (The pitch does not matter–whatever is spontaneous and natural.) This makes the repetition stronger and of deeper effect, because intoning unifies the mind and naturally concentrates it.

The Practice of Soham Yoga Meditation

1. Sit upright, comfortable and relaxed, with your hands on your knees or thighs or resting, one on the other, in your lap.
2. Turn your eyes slightly downward and close them gently. This removes visual distractions and reduces your brain-wave activity by about seventy-five percent, thus helping to calm the mind. During meditation your eyes may move upward and downward naturally of their own accord. This is as it should be when it happens spontaneously. But start out with them turned slightly downward without any strain.
3. Be aware of your breath naturally (automatically) flowing in and out. Your mouth should be closed so that all breathing is done through the nose. This also aids in quieting the mind. Though your mouth is closed, the jaw muscles should be relaxed so the upper and lower teeth are not clenched or touching one another, but parted. Breathe naturally, spontaneously. Your breathing should always be easeful and natural, not deliberate or artificial.
4. Then in a very quiet and gentle manner begin *mentally* intoning Soham in time with your breathing. (Remember: Soham is pronounced like our English words *So* and *Hum*.)

    Intone *Soooooo*, prolonging a single intonation throughout each inhalation, and *Huuummm*, prolonging a single intonation throughout each exhalation, "singing" the syllables on a single note.

    There is no need to pull or push the mind. Let your relaxed attention sink into and get absorbed in the mental sound of your inner intonings of Soham.

    Fit the intonations to the breath—not the breath to the intonations. If the breath is short, then the intonation should be short. If the breath is long, then the intonation should be long. It does not matter if the inhalations and exhalations are not of equal length. Whatever is natural and spontaneous is what is right.

Your intonation of *Soooooo* should begin when your inhalation begins, and *Huuummm* should begin when your exhalation begins. In this way your intonations should be virtually continuous, that is:

SooooooHuuummmSooooooHuuummmSooooooHuuummmSoooooo-Huuummm.

Do not torture yourself about this—basically continuous is good enough.

5. For the rest of your meditation time keep on intoning Soham in time with your breath, calmly listening to the mental sound.

6. In Soham meditation we do not deliberately concentrate on any particular point of the body such as the third eye, as we want the subtle energies of Soham to be free to manifest themselves as is best at the moment. However, as you meditate, you may become aware of one or more areas of your brain or body at different times. This is all right when such sensations come and go spontaneously, but keep centered on your intonations of Soham in time with your breath.

7. In time your inner mental intonations of Soham may change to a more mellow or softer form, even to an inner whispering that is almost silent, but the syllables are always fully present and effective. Your intonations may even become silent, like a soundless mouthing of Soham or just the thought or movement of Soham, yet you will still be intoning Soham in your intention. And of this be sure: *Soham never ceases.* Never. You may find that your intonations of Soham move back and forth from more objective to more subtle and back to more objective. Just intone in the manner that is natural at the moment.

8. In the same way you will find that your breath will also become more subtle and refined, and slow down. Sometimes the breath may not be perceived as movement of the lungs, but just as the subtle pranic energy movement which causes the physical breath.

Your breath can even become so light that it seems as though you are not breathing at all, just *thinking* the breath (or almost so).

9. Thoughts, impressions, memories, inner sensations, and suchlike may also arise during meditation. Be calmly aware of all these things in a detached and objective manner, but keep your attention centered in your intonations of Soham in time with your breath. Do not let your attention become centered on or caught up in any inner or outer phenomena. Be calmly aware of all these things in a detached and objective manner. They are part of the transforming work of Soham, and are perfectly all right, but keep your attention centered in your intonations of Soham in time with your breath. Even though something feels very right or good when it occurs, it should not be forced or hung on to. The sum and substance of it all is this: It is not the experience we are after, but the effect. Also, since we are all different, no one can say exactly what a person's experiences in meditation are going to be like.

10. If you find yourself getting restless, distracted, fuzzy, anxious or tense in any degree, just take a deep breath and let it out fully, feeling that you are releasing and breathing out all tensions, and continue as before.

11. Remember: Soham Yoga meditation basically consists of four things: a) sitting with the eyes closed; b) being aware of our breath as it moves in and out, and c) mentally intoning Soham in time with the breath and d) listening to those mental intonations: all in a relaxed and easeful manner, without strain.

Breath and sound are the two major spiritual powers possessed by us, so they are combined for Soham Yoga practice. It is very natural to intone Soham in time with the breathing. The way is simple and easy.

12. At the end of your meditation time, keep on intoning Soham in time with your breath as you go about your various activities, listening to the inner mantric sound, just as in meditation. One

of the cardinal virtues of Soham sadhana is its capacity to be practiced throughout the day. The *Yoga Rasyanam* in verse 303 says: "Before and after the regular [meditation] practice, the repetition of Soham should be continuously done [in time with the breath] while walking, sitting or even sleeping…. This leads to ultimate success."

Can it be that simple and easy? Yes, because it goes directly to the root of our bondage which is a single–and therefore simple–thing: loss of awareness. Soham is the seed (bija) mantra of nirvanic consciousness. You take a seed, put it in the soil, water it and the sun does the rest. You plant the seed of Soham in your inner consciousness through japa and meditation and both your Self and the Supreme Self do the rest. By intentionally intoning *So* and *Ham* with the breath we are linking the conscious with superconscious mind, bringing the superconscious onto the conscious level and merging them until they become one. It is divinely simple!

Soham Yoga Sadhana in three sentences

The two supreme yogis of India's history, Matsyendranath and Gorakhnath, and the Yoga Chudamani Upanishad have made three statements that are most important for the yogi, for they present the essence of Soham Sadhana.

1. The inhalation comes in with the subtle sound of *So*, and the exhalation goes out with the subtle sound of *Ham*.
2. There is no knowledge equal to this, nor has there ever been in the past or shall be in the future any knowledge equal to this.
3. There is no japa equal to this, nor has there ever been in the past or shall be in the future any japa equal to this.

The implication is that the unequaled, and therefore supreme, knowledge and the unequaled and supreme yoga practice are the mental intonations of *So* throughout the inhalation and *Ham* throughout the exhalation. And therefore that intoning *So* and *Ham* in time with the breath is the totality of Soham Yoga practice.

Such gimmicks as thinking the breath is going up the spine with the intonation of *So* and down the spine with the intonation of *Ham*, or intoning Soham at the chakras, are not Soham Sadhana. Consequently, the Soham yogi's attention should be only on the movement of his breath and his mental intonations of *So* and *Ham* in time with it.

These three statements of Matsyendranath, Gorakhnath and the Yoga Chudamani Upanishad also imply that the difference between Soham Yoga and other yogas is the difference between lightning and lightning bugs.

How is this? Because, as we have seen in the previous chapter, according to the Isha and Brihadaranyaka Upanishads the fundamental nature of both the Supreme Self (Ishwara) and the Individual Self (Jiva) of each one of us, is Soham. Soham Sadhana takes us directly and immediately into the consciousness of the Self and the Supreme Self, simultaneously. Other yoga practices do not do this, but go about it in a roundabout manner, taking many years (if not decades) before even beginning to do what Soham Sadhana does from the very first.

In Soham Yoga only the sufficient time to experience the full range of Self-experience and become permanently established in that experience is necessary for the Soham yogi to become liberated. As soon as he truly knows: "I am Soham," the Great Work is complete. For Ishwarapranidhana not only means offering the life to God, it also literally means offering the breath (prana) to God. This is done by intoning *So* during inhalation and *Ham* during exhalation, both in meditation and the rest of the day and night. In this way Soham Bhava, God-consciousness, is attained.

What can you expect?

Yoga and its practice is a science and the yogi is the laboratory in which that science is applied and tested. At first the aspirant takes the word of a book, a teacher or other aspirants that a yoga method is worthwhile, but eventually it is his personal experience alone that should determine his evaluation of any yoga practice. Because each person is unique in his makeup there can be a tremendous difference in each one's experience of yoga. Nevertheless, there are certain principles which can be stated.

If a yogi is especially sensitive or has practiced the method in a previous life, he may get obviously beneficial results right away. Yet for many people it takes a while for a practice to take hold and produce a steadily perceptible effect. One yogi I knew experienced satisfactory effects immediately. Then to his puzzlement for some days it seemed that absolutely nothing was happening, that his meditation was a blank. But he had the deep conviction (no doubt from a past life as a yogi) that Soham sadhana was the right and true way for him. So he kept on meditating for hours at a time. Then one morning during the final hour of meditation results began coming in the form of experiences that he had not had before. All doubt was dispelled, and he knew he was on the right track. From then onward everything was satisfactory, though there were alternating periods of active experiences and simple quiet observation of inner rest.

Experiences, as I say, can be different for everyone, but certainly peace and refinement of consciousness can be expected. Many things will occur that simply cannot be described because ordinary human language has no words for them. The real test is the yogi's state of mind outside meditation. This he should watch carefully. And he must make sure that he is always practicing correctly. Fortunately, Soham sadhana is simple and easy to do.

Warning: Do Not Interfere!

We are used to directing and controlling as much of our life as possible. But what applies to the external life as wisdom is not necessarily so in the internal life of meditation. The very simple twelve points given previously when followed exactly in a relaxed and calm manner will produce the inner environment in which Soham can do its divine work of revealing itself as the consciousness that is the yogi's true Self. If there is any interference in the form of trying to change something or direct the meditation or experience in any way, the process is interrupted and will produce no results. Naturally, since the practice is so incredibly simple and we have read all kinds of propaganda about "powerful" yogas and the chills and thrills they produce and the "profound insights" and even visions of higher worlds, etc. and etc. that supposedly result from them, we wonder if there surely isn't "more than this to it" and consider trying out such gimmicks as intoning Soham at the chakras, integrating it with some artificial form of pranayama, concentrating on the spine while visualizing/imagining currents moving up and down the spine, and other "enhancements" that may entertain but will only be obstacles to success in Soham sadhana.

The truth is that Soham intoned in time with the breath immediately begins producing a tremendous number of yogic kriyas, but kriyas that are so subtle and natural that they are usually not perceived. It takes real refinement of the mental energies to experience much of what Soham effects in the entire being of the yogi. I have been astonished at how profound the effects of Soham sadhana are, and some of my experiences have been really incredible, but I have had decades of yogic practice behind me to enable me to experience and understand the workings of Soham. I am not describing any of these experiences lest when you encounter them yourself you wonder if your experience is only autosuggestion based on my description.

Be wise and just breathe and intone Soham in time with it with eyes closed during mediation and open during the rest of the day's activity. Nothing else, but just being aware of that process and listening to the inner intonations of Soham is the secret and the assurance of success. And that is all. Soham must not be interfered with–it really cannot be, so any attempt will interrupt and spoil the practice and drag you back on the path of samsara, however "yogic" it may seem to you.

Simplicity of practice

The simpler and more easeful the yoga practice, the more deeply effective it is. This is a universal principle in the realm of inner development and experience. How is this? In the inner world of meditation things are often just the opposite to the way they are in the outer world. Whereas in the outer world a strong aggressive force is most effective in producing a change, in the inner world it is subtle, almost minimal force or movement that is most effectual–even supremely powerful. Those familiar with homeopathic medicine will understand the concept that the more subtle an element is, the more potentially effective it is. In meditation and japa the lightest touch is usually the most effective. This being so, the simple subtle intonations of Soham are the strongest and most effective form of mantric invocation.

An incident that took place during one of the crusades illustrates this. At a meeting between the leaders of the European forces and Saladin, commander of the Arab armies, one of the Europeans tried to impress and intimidate Saladin by having one of his soldiers cleave a heavy wooden chair in half with a single downstroke of his broadsword. In response, Saladin ordered someone to toss a silk scarf as light and delicate as a spider's web into the air. As it descended, he simply held his scimitar beneath it with the sharp edge upward. When the scarf touched the edge, it sheared in half and fell on either side of the blade without even a whisper as he held it completely still. This is like the power of the subtle and simple practice of Soham Yoga meditation.

Subtlety of practice

Soham sadhana is extraordinarily powerful, yet until we become attuned to it by some time of practice it may seem very mild, just a kind of yogic sitting-up exercise. But it is a mighty tool of yoga alchemy. The secret of its power and effectiveness is its subtlety–the very thing that may cause it to be disregarded and not recognized for its intense value, for it is the subtle energies that are able to work lasting changes in our awareness. The more evolved consciousness or energy becomes, the more refined and subtle it becomes–truly spiritual.

It is the very subtle energies that are able to work lasting changes in our awareness. The more evolved consciousness or energy becomes, the more refined and subtle it becomes. Thus it is the highest level of spiritual powers alone that are able to effect our ascent in consciousness.

Tension of any kind interferes with these energies. It is important, then, to keep in mind that often when things seem stuck in meditation and not moving as they should, or when the mind does not calm down, it is often because we are not relaxed sufficiently and are not allowing our inner intonations of Soham to become as subtle as they should be. For the subtler the intonations, the more effective and on target they are.

Even so, I do not mean to give you the impression that your inner intonations of Soham should become feeble or weak in the sense of becoming tenuous–only barely within your mental grasp, and liable to slip away and leave you blank. Not at all. The inner sound of the intonations may become subtler and subtler, but they do not at all become weaker–only gentler and more profound and therefore more effective.

An exception

In point 6 of the Soham Meditation instructions I said that "we do not deliberately concentrate on any particular point of the body such as the third eye, as we want the subtle energies of Soham to be free to manifest themselves as is best at the moment." There is an exception to that. On occasion, such as at the very beginning of meditation or when during the rest of the day you find your attention drifting from the breath and Soham, it can be helpful to make yourself very gently (lest you give yourself a headache from tension) aware of your entire brain (Sahasrara) area, feeling that the breath and Soham intonations are taking place there.

A short time of this awareness (which can arise spontaneously as well) is sufficient, because correct practice will result in Sahasrara awareness naturally.

A final word

All the theory and eulogy in the world regarding a meditation method mean virtually nothing. *But practice is everything.* In yoga more than anything else, practice certainly does Make Perfect. And the practice is so marvelously simple. Consequently, as a friend I urge you in every sense of the expression to literally take this practice to heart. Meditation produces steady spiritual growth if there is steady practice.

The secret of success is regularity in meditation. If you meditate regularly, every day, great will be the result.

So it really is all up to you. The sane and sober voice of the sages and scriptures of India assures us that through the simple japa and meditation of Soham all possible spiritual attainments will be realized.

Sri Gajanana Maharaj On Soham With The Breath

Abbot George Burke (Swami Nirmalananda Giri)

It is consistently found in books on yoga that the expression "ajapa japa" refers to the production of "So" by the inhalation and "Ham" by the exhalation. And the "practice" of ajapa japa is always the mental japa of Soham in time with the breathing. The word "Soham" is certainly a mantra, but it is only ajapa japa when done with the breath: "So" throughout the inhalation and "Ham" throughout the exhalation, the breath being natural and spontaneous, not deliberate. Therefore, when in *Soham Yoga: The Yoga of the Self* and *Light of Soham* the expression "ajapa japa" is found, it means the joining of Soham with the breath, not just the repetition of Soham over and over like an ordinary mantra, for then it would be ordinary mantra japa, *not* ajapa japa.

245

Here are Sri Gajanana Maharaj's words on the subject. The words in italics are mine.

As this Soham Mantra is the mantra of all the Nine Nathas and as it is also the mantra signifying the action of breathing of all creatures, an aspirant who takes to it is sure to make some progress in this very birth and to get experiences showing his progress.

Since Soham is the mantra of the breath, the way to get experience and progress is to do its japa in time with the breath.

Now let us see the real significance of "Soham." All creatures are taking in and giving out breath. The number of breaths in the whole day amounts to twenty-one thousand and six hundred. The taking in of the breath generates the sound "So" and the giving out generates the sound of "Ham." Thus the sound of "Soham" is being continuously generated in every creature, although very few are conscious of it. To be conscious of this sound is the real "Sudarshana" of "Soham," which means "I am He." "Soham," therefore, is the sign showing the oneness of Jiva (human soul) and Shiva (Supreme Soul).... This is the real Dhyana-Yoga or Raja-Yoga.

Soham is inseparable from the breath. The breath and Soham are one, not two. Obviously japa of Soham with the breath is the way to become conscious of the perpetual sound. Awareness of this japa of Soham in time with the breath is the Sudarshana Chakra of the Self.

When the power of breath gets an upward turn, the breath proceeds upwards through the Sushumna and... proceeds to the brahmarandhra at the centre of the brain. The Soham consciousness then merges in the unknowable Supreme Self and the sadhaka attains perfection.

The "power of breath" gets an upward turn by the japa of Soham being done in time with the breath.

Maharaj quotes the following verse of Mahipati: "The seed was sown by the sadguru in the ear and the crop began to grow in the eyes in the form of light. The breath and mind were made one and I became as it were mad with joy."

The seed is Soham, and the breath and mind are "made one" by Soham japa in time with the breath.

Sri Narayana Saraswati, after hearing the vision of Sri Gajanana Maharaj in which he was initiated by Sri Matsyendranath, blessed him and said: "I shall always manifest myself to you in your breath" *obviously through Soham japa in time with the breath.*

"Kabir has said, 'If you want to know the Eternal, you won't find Him in the Vedas, the Shastras or in the Koran, in the Temples or in the Mosques. Penance, pilgrimage, breath-control, or living on merely Neem leaves would not lead you to Him. You can find Him only in your breath (Soham- "So" when taking in and "Ham" when giving out the breath).'"

The words in parentheses are Maharaj's, and underline the blessing of Sri Narayana Saraswati: "I shall always manifest myself to you in your breath."

My guru showered his grace upon me and gave me the ajapa japa mantra of Soham. This grace has deeply entered the innermost recesses of my heart.

[My guru] blessed me by giving me the mantra of Soham. This mantra is the inner, subtle sound produced by the incoming and outgoing breaths. Everyone is breathing and producing this sound, but no one is conscious of it. Hence no one practices this japa. But if anyone carries on the practice by fixing his attention upon this japa, he will be sure to obtain its fruit. I carried on the japa with perseverance and firm faith, and later this practice became my nature.

The way to be conscious of the inner sound of Soham is to repeat it in time with the breath—"So" when inhaling and "Ham" when exhaling. "This japa" is the japa of Soham in time with the breath. And that is the japa Maharaj speaks of in the final sentence.

The mantra Soham was hidden in the Avyakta in the deep recesses of my own soul. This treasure was with me but I had forgotten the place where it was hidden. The saints pointed out to me that place and from that time I have been continuously contemplating on the Self.

The place where Soham was hidden is the breath. Contemplation on the Self is done in the breath by Soham japa in time with the breath.

This Soham is ever present in every being in the form of his own Self. This Soham is continuously going on, it never stops.

Soham is present in all as the continuous breath. By repeating Soham in time with the breath the Soham-Self becomes known.

Even while we are conscious of worldly objects our meditation on Soham must be ceaselessly going on.... Thus, the state of ajapa-japa is reached.

Everyone knows that "ajapa-japa" means the inner sound of Soham in time with the breath. Only through conscious Soham japa also in time with the breath can the state of ajapa-japa be reached. Maharaj continues:

When this is reached we experience the state of samadhi even while we are doing worldly activities. The mind itself becomes one with Soham and the truth of the following words is realized: "The mind has become fixed and motionless in one place. Atmic bliss has, therefore, been realized to the full. Nothing remains lacking."

The one place is which the mind is fixed and motionless is the breath. This is made possible by japa of Soham in with and in the breath.

As long as the breath goes on, life goes on, and the activities of the body go on. The saints have explained the meaning of the incoming and outgoing breath, and <u>Soham is the sound which is produced by the incoming and outgoing breath. This Soham sound is ceaselessly being repeated in our body whether we are conscious of it or not. If we become conscious of this internal Soham, we shall experience peace of mind.</u> If we fully understand this Soham, we shall attain complete bliss, which is the real nature of Soham, and become one with it.

The underlined portion refers to Soham japa with the breath. And as Maharaj says we are to "become conscious of this internal Soham." This is done by the japa of Soham with the breath.

My brothers and sisters should remember that a liking for and devotion to Vithal (God) is the result of the accumulation of great merit in previous lives. If you have this liking, Vithal in the form of Soham who has His dwelling in the outgoing and incoming breath of every human being, will be realized by you. I say this from my own experience. You may have no faith in me but you should have faith in this Soham.

Vithal and Soham have their "dwelling in the outgoing and incoming breath of every human being." Therefore this realization requires the joining of Soham to the outgoing and incoming breath. That alone is "this Soham" in which we are to have faith.

The ajapa japa is automatically going on in the breath (So in taking the breath in, and Ham in giving out). When one repeats this japa of Soham consciously then it is called ajapa japa. If one fixes his attention on the sound produced by the breath, the three nerves–Ida, Sushumna, and Pingala, become free in their actions.

Soham is the pure Sudarshana, which removes all distinctions and gives the experience of Unity in diversity. He who has this Sudarshana in his hand becomes himself Lord Sri Krishna. The four Vedas, the six shastras and the eighteen Puranas describe nothing else except the Sudarshana.... The Sudarshana is situated in your breath. It destroys the three kinds of pains which beset a human being.

The Sudarshana is the Soham Breath itself, the japa of Soham in time with the breath.

The following are words of Sri Gajanana Maharaj spoken to Mr. Vishwanath Gopal Vaidya at various times.

Disciples ask the guru, "Where is the 'Soham Sudarshana'? Please explain it to me." Listening to the disciple's query, the guru says, "The Soham Sudarshana is in the breath, which eliminates the three types of anxieties, namely: those pertaining to this physical body, those pertaining to this material world and those pertaining to the attainment of moksha. Soham Sudarshana is when the mind is moving in the interior ajapa by the repetition of Soham in time with the breath.

When the jiva, the individual Self, and Shiva, the Supreme Self, merge inwardly through the japa of Soham, that is the means whereby you can become immortal when perfectly established in that state. Understand that this Soham Hansa (Swan of Soham) state is the ultimate state in yoga.

Meditate on the sounds of the inner, mental repetition of Soham until they reveal the Self.

To what I am going to tell you, listen carefully. Keep your awareness within the head [the brain, the sahasrara chakra, the thousand-petalled lotus]. There you will find the Gurupada, the feet of the Inner Guru, the Self. Be absorbed in the subtle sound of your mental intonations of Soham in time with the breath.

[In *Soham Yoga: The Yoga of the Self,* there is a citation in the third chapter from a talk by Swami Muktananda in which he speaks of this very same teaching of the Nath Yogis about the Gurupada in the sahasrara. *Editor's note.*]

Mr. Vaman Keshav Mahegaonkar, a disciple of Gajanana Maharaj, told the following:

Once in meditation I saw Sri Dattatreya, who asked me whether I had understood the meaning of Soham. According to my understanding I replied, "'So' means 'He'–that is, God–and 'Ham' means 'I am.' Hence Soham means that God is my Self." Hearing this reply Sri Dattatreya nodded His head in approval, but asked me again whether I knew any other meaning of that mantra. I, however, could not answer this question. Then Sri Dattatreya told me with His own lips that "So" meant taking in of the breath and "Ham" meant letting out of the breath. Hence, he said, Soham meant Taking In and Letting Out. What is to be taken in and what is to be let out? The answer to that is that bad qualities, passions, egotism etc., are to be let out and then good qualities–that is, good morals, faith in truth and devotion to God–are to be taken in. First of all bad qualities are to be let out and then good qualities are to be taken in. Soham can be interpreted in this manner also.

Mr. Balkrishna Mahadeo Gadkari, another disciple of Gajanana Maharaj, wrote:

I first got the darshan of Sri Gajanana Maharaj in the month of May, 1929. After I had the good fortune of being in his company for four or five days, he had me sit near him and placed the right palm of his hand on my head. He told me to shut my eyes and fix my mind inside on the movements of breath, and he favored me with the japa of Soham. When I had repeated the japa of Soham for five minutes, he in his great mercy manifested to me a strong light and said, "This is the light of your own Self. By means of the Soham japa you will be able to see it constantly."

At the end of *Atmaprabha*, Sri Gajanana Maharaj concludes: "With these words I stop and enter into the deep and changeless love and joy of the ajapa japa of Soham." As we see from all the foregoing, the *ajapa japa* of Soham is "done" in time with the breath.

Sri Ramana Maharshi on Soham Sadhana

(by Swami Nirmalananda Giri, Editor)

The contents of *Atmaprabha* were given in response to invitations in 1943 and 1945 for Sri Gajanana Maharaj to attend or send a written message to the Jayanti Utsav (Birthday Celebration) of Sri Ramana Maharshi. The request was not just because of the reputation of Gajanana Maharaj as a great yogi, but because of the Soham Sadhana he advocated, which was in complete consonance with the teachings of the Maharshi.

Someone asked Bhagavan Sri Ramana Maharshi: "What is the purport of the teaching that one should meditate, through the 'I am he' [Soham] thought, on the truth that one is not different from the self-luminous Reality that shines like a flame?"

Bhagavan replied: "The purport of teaching that one should meditate with the 'I am he' thought is this: *sah-aham*: So'ham; *sah* the supreme Self, *aham* the Self that is manifest as 'I.' If one meditates for a long time, without disturbance, on the Self ceaselessly, with the 'So'ham–I am he' thought which is the technique of reflection on the Self, the darkness of ignorance which is in the heart and all the impediments which are but the effects of ignorance will be removed, and the plenary wisdom will be gained.... The body is the temple; the jiva is God (Shiva). If one worships him with the 'So'ham–I am he' thought, one will gain release" (*Collected Works* [Section] 29).

Once Sri Ramana Maharshi was shown the Sanskrit text of *Devi-kallotara Jnanachara Vichara Padalam* (A Study of the Exposition of

Supreme Wisdom and Conduct to Goddess Ishwari by Lord Shiva) written on palm leaves. He said that this writing was very, very important, and himself translated it into Tamil with his commentary. Sri T. K. Jayaram then translated it into English, including the following:

"[Shiva said to Parvati:] The means by which this mind, which is restless and moves about quicker than the wind, can be brought under control, is indeed the means to obtain liberation; is indeed what is good for those who seek permanent Reality; it itself is pure Consciousness and the state of firmness; moreover, it alone is the righteous duty to be followed by discerning aspirants; it alone is the pilgrimage to holy waters; it alone is charity; it alone is austerities. Know that there is no doubt about this." (8-9)

Bhagavan's comment: Now all your pilgrimages are over. Soham Sadhana is the last pilgrimage.

"Repeatedly say thus: I am He, the eternal, Omnipresent Reality which is Brahman. Meditating thus for a long time, whoever abides imperturbably, will become the Supreme Brahman, thereby attaining immortality." (60)

Bhagavan's comment: This is the secret of the Nath Panth. Here comes "I Am He" or "He I Am"–Soham. Our system also says this. Meditate thus for a long time on the Self. You have to say repeatedly: "He I Am"–Soham. This sixtieth verse is very important.

DID YOU ENJOY READING THIS BOOK?

Thank you for taking the time to read *Light of Soham*. If you enjoyed it, please consider telling your friends or posting a short review at Amazon.com, Goodreads, or the site of your choice.

Word of mouth is an author's best friend and much appreciated

There is a whole book on the subject of Soham Yoga entitled: Soham Yoga: The Yoga of the Self, *which we recommend you read.*

Get your FREE Meditation Guide

Sign up for the Light of the Spirit Newsletter and get *Learn How to Meditate Effectively.*

Get free updates: newsletters, blog posts, and podcasts, plus exclusive content from Light of the Spirit Monastery.

Visit: https://ocoy.org/newsletter-registration

GLOSSARY

Abhyasa: Sustained (constant) spiritual practice.

Abhyasa Yoga: Yoga, or union with God, through sustained spiritual practice.

Abhyasin: Yoga-practitioner.

Acharya: Preceptor; teacher; spiritual teacher/ guide; guru.

Adesha: A divine command from within the being; teaching, as is upadesha– teaching received while sitting near (upa).

Adhimatra: The degree of vairagya when worldly enjoyment becomes a source of pain.

Adhishthana(m): Seat; basis; substratum; ground; support; abode; the body as the abode of the subtle bodies and the Self; underlying truth or essence; background.

Adhyatma: The individual Self; the supreme Self; spirit.

Adhyatmika: Adhyatmic; pertaining to the Self (Atman or Jivatman), individual and Supreme (Paramatman).

Advaita: Non-dualism; non-duality; literally: not [a] two [dvaita].

Advaita Nishtha: Establishment in the state of non-duality.

Advaita vada: The theory that Brahman is the only existence; monism; Vedanta.

Advaita Vedanta: The teaching that there is only One Reality (Brahman-Atman), as found in the Upanishads. Non-dualistic philosophy, especially that of Shankara.

Advaitic: Non-dual; having to do with the philosophy of Advaita (Non-Dualism).

Advaitin: A proponent of Advaita philosophy.

Advaitist: A proponent of Advaita philosophy.

Aham: I; I-awareness; the ego; the individual soul; self-consciousness; the pure inner Self.

Aham Brahmasmi: "I am Brahman." The Mahavakya (Great Saying) of the Brihadaranyaka Upanishad.

Ahamkara: See Ahankara.

Ahankara: Ego; egoism or self-conceit; the self-arrogating principle "I," "I" am-ness; self-consciousness.

Ahimsa: Non-injury in thought, word, and deed; non-violence; non-killing; harmlessness.

Ajapa Japa: A yogic term that means the natural, spontaneous sound of the breath that goes on perpetually through the simple act of breathing. This sound is extremely subtle, and though non-verbal is the highest form of mantra. The Mantra "Soham" (I am That) which is produced by the breath itself, without any conscious effort at repeating it: the inhalation sounding 'So' and the exhalation 'ham.'

Ajapa Gayatri: Soham Mantra.

Ajna chakra: "Command Wheel." Energy center located at the point between the eyebrows, the "third eye." The seat of the mind. The medulla center opposite the point between the eyebrows, having two "petals" or rays.

Akarma: Inaction; non-doing.

Amrita: That which makes one immortal. The nectar of immortality that emerged from the ocean of milk when the gods churned it.

Ananda: Bliss; happiness; joy. A fundamental attribute of Brahman, which is Satchidananda: Existence, Consciousness, Bliss.

Anna: In the old currency, there were sixteen annas in a rupee. In the modern currency, twenty-five and fifty pice coins are called four and eight annas, respectively, but it is not really so.

Apana: The prana that moves downward, producing the excretory functions in general; exhalation.

Anugraha: Divine grace; attraction; favor; kindness, conferring benefits; assistance.

Arati: A ceremony of worship in which lights, incense, camphor, and other offerings representing the five elements and the five senses–the totality of the human being–are waved before an image or symbol of the Divine.

Arta(m): Pain(ed); distress(ed); affliction (afflicted); one who is seeking/asking for relief from personal troubles or suffering.

Arya(n): One who is an Arya–literally, "one who strives upward." Both Arya and Aryan are exclusively psychological terms having nothing whatsoever to do with birth, race, or nationality. In his teachings Buddha habitually referred to spiritually qualified people as "the Aryas." Although in English translations we find the expressions: "The Four Noble Truths," and "The Noble Eightfold Path," Buddha actually said: "The Four Aryan Truths," and "The Eightfold Aryan Path."

Asana: Posture; seat; meditation posture; Hatha Yoga posture.

Ashram(a) (1): A place for spiritual discipline and study, usually a monastic residence.

Ashram(a) (2): stage of life. In Hinduism life is divided ideally into four stages (ashramas): 1) the celibate student life (brahmacharya); 2) the married household life (grihasta); 3) the life of retirement (seclusion) and contemplation (vanaprastha); 4) the life of total renunciation (sannyasa).

Ashrama-dharma: Duties pertaining to the four orders or stages of life.

Ashramite: Resident of an ashram.

Atishudra: One who has no caste standing; an outcaste; an aboriginal, a member of an indigenous people.

Atma(n): The individual spirit or Self that is one with Brahman; the essential being, nature or identity of each sentient being.

Atmabala: Soul-force.

Atmajnana: Direct knowledge of the Self; Brahma-Jnana.

Atmajnani: One who has atmajnana.

Atmananda: The bliss of the Self (Atman).

Atmaprabha: Light of the Self; shining by one's own light; self-illuminated or Self-illuminated: illuminated by one's own true Self. Light of the Self; shining by one's own light; self-illuminated or Self-illuminated: illuminated by one's own true Self.

Atmapratiti: Realization/experience of the Self.

Atmarama: Satisfied–delighted–in the Self.

Atmasakshatkara: "Direct sight of the Self;" realization of the true nature of the Self; Self-realization.

Atmatattwa: The principle of the Self; the true nature of the Self; the reality of the Self.

Atmic: Having to do with the atma–spirit or Self.

Avadhuta: "Cast off" (one who has cast off the world utterly). A supreme ascetic and jnani who has renounced all worldly attachments and connections and lives in a state beyond body consciousness, whose behavior is not bound by ordinary social conventions. Usually they wear no clothing. They embody the highest state of asceticism or tapas.

Avatar(a): A fully liberated spirit (jiva) who is born into a world below Satya Loka to help others attain liberation. Though commonly referred to as a divine incarnation, an avatar actually is totally one with God, and therefore an incarnation of God-Consciousness.

Avyakta(m): Unmanifest; invisible; when the three gunas are in a state of equilibrium,.. the undifferentiated.

Baba: A title often given to sadhus, saints and yogis, meaning "father." Little boys are sometimes affectionately called "baba" by adults.

Balkrishna: The child/boy Krishna.

Bandha: "Lock;" bond; bondage; tie or knot; a Hatha Yoga exercise.

Bhagavad Gita: "The Song of God." The sacred philosophical text often called "the Hindu Bible," part of the epic Mahabharata by Vyasa; the most popular sacred text in Hinduism.

Bhagavatam: The Srimad Bhagavatam.

Bhajan: Devotional singing; a devotional song; remembrance (of God).

Bhakta: Devotee; votary; a follower of the path of bhakti, divine love; a worshipper of the Personal God.

Bhakti: Devotion; dedication; love (of God).

Bhakti Marga: The path of devotion leading to union with God.

Bhakti Yoga: The yoga of attaining union with God through the prescribed spiritual discipline of the path of devotion.

Bhakti Yogi: One who practices Bhakti Yoga.

Bindu: Point; dot; seed; source; the creative potency of anything where all energies are focused.

Brahmajnana: Direct, transcendental knowledge of Brahman; Self-realization.

Brahman: The Absolute Reality; the Truth proclaimed in the Upanishads; the Supreme Reality that is one and indivisible, infinite, and eternal; all-pervading, changeless Existence; Existence-knowledge-bliss Absolute (Satchidananda); Absolute Consciousness; it is not only all-powerful but all-power itself; not only all-knowing and blissful but all-knowledge and all-bliss itself.

Brahmanishtha: Remaining steadfast in the Absolute (Brahman). One who is firmly established in the Supreme being, in the direct knowledge of Brahman, the Absolute Reality.

Brahmarandhra: "The hole of Brahman," the subtle (astral) aperture in the crown of the head. Said to be the gateway to the Absolute (Brahman) in the thousand-petaled lotus (sahasrara) in the crown of the head. Liberated beings are said to exit the physical body through this aperture at death.

Brahmavidya: Science of Brahman; knowledge of Brahman; learning pertaining to Brahman or the Absolute Reality.

Brahmin (Brahmana): A knower of Brahman; a member of the highest Hindu caste traditionally consisting of priests, pandits, philosophers, and religious leaders.

Buddhi: Intellect; intelligence; understanding; reason; the thinking mind; the higher mind, which is the seat of wisdom; the discriminating faculty.

Buwa: The Marathi word for Baba.

Chaitanya: Consciousness; intelligence; awareness; the consciousness that knows itself and knows others; Pure Consciousness.

Chakra: Plexus; center of psychic energy in the human system, particularly in the spine or head.

Charvaka: The Indian materialistic school, also known as Lokayata ("restricted to the world of common experience"). Its central teaching is that matter is the only reality, and sense perception is the only valid means of knowledge or proof. Therefore sense satisfaction is the only goal.

Chaturvarga: Fourfold aims, viz., dharma, artha, kama, and moksha.

Chit: Consciousness (that is spirit or purusha); "to perceive, observe, think, be aware, know;" pure unitary Consciousness. The principle of universal intelligence or consciousness.

Chitta: The subtle energy that is the substance of the mind, and therefore the mind itself; mind in all its aspects; the field of the mind; the field of consciousness; consciousness itself; the subconscious mind.

Collyrium (Khol): A black substance put around the eyes. Though used cosmetically, it is considered to have medicinal properties that protect the eyes from infection or disease. It is often put around children's eyes for this purpose.

Crore: Ten million.

Dakshina: Gift; priestly gift; sacrificial fee; donation; an offering given as a gift of gratitude.

Darshan: Literally "sight" or "seeing;" vision, literal and metaphysical; a system of philosophy (see Sad-darshanas). Darshan is the seeing of a holy being as well as the blessing received by seeing such a one.

Datta: Dattatreya.

Dattatreya: A famous sage, son of the Rishi Atri and Anasuya. His birth was a divine boon, hence his name: Datta–"given"–and atreya–"son of Atri." Considered a divine incarnation and known as the Lord of Avadhutas, he is often revered as the embodiment of the Supreme Guru. He is credited with the authorship of the Avadhuta Gita, the Jivanmukti Gita, and the Tripura Rahashya.

Devi: Goddess; the Supreme Shakti (Divine Power) or Divine Mother, or a demigoddess.

Dharana: Concentration of mind; fixing the mind upon a single thing or point. "Dharana is the confining [fixing] of the mind within a point or area" (Yoga Sutras 3:1).

Dharma: The righteous way of living, as enjoined by the sacred scriptures and the spiritually illumined; law; lawfulness; virtue; righteousness; norm.

Dharmashala: A place for pilgrims to stay, either free of charge or at a minimal cost.

Dhoti: A long piece of material worn around the waist by traditionally-dressed men in India, rather like a long skirt.

Dhyana(m)/Dhyana Yoga: Meditation; contemplation.

Divyadrishti: Divine vision.

Diwali: The Hindu autumnal Festival of Lights celebrated everywhere in India and abroad.

Durga: "Incomprehensible One;" "Difficult to reach;" the Universal Mother; she rides a lion (or tiger) and carries a weapon in each of her eight arms symbolizing the powers of the Self against ignorance and evil. She is invoked against all forms of evil–physical and metaphysical. Considered the consort, the shakti, of Shiva.

Dvaita/Dwaita: Dual; duality; dualism.

Ekagrata: One-pointedness of the mind; concentration.

Eknath: A renowned Vaishnava saint of Western India (Maharashtra).

Four Sadhanas: (1) the discrimination between eternal and non-eternal things; (2) disinterestedness regarding enjoyments in this as well as the next world; (3) possession of self-control, peace of mind, etc.; (4) a keen desire for liberation or moksha.

Ganapati: "Lord of the Ganas" (the spirits that always accompany Shiva). See Ganesha.

Ganesha: The elephant-headed son of Shiva and Parvati; the remover of obstacles; lord (pati) of the ganas (spirits that always accompany Shiva); god of wisdom; god of beginnings; the granter of success in spiritual and material life; in ritual worship he is worshipped first, and is therefore known as Adi-deva, the First God.

Gayatri Mantra: A Rig Vedic mantra in the gayatri meter invoking the solar powers of evolution and enlightenment, recited at sunrise and sunset.

Gerua: The brownish-orange mud used to dye the clothing of Hindu monastics; the color produced by dyeing with gerua is also itself called gerua.

Ghee: Clarified butter.

Gita: The Bhagavad Gita.

Gorakhnath/Gorakshanath: A master yogi of the Nath Yogi (Nath Pantha) tradition. His dates are not positively known, but he seems to have lived for many centuries and travelled throughout all of India, Bhutan, Tibet, and Ladakh teaching philosophy and yoga.

Grihastha: One who is living in the second stage (ashrama) of Hindu social life; married householder's life.

Guna: Quality, attribute, or characteristic arising from nature (Prakriti) itself; a mode of energy behavior. As a rule, when "guna" is used it is in reference to the three qualities of Prakriti, the three modes of energy behavior that are the basic qualities of nature, and which determine the inherent characteristics of all created things. They are: 1) sattwa–purity, light, harmony; 2) rajas–activity, passion; and 3) tamas–dullness, inertia, and ignorance.

Guru: Teacher; preceptor; spiritual teacher or acharya.

Indra: King of the lesser "gods" (demigods); the ruler of heaven (Surendra Loka); the rain-god.

Indraloka: Indra's world; Indra's heaven.

Indriya: Organ. The five organs of perception (jnanendriyas) are the ear, skin, eye, tongue, and nose. The five organs of action (karmendriyas) are the voice, hand, foot, organ of excretion, and the organ of generation.

Ishwara: "God" or "Lord" in the sense of the Supreme Power, Ruler, Master or Controller of the cosmos. "Ishwara" implies the powers of omnipotence, omnipresence and omniscience.

Ishwarasayujya: Union with Ishwara.

Japa: Repetition of a mantra.

Jijnasa: Desire to know.

Jijnasu: One who aspires after knowledge; spiritual aspirant.

Jiva: Individual spirit.

Jivanmukta: One who is liberated here and now in this present life.

Jivanmukti: Liberation in this life.

Jivatma(n): Individual spirit; individual consciousness.

Jnana(m): Knowledge; knowledge of Reality–of Brahman, the Absolute; also denotes the process of reasoning by which the Ultimate Truth is attained.

The word is generally used to denote the knowledge by which one is aware of one's identity with Brahman.

Jnana Marga: The path of discriminative knowledge leading to union with God.

Jnana Yoga: The path of knowledge; meditation through wisdom; constantly and seriously thinking on the true nature of the Self as taught by the upanishads.

Jnana yogi: One following the path of knowledge–jnana yoga.

Jnanadev(a): Jnaneshwar.

Jnanendriyas: The five organs of perception: ear, skin, eye, tongue, and nose.

Jnaneshwar: A thirteenth-century saint of Maharashtra, a poet, philosopher and yogi of the Nath Yogi Panth or tradition.

Jnaneshwari: The renowned commentary on the Bhagavad Gita written by Sri Jnaneshwar.

Jnani: A follower of the path of knowledge (jnana); one who has realized–who knows–the Truth (Brahman).

Kabir: An Indian mystic of the fifteenth and sixteenth centuries.

Kaivalya: Transcendental state of Absolute Independence; state of absolute freedom from conditioned existence; moksha; isolation; final beatitude; emancipation.

Kaivalya-mukti (moksha): Liberation in which the yogi becomes one with Brahman while living (jivanmukti); final emancipation.

Kali: "The Black One;" the black-skinned goddess who emerged from the body of Goddess Durga to defeat the demons that were attacking her. She wears a garland of skulls (or severed heads) around her neck and a skirt of severed arms–both symbolizing the sense of egotism. In one hand she wields the sword of spiritual wisdom (prajna) and in the other carries a severed head (ego). Despite her fearsome appearance, her two other hands are held in the gestures (mudras) that indicate: "Fear not" and "Draw near."

Kali Yuga: The dark age of spiritual and moral decline, said to be current now. See Yuga.

Kama: Desire; passion; lust.

Kamadhenu: Wish-fulfilling cow produced at the churning of the milk ocean.

Karma: Karma, derived from the Sanskrit root kri, which means to act, do, or make, means any kind of action, including thought and feeling. It also means the effects of action. Karma is both action and reaction, the metaphysical equivalent of the principle: "For every action there is an equal and opposite reaction." "Whatsoever a man soweth, that shall he also reap" (Galatians 6:7). It is karma operating through the law of cause and effect that binds the jiva or the individual soul to the wheel of birth and death. There are three forms of karma: sanchita, agami, and prarabdha. Sanchita karma is the vast store of accumulated actions done in the past, the fruits of which have not yet been reaped. Agami karma is the action that will be done by the individual in the future. Prarabdha karma is the action that has begun to fructify, the fruit of which is being reaped in this life.

Karma Marga: The path of selfless action leading to union with God.

Karma Yoga: The Yoga of selfless (unattached) action; performance of one's own duty; service of humanity.

Karmakhanda: The ritual portion of the Veda. The philosophy that Vedic ritual is the only path to perfection.

Karmakhandi(n): One who follows the Karma-kanda as philosophy and practice.

Karmendriyas: The five organs of action: voice, hand, foot, organ of excretion, and the organ of generation.

Katha: Tale or story; history or narrative.

Kayastha: A kayastha is a member of the Kayastha caste that is traditionally believed to be been keepers of public records and accounts, writers and state administrators. Yet their actual place in the caste system has never been really determined. In north central India the term "Kayastha" is a polite and non-commital term used to refer to non-Brahmins.

Kirtan(a): Singing the names and praises of God; devotional chanting.

Krama: Order; sequence; sequential order or progression; stage; underlying process; natural law—all these are inherent in their substratum or dharmi.

Krama mukti: Attainment of liberation in stages; gradual liberation; passing from this world to a higher world beyond rebirth and from there attaining liberation.

Krishna: An avatar born in India about three thousand years ago, Whose teachings to His disciple Arjuna on the eve of the Great India (Mahabharata) War comprise the Bhagavad Gita.

Kriyamana: Literally: "what is being done;" the effect of the deeds of the present life to be experienced in the future; same as Agami.

Krodha: Anger, wrath; fury.

Kukarma: Negative, bad or evil action.

Kumbhaka: Retention of breath; suspension of breath.

Kundalini: The primordial cosmic conscious/energy located in the individual; it is usually thought of as lying coiled up like a serpent at the base of the spine.

Lakh: One hundred thousand.

Lakshmi: The consort of Vishnu; the goddess of wealth and prosperity.

Laya: Dissolution; merging.

Laya Yoga: Dissolution; merging; process of absorption of the individual soul into the Supreme Soul; another name of Nada-yoga or Kundalini-yoga.

Lila: Play; sport; divine play; the cosmic play. The concept that creation is a play of the divine, existing for no other reason than for the mere joy of it. The life of an avatar is often spoken of as lila.

Linga: Mark; gender; sign; symbol. Usually a reference to a column-like or egg-shaped symbol of Shiva.

Lobha: Greed; covetousness.

Madhyama: Moderate; the middle stage of sound as it develops from silent to fully audible or spoken. Sound in its subtle form as it exists in the mind/psyche before its gross manifestation.

Mahabharata: The world's longest epic poem (110,00 verses) about the Mahabharata (Great Indian) War that took place about three thousand years ago. The Mahabharata also includes the Bhagavad Gita, the most popular sacred text of Hinduism.

Mahabhava: Supreme love and yearning for God, exemplified by Sri Radha.

Mahabodha: The Great Awakening.

Mahalaya: The Great Dissolution, Great Merging; process of absorption of the individual soul into the Supreme Soul.

Mahant: The head of an ashram; an abbot.

Maharaj(a): "Great king;" lord; master; a title of respect used to address holy men.

Maharashtra: One of the largest–and the wealthiest–states in India, whose capital is Mumbai (Bombay). Considered the land of yogis, especially of the Nath Sampradaya.

Mahasamadhi: Literally "the great union [samadhi]," this refers to a realized yogi's conscious departure from the physical body at death.

Mahashivaratri: "The Great Night of Shiva." The major, night-long festival of the worship of Shiva that occurs on the fourteenth day of the dark half of the lunar month known as Phalguna (usually in February, but every third year when an extra month is added to the lunar calendar, it may occur in March).

Mahatma: Literally: "a great soul [atma]." Usually a designation for a sannyasi, sage or saint.

Mahavakya: Literally: "Great Saying." The highest Vedantic truth, found in the Upanishads expressing the highest Vedantic truths or the identity between the individual soul and the Supreme Soul. There are four Mahavakyas: 1) Prajñanam Brahma–"Consciousness is Brahman" (Aitareya Upanishad 3.3); 2) Ayam Atma Brahma–"This Self is Brahman" (Mandukya Upanishad 1.2); 3) Tat Twam Asi–"Thou art That" (Chandogya Upanishad 6.8.7); 4) Aham Brahmasmi–"I am Brahman" (Brihadaranyaka Upanishad 1.4.10).

Manas(a): The sensory mind; the perceiving faculty that receives the messages of the senses.

Mantra(m): Sacred syllable or word or set of words through the repetition and reflection of which one attains perfection or realization of the Self. Literally, "a transforming thought" (manat trayate). A mantra, then is a sound formula that transforms the consciousness.

Mantra Yoga: The Yoga of the Divine Word; the science of sound; the path to divine union through repetition of a mantra–a sound formula that transforms the consciousness.

Marathi: The language of Maharashtra.

Math: A monastery.

Matsyendranath: Guru of Gorakhnath and the first publicly known Nath Yogi, having become a disciple of Adinath who is considered an avatar of Shiva. As with Gorakhnath, we have no dates for him.

Maya: The illusive power of Brahman; the veiling and the projecting power of the universe, the power of Cosmic Illusion. "The Measurer"–a reference to the two delusive "measures," Time and Space.

Mayic: Having to do with Maya.

Moksha: Release; liberation; the term is particularly applied to the liberation from the bondage of karma and the wheel of birth and death; Absolute Experience.

Mudhavastha: State of ignorance or forgetfulness of one's real nature.

Mudra: A position–usually of the hands/fingers–which inherently produces a desired state in the subtle energy levels (prana) according to the Tantric system; a Hatha Yoga posture; a position of the eyes in meditation.

Mukta: One who is liberated–freed–usually in the sense of one who has attained moksha or spiritual liberation.

Mukta purusha: A person liberated from all kinds of bondage; One freed from birth and death.

Mukti: Moksha; liberation.

Muktidata: Giver of liberation (mukti; moksha).

Muladhara chakra: "Seat of the root." Energy center located at the base of the spine. Seat of the Earth element.

Mumukshu: Seeker after liberation (moksha).

Mumukshutwa: Intense desire or yearning for liberation (moksha).

Nadi: A channel in the subtle (astral) body through which subtle prana (psychic energy) flows; a physical nerve. Yoga treatises say that there are seventy-two thousand nadis in the energy system of the human being.

Naivedya: Edible offerings to the deity in a temple or household shrine.

Nama: Name. The Divine Name.

Nath(a): Master; lord; ruler; protector.

Nath Pantha (Nathas): Various associations of yogis who trace their roots back to Matsyendranath and the Nath Yogi Sampradaya.

Nath Yogi: A member of the Nath Yogi Sampradaya.

Nath Sampradaya: An ancient order of yogis claiming Matsyendranath, Gorakhnath, Patanjali, Jnaneshwar and Jesus (Isha Nath) among their master teachers.

Navaratri Puja: Nine days' worship of the goddess Durga in the month of Ashwin (September-October).

Nine Nathas: Nine great Masters of the Nath Yogi Sampradaya, including Matsyendranath and Ghoraknath.

Niranjana: Without blemish; spotless.

Niranjanawastha: The state of absolute purity.

Nirguna: Without attributes or qualities (gunas).

Nirguna Brahman: The impersonal, attributeless Absolute beyond all description or designation.

Nirvikalpa: Indeterminate; non-conceptual; without the modifications of the mind; beyond all duality.

Nirvikalpa Samadhi: Samadhi in which there is no objective experience or experience of "qualities" whatsoever, and in which the triad of knower, knowledge and known does not exist; purely subjective experience of the formless and qualitiless and unconditioned Absolute. The highest state of samadhi, beyond all thought, attribute, and description.

Nishkama: Free from wish or desire; desirelessness; selfless, unselfish; action without expectation of fruits.

Nishkama bhava: Motiveless, spontaneous feeling; the attitude of non-expectation of fruits of action.

Nishkama karma: Desireless action; disinterested action; action dedicated to God without personal desire for the fruits of the action; selfless action.

Nishkama Karma Yoga: Action without expectation of fruits, and done without personal interest or egoism.

Niyama: Observance; the five Do's of Yoga: 1) Shaucha: purity, cleanliness; 2) Santosha: contentment, peacefulness; 3) Tapas: austerity, practical (i.e., result-producing) spiritual discipline; 4) Swadhyaya: self-study, spiritual study; 5) Ishwarapranidhana: offering of one's life to God.

Ojas: Vitality; vigor; luster; splendor; energy; spiritual energy. The highest form of energy in the human body. In the spiritual aspirant who constantly practices continence and purity, other forms of energy are transmuted into ojas and stored in the brain, manifesting as spiritual and intellectual power.

Padmasana: Lotus posture; considered the best posture for meditation.

Panchanga: The traditional Indian (Hindu) calendar. "It provides precise information about astrological factors, planets, and stars which influence and alter the nature of the subtle environment" (A Concise Dictionary of Indian Philosophy).

Pandharpur: The major pilgrim city for Vaishnavas in Maharashtra, site of the famous Vithoba (or Vithala) Temple of Lord Krishna.

Pandit(a): Scholar; pundit; learned individual; a man of wisdom.

Punya: Merit; virtue; meritorious acts; virtuous deeds.

Panduranga: Krishna, in the form worshipped in the Vithoba Temple in Pandharpur.

Pantha: Road; path; way. Often this is used to designate a spiritual tradition or an association of followers of a particular spiritual tradition or path, such as the Nath Pantha, Kabir Pantha, etc.

Para(ma): Highest; universal; transcendent; supreme.

Paramartha: The highest attainment, purpose, or goal; absolute truth; Reality.

Paramatma(n): The Supreme Self, God.

Param[a]samvit: Supreme consciousness; supreme knowledge.

Paravairagya: Highest type of dispassion; the mind turns away completely from worldly objects and cannot be brought back to them under any circumstances.

Pashyanti: The first prearticulated aspect of sound; sound in a subtle form as it starts to manifest before reaching the mind; the first perceptible form of sound.

Patanjali: A yogi of ancient India, a Nath Yogi and the author of the Yoga Sutras.

Pice: A monetary unit. There were sixty-four pice in the old rupee, but now there are one hundred.

Pitri: A departed ancestor, a forefather.

Pitriloka: The world occupied by the divine hierarchy of ancestors.

Prachiti: Investigation; examination.

Prajna: Consciousness; awareness; wisdom; intelligence.

Prakriti: Causal matter; the fundamental power (shakti) of God from which the entire cosmos is formed; the root base of all elements; undifferentiated matter; the material cause of the world. Also known as Pradhana. Prakriti can also mean the entire range of vibratory existence (energy).

Prana: Life; vital energy; life-breath; life-force; inhalation. In the human body the prana is divided into five forms: 1) Prana, the prana that moves upward; 2) Apana: The prana that moves downward, producing the excretory functions in general. 3) Vyana: The prana that holds prana and apana together and produces circulation in the body. 4) Samana: The prana that carries the grosser material of food to the apana and brings the subtler material to each limb; the general force of digestion. 5) Udana: The prana which brings up or carries down what has been drunk or eaten; the general force of assimilation.

Pranashakti: Subtle vital power.

Pranavayu: The upward moving prana in the body, controller of the heart and lungs.

Pranayama: Control of the subtle life forces, often by means of special modes of breathing. Therefore breath control or breathing exercises are usually mistaken for pranayama. It also means the refining (making subtle) of the breath, and its lengthening through spontaneous slowing down of the respiratory rate.

Prarabdha: Karma that has become activated and begun to manifest and bear fruit in this life; karmic "seeds" that have begun to "sprout."

Prasad(am): Grace; food or any gift that has been first offered in worship or to a saint; that which is given by a saint.

Prashanta: Calmed; quiet; tranquilized; tamed; intensified peace.

Pratiti: Perception; apprehension; insight; complete understanding; conviction; faith, confidence, belief, trust, credit; fame, respect; delight.

Pratyaksha: Perception; direct perception; intuition.

Pratyakshapramana: Proof of direct perception or intuition.

Prayaschitta: Atonement (through various prescribed acts); expiation; mortification.

Prema: Love; divine love (for God).

Pundit: Scholar; pandita; learned individual.

Puraka: Inhalation of breath.

Purana: Literally "The Ancient." The Puranas are a number of scriptures attributed to the sage Vyasa that teach spiritual principles and practices through stories about sacred historical personages which often include their teachings given in conversations.

Purusha: "Person" in the sense of a conscious spirit. Both God and the individual spirits are purushas, but God is the Adi (Original, Archetypal) Purusha, Parama (Highest) Purusha, and the Purushottama (Highest or Best of the Purushas).

Raja Yoga: See Dhyana Yoga.

Rajas: Activity, passion, desire for an object or goal.

Rajasa: See Rajasic.

Rajasic: Possessed of the qualities of the raja guna (rajas). Passionate; active; restless.

Ram: A title of Brahman the Absolute. Though sometimes used as a contraction of the name of Rama, many yogis insist that it is properly applied to Brahman alone and employ it as a mantra in repetition and meditation to reveal the Absolute. Interestingly, Ram (Rahm) is also a title of God in Hebrew.

Rama: An incarnation of God–the king of ancient Ayodhya in north-central India. His life is recorded in the ancient epic Ramayana.

Ramana Maharshi: A great twentieth-century sage from Tamil Nadu, who lived most of his life at or on the sacred mountain of Arunachala in the town of Tiruvannamalai.

Rishi: Sage; seer of the Truth.

Ritambhara: Full of experience; cosmic harmony; the first stage of savikalpa samadhi.

Ritambharaprajna: Truth consciousness; consciousness that is full of truth. That power or truth obtained in the super-reflective state of samadhi; cosmic experience. The repeated experience of nirodha in samadhi eventually itself becomes the dynamic truth-bearing samskara, ritambhara prajna, which blocks other samskaras, vrittis, etc., giving birth to seedless (nirbija) samadhi.

Rudraksha: "The Eye of Shiva;" a tree seed considered sacred to Shiva and worn by worshippers of Shiva, Shakti, and Ganesha, and by yogis, usually in a strand of 108 seeds. Also used as a rosary to count the number of mantras repeated in japa.

Sadagati: Everlasting happiness; final beatitude.

Sadguru: True guru, or the guru who reveals the Real: Sat; God.

Sadhaka: One who practices spiritual discipline—sadhana—particularly meditation.

Sadhana: Spiritual practice.

Sadhana-chatushtaya: The fourfold aids to spiritual practice: 1) Viveka, the ability to discriminate between the transient and the eternal (nitya-anity-as-tu-viveka); 2) Vairagya, the absence of desire for securing pleasure or pain either here or elsewhere (iha-anutra-artha-phala-vairagya); 3) Shad-Sampat (The Sixfold Virtue): Sama, the serenity or tranquillity of mind which is brought about through the eradication of desires; Dama, the rational control of the senses; Uparati, satiety or resolutely turning the mind away from desire for sensual enjoyment; Titiksha, the power of endurance (an aspirant should patiently bear the pairs of opposites such as heat and cold, pleasure and pain, etc.; Shraddha, intense faith, lasting, perfect and unshakable; Samadhana, fixing the mind on Brahman or the Self, without allowing it to run towards objects; 4) Mumukshutwa, the intense desire for liberation.

Sadhu: Seeker for truth (sat); a person who is practicing spiritual disciplines; a good or virtuous or honest man, a holy man, saint, sage, seer. Usually this term is applied only to monastics.

Saguna: Possessing attributes or qualities (gunas).

Saguna Brahman: Brahman with attributes, such as mercy, omnipotence, omniscience, etc.; the Absolute conceived as the Creator, Preserver, and Destroyer of the universe; also the Personal God according to the Vedanta.

Sahaja: Natural; innate; spontaneous; inborn.

Sahaja Nirvikalpa Samadhi: Natural, non-dual state of Brahmic Consciousness.

Sahaja samadhi: See Sahaja Nirvikalpa Samadhi.

Sahajanishtha: Natural and normal establishment; establishment in one's own essential nature of Satcidananda.

Sahajavastha: Superconscious state that has become natural and continuous.

Sahasrara: The "thousand-petalled lotus" of the brain. The highest center of consciousness, the point at which the spirit (atma) and the bodies (koshas) are integrated and from which they are disengaged.

Sahasr(ar)adala: The Sahasrara chakra located in the center of the brain according to the Nath Panth tradition.

Sakama: Action with expectation of fruits.

Sakshatakara: Self-realization; direct experience; experience of Absoluteness; Brahmajnana.

Sakshi(n): a witness; the Witness Self; the kutashtha which passively observes the actions of the body and the senses; seer; the intuitive faculty.

Sakshiavastha: Permanent establishment in the Witness State.

Sakshibhava: The attitude of remaining as a witness.

Sakshitwa: Establishment in the consciousness of being the Witness Self; looking upon oneself as merely the observer.

Samadhi (1): The state of superconsciousness where Absoluteness is experienced attended with all-knowledge and joy; Oneness; here the mind becomes identified with the object of meditation; the meditator and the meditated, thinker and thought become one in perfect absorption of the mind. See

Samprajñata Samadhi, Asamprajñata Samadhi, Savikalpa Samadhi, and Nirvikalpa Samadhi.

Samadhi (2): The tomb or memorial of a saint.

Samarth Ramdas: A renowned saint and poet of Maharastra; guru of the great warrior-king Shivaji; rishi of the mantra: Sri Ram Jai Ram Jai Jai Ram.

Samata: Balanced state of mind.

Samatva: Equanimity (under all conditions); equanimity of outlook (making no distinction between friend and foe, pleasure and pain, etc.)

Sampradaya: Tradition; philosophical school; literally: "hand-ed-down instruction."

Samprajnata: A stage in samadhi wherein one is conscious of an object; that mind functions in this stage and concentrates on an object of knowledge (perception).

Samprajñata samadhi: State of superconsciousness, with the triad of meditator, meditation and the meditated; lesser samadhi; cognitive samadhi; samadhi of wisdom; meditation with limited external awareness. Savikalpa samadhi.

Samsara: Life through repeated births and deaths; the wheel of birth and death; the process of earthly life.

Samskara: Impression in the mind, either conscious or subconscious, produced by action or experience in this or previous lives; propensities of the mental residue of impressions; subliminal activators; prenatal tendency. See Vasana.

Samyama: Self-control; perfect restraint; an all-complete condition of balance and repose. The combined practice of the last three steps in Patanjali's Ashtanga Yoga: concentration (dharana), meditation (dhyana), and union (samadhi). See the Vibhuti Pada of the Yoga Sutras.

Sanchita karma: The vast store of accumulated actions done in the past, the fruits of which have not yet been reaped.

Sandhya: A ritual done at the "junctions" (sandhyas) of the day—dawn, noon, and sunset—during which the Savitri Gayatri is repeated.

Sankalpa: A life-changing wish, desire, volition, resolution, will, determination, or intention—not a mere momentary aspiration, but an empowering act of will that persists until the intention is fully realized. It is an act of spiritual, divine creative will inherent in each person as a power of the Atma.

Sankhya: One of the six orthodox systems of Hindu philosophy whose originator was the sage Kapila, Sankhya is the original Vedic philosophy, endorsed by Krishna in the Bhagavad Gita (Gita 2:39; 3:3, 5; 18:13, 19), the second chapter of which is entitled "Sankhya Yoga." A Ramakrishna-Vedanta Wordbook says: "Sankhya postulates two ultimate realities, Purusha and Prakriti. Declaring that the cause of suffering is man's identification of Purusha with Prakriti and its products, Sankhya teaches that liberation and true knowledge are attained in the supreme consciousness, where such identification ceases and Purusha is realized as existing independently in its transcendental nature." Not surprisingly, then, Yoga is based on the Sankhya philosophy.

Sannyas(a): Renunciation; monastic life. Sannyasa literally means "total throwing away," in the sense of absolute rejection of worldly life, ways and attitudes. True sannyas is based on viveka and vairagya. It is not just a mode of external life, but a profound insight and indifference to the things of the world and the world itself–not the world of God's creation, but the world of human ignorance, illusion, folly and suffering which binds all sentient beings to the wheel of continual birth and death. The sannyasi's one goal is liberation through total purification and enlightenment. His creed is Shankara's renowned Vedanta in Half a Verse: "Brahman is real. The world is illusion. The jiva is none other than Brahman."

Sannyasi(n): A renunciate; a monk.

Saraswati: The goddess of speech, wisdom, learning and the arts–particularly music.

Sat: Existence; reality; truth; being; a title of Brahman, the Absolute or Pure Being.

Sat Chakras: The six chakras: Muladhara, Swadhishthana, Manipura, Anahata, Vishuddha and Ajna, located at the base of the spine, in the spine a little less than midway between the base of the spine and the area opposite the navel in the spine, the point in the spine opposite the navel, the point in the spine opposite the midpoint of the sternum bone, the point in the spine opposite the hollow of the throat, and the point between the eyebrows, respectively.

Satchidananda: Existence-Knowledge-Bliss Absolute; Brahman.

Sattwa: Light; purity; harmony, goodness, reality.

Sattwa Guna: Quality of light, purity, harmony, and goodness.

Sattwic: Partaking of the quality of Sattwa.

Satya Loka: "True World," "World of the True [Sat]", or "World of Truth [Satya]." This highest realm of relative existence where liberated beings live who have not entered back into the Transcendent Absolute where there are no "worlds" (lokas). From that world they can descend and return to other worlds for the spiritual welfare of others, as can those that have chosen to return to the Transcendent.

Savikalpa Samadhi: Samadhi in which there is objective experience or experience of "qualities" and with the triad of knower, knowledge and known; lesser samadhi; cognitive samadhi; samadhi of wisdom; meditation with limited external awareness. Samprajñata samadhi.

Sayujya: Closely united with; united with God; becoming one with God.

Sayujyata: The state of being in Sayujya.

Shabda: Sound; word.

Shabda Brahman: Sound-God; Brahman in the Form of Sound; Omkara; the Vedas.

Shakta: A worshipper of Shakti, the Divine Feminine.

Shakti: Power; energy; force; the Divine Power of becoming; the apparent dynamic aspect of Eternal Being; the Absolute Power or Cosmic Energy; the Divine Feminine.

Shalagrama: A flat-round or disk-like stone with rounded edges, found only in the Mandakini River in the region of Tibet, considered to be a manifestation of Vishnu and his avataras.

Shankara: "The Auspicious One." A title of Shiva.

Shastra: Scripture; spiritual treatise.

Shastri: One who is a scholar and teacher of the scriptures (shastras).

Shastric: Scriptural or having to do with the scriptures.

Shesha: The endless; the infinite; The name of the snake (naga) upon which Vishnu reclines.

Shesha Narayana: The form of Vishnu reclining upon Shesha, the infinite (endless) snake (naga).

Shishya: Disciple; student.

Shiva: A name of God meaning "One Who is all Bliss and the giver of happiness to all." Although classically applied to the Absolute Brahman, Shiva can also refer to God (Ishwara) in His aspect of Dissolver and Liberator (often mistakenly thought of as "destroyer").

Shivatma(n): The Paramatman who is the root cause of all the activities in the Universe.

Shravana: Hearing; study; listening to reading of the scriptures or instruction in spiritual life.

Shudra: A member of the laborer, servant caste.

Siddha: A perfected–liberated–being, an adept, a seer, a perfect yogi.

Siddha Nama: The Perfect Name; a title of the Soham Mantra.

Siddha Purusha: A Siddha.

Siddhi: Spiritual perfection; psychic power; power; modes of success; attainment; accomplishment; achievement; mastery; supernatural power attained through mantra, meditation, or other yogic practices. From the verb root sidh–to attain.

Vinayaka: Remover of Obstacles, a title of Ganesha.

Smriti: Memory; recollection; "that which is remembered;" code of law. In this latter sense, Smriti is used to designate all scriptures except the Vedas and Upanishads (which are considered of greater authority: Shruti).

Soham: "That am I;" the ultimate Atma mantra, the mantra of the Self; the Ajapa Gayatri formula of meditation in which "So" is intoned mentally during natural inhalation and "Ham" is intoned mentally during natural exhalation. Soham is pronounced "Sohum," as the short "a" in Sanskrit is pronounced like the American "u" in "up."

Sphota: The Sanskrit original of our English word "spot;" manifester; the idea which bursts or flashes–including the Pranava which burst or flashes forth from the Absolute and becomes transformed into the Relative.

Srimad Bhagavatam: One of the eighteen scriptures known as Puranas which are attributed to Vyasa.

Sudarshana: Sudarshana Chakra.

Sudarshana Chakra: The invincible weapon of Lord Vishnu which is able to cut through anything, and is a symbol of the Lord's power of cutting through all things which bind the jiva to samsara. Thus it is the divine power of liberation (moksha).

Sukarma: Good action; good deed; virtuous; diligent.

Sukhadeva: The son of the rishi Vyasa who is considered the ultimate example of total moral purity on all levels, including his mind and thoughts.

Sushumna: A subtle passage in the midst of the spinal column, corresponding to the spinal cord, that extends from the base of the spine to the brahma-randhra at the top of the head.

Swarajya: "Self-rule;" independence; freedom; absolute freedom.

Swarga: Heaven-world; the celestial region.

Swarupa: "Form of the Self." Natural–true–form; actual or essential nature; essence. A revelatory appearance that makes clear the true nature of some thing.

Swarupajnana: Knowledge which is of the nature of the Self; knowledge of one's essential nature; knowledge of pure consciousness, which is the highest end in life.

Tamas: Dullness, darkness, inertia, folly, and ignorance.

Tamasic: Possessed of the qualities of the tamo guna (tamas). Ignorant; dull; inert; and dark.

Tantra: A manual of, or a particular path of, sadhana laying great stress upon japa of a mantra and other esoteric practices relating to the powers latent in the human complex of physical, astral, and causal bodies in relation to the cosmic Power usually thought as the Divine Feminine.

Tantrika: Tantric; Pertaining to Tantra.

Tapas: See tapasya.

Tapasya: Austerity; practical (i.e., result-producing) spiritual discipline; spiritual force. Literally it means the generation of heat or energy, but is always used in a symbolic manner, referring to spiritual practice and its effect, especially the roasting of karmic seeds, the burning up of karma.

Tola: Three-eights of an ounce.

Trikalajnana: Knowledge of the past, present and the future.

Trikalajnani: One who knows the past, present and the future.

Trishudhi: The combination of mind, intellect and body.

Tukaram: A poet-saint of seventeenth century India (Maharashtra) devoted to Krishna in his form of Panduranga (Vittala).

Tulasi (Tulsi): The Indian basil plant sacred to Vishnu. Considered a manifestation of the goddess Lakshmi. Its leaves are used in worship of Vishnu and his avataras, and its stems and roots are formed into rosary beads used for counting the repetition of the mantras of Vishnu and his avataras. The leaves of tulasi are also used for purification and even medicinally.

Turiya: The state of pure consciousness. A Ramakrishna-Vedanta Wordbook defines it as: "The superconscious; lit., 'the Fourth,' in relation to the three ordinary states of consciousness—waking, dreaming, and dreamless sleep—which it transcends."

Turiya-Turiya: "The consciousness of Consciousness;" the Absolute Consciousness of God, the Consciousness behind our individualized consciousness (turiya).

Tyaga: Literally" leaving; separation; abandonment; renunciation in the sense of dissociation of the mind from worldly objects and the seeds of desire; in the Gita, the relinquishment of the fruit of action.

Tyagi: A renouncer, an ascetic.

Unmana: "That which transcends the mind;" the "mindless" state of a yogi that is really the state beyond the mind.

Unmani: One who is in the state of unmana.

Upadesha: Spiritual instruction; the instructions given by the guru at the time of initiation; initiation itself.

Upanayana(m): Investure with the sacred thread (yajnopavita) and initiation into the Gayatri mantra.

Upanishads: Books (of varying lengths) of the philosophical teachings of the ancient sages of India on the knowledge of Absolute Reality. The upanishads contain two major themes: (1) the individual self (atman) and the Supreme Self (Paramatman) are one in essence, and (2) the goal of life is the realization/manifestation of this unity, the realization of God (Brahman). There are eleven principal upanishads: Isha, Kena, Katha, Prashna, Mundaka, Mandukya, Taittiriya, Aitareya, Chandogya, Brihadaranyaka, and Shvetashvatara, all of which were commented on by Shankara, Ramanuja and Madhavacharya, thus setting the seal of authenticity on them.

Upasana: "Sitting near" or "drawing near;" worship; adoration; contemplation of God or deity; devout meditation; both teaching and learning.

Vaikhari: Sound that is spoken and heard.

Vairagya: Non-attachment; detachment; dispassion; absence of desire; disinterest; or indifference. Indifference towards and disgust for all worldly things and enjoyments.

Vaishnava: A devotee of Vishnu.

Vaishnavism: A religious sect of Hinduism, whose members follow the path of devotion to God as Vishnu or one of Vishnu's avatars—especially Sri Rama, Sri Krishna, and (in Bengal) Sri Chaitanya.

Vak: Speech.

Vani: Speech; voice; sound; music; language; words.

Varna: Caste. (Literally: color.) In traditional Hindu society there were four divisions or castes according to the individual's nature and aptitude: Brahmin, Kshatriya, Vaishya, and Shudra.

Varnashrama: Related to the four castes and the four stages (ashramas) of Hindu life; the laws of caste and ashrama.

Varnashram dharma: The observance of caste and ashram.

Vasana: Subtle desire; a tendency created in a person by the doing of an action or by experience; it induces the person to repeat the action or to seek a repetition of the experience; the subtle impression in the mind capable of developing itself into action; it is the cause of birth and experience in general; an aggregate or bundle of samskaras—the impressions of actions that remain unconsciously in the mind.

Vasana(s): A bundle or aggregate of such samskaras.

Vayu: Air; vital breath; prana.

Vedanta: Literally, "the end of the Vedas;" the Upanishads; the school of Hindu thought, based primarily on the Upanishads, upholding the doctrine of either pure non-dualism or conditional non-dualism. The original text of this school is Vedanta-darshana, the Brahma Sutras compiled by the sage Vyasa.

Vedantin: A follower of Vedanta.

Vedas: The oldest scriptures of India, considered the oldest scriptures of the world, that were revealed in meditation to the Vedic Rishis (seers). Although in modern times there are said to be four Vedas (Rig, Sama, Yajur, and Atharva), in the upanishads only three are listed (Rig, Sama, and Yajur). In actuality, there is only one Veda: the Rig Veda. The Sama Veda is only a collection of Rig Veda hymns that are marked (pointed) for singing. The Yajur Veda is a small book giving directions on just one form of Vedic sacrifice. The Atharva Veda is only a collection of theurgical mantras to be recited for the cure of various afflictions or to be recited over the herbs to be taken as medicine for those afflictions.

Vedic: Having to do with the Vedas.

Videhakaivalya mukti: Disembodied salvation.

Videhamukti: Disembodied salvation; salvation attained by the realized soul after shaking off the physical sheath as opposed to jivanmukti which is liberation even while living.

Vidya: Knowledge; both spiritual knowledge and mundane knowledge.

Vijnana: The highest knowledge, beyond mere theoretical knowledge (jnana); transcendental knowledge or knowing; experiential knowledge; a high state of spiritual realization–intimate knowledge of God in which all is seen as manifestations of Brahman; knowledge of the Self.

Vikalpa: Imagination; fantasy; mental construct; abstraction; conceptualization; hallucination; distinction; experience; thought; oscillation of the mind.

Vinayaka: Remover of Obstacles, a title of Ganesha.

Vishwaprana: The universal life force (prana).

Vithoba: See Vitthala.

Vitthala: A title of Krishna, meaning "the one standing on a brick," a reference to the image of Krishna worshipped in Pandharpur in Western India.

Vritti: Thought-wave; mental modification; mental whirlpool; a ripple in the chitta (mind substance).

Vyasa: One of the greatest sages of India, commentator on the Yoga Sutras, author of the Mahabharata (which includes the Bhagavad Gita), the Brahma Sutras, and the codifier of the Vedas.

Yajna: Sacrifice; offering; sacrificial ceremony; a ritual sacrifice; usually the fire sacrifice known as agnihotra or havan.

Yama (1): Restraint; the five Don'ts of Yoga: 1) ahimsa–non-violence, non-injury, harmlessness; 2) satya–truthfulness, honesty; 3) asteya–non-stealing, honesty, non-misappropriativeness; 4) brahmacharya–continence; 5) aparigraha–non-possessiveness, non-greed, non-selfishness, non-acquisitiveness. These five are called the Great Vow (Observance, Mahavrata) in the Yoga Sutras.

Yama (2): Yamaraja; the Lord of Death, controller of who dies and what happens to them after death.

Yama Duta: A messenger of Yama; who who comes to take the soul from the body at the time of death.

Yoga: Literally, "joining" or "union" from the Sanskrit root yuj. Union with the Supreme Being, or any practice that makes for such union. Meditation that unites the individual spirit with God, the Supreme Spirit. The name of the philosophy expounded by the sage Patanjali, teaching the process of union of the individual with the Universal Soul.

Yoga Shastra: The scriptures and writings of various authorities dealing specifically with the theory and practice of yoga, especially the Yoga Sutras (Yoga Darshan) of Patanjali.

Yoga Sutras: The oldest known writing on the subject of yoga, written by the sage Patanjali, a yogi of ancient India, and considered the most authoritative text on yoga. Also known as Yoga Darshana, it is the basis of the Yoga Philosophy which is based on the philosophical system known as Sankhya.

Yuga: Age or cycle; aeon; world era. Hindus believe that there are four yugas: the Golden Age (Satya or Krita Yuga), the Silver age (Treta Yuga), The Bronze Age (Dwapara Yuga), and the Iron Age (Kali Yuga). Satya Yuga is four times as long as the Kali Yuga; Treta Yuga is three times as long; and Dwapara Yuga is twice as long. In the Satya Yuga the majority of humans use the total potential–four-fourths–of their minds; in the Treta Yuga, three-fourths; in the Dwapara Yuga, one half; and in the Kali Yuga, one fourth. (In each Yuga there are those who are using either more or less of their minds than the general populace.) The Yugas move in a perpetual circle: Ascending Kali Yuga, ascending Dwapara Yuga, ascending Treta Yuga, ascending Satya Yuga, descending Satya Yuga, descending Treta Yuga, descending Dwapara Yuga, and descending Kali Yuga–over and over. Furthermore, there are yuga cycles within yuga cycles. For example, there are yuga cycles that affect the entire cosmos, and smaller yuga cycles within those greater cycles that affect a solar system. The cosmic yuga cycle takes 8,640,000,000 years, whereas the solar yuga cycle only takes 24,000 years. At the present time our solar system is in the ascending Dwapara Yuga, but the cosmos is in the descending Kali Yuga. Consequently, the more the general mind of humanity develops, the more good can be accomplished by the positive, and the more evil can be accomplished by the negative. Therefore we have more contrasts and polarization in contemporary life than previously before 1900.

ABOUT THE AUTHOR

Abbot George Burke (Swami Nirmala-nanda Giri) is the founder and director of the Light of the Spirit Monastery (Atma Jyoti Ashram) in Cedar Crest, New Mexico, USA.

In his many pilgrimages to India, he had the opportunity of meeting some of India's greatest spiritual figures, including Swami Sivananda of Rishikesh and Anandamayi Ma. During his first trip to India he was made a member of the ancient Swami Order by Swami Vidyananda Giri, a direct disciple of Paramhansa Yogananda, who had himself been given sannyas by the Shankaracharya of Puri, Jagadguru Bharati Krishna Tirtha.

In the United States he also encountered various Christian saints, including Saint John Maximovich of San Francisco and Saint Philaret Voznesensky of New York. He was ordained in the Liberal Catholic Church (International) to the priesthood on January 25, 1974, and consecrated a bishop on August 23, 1975.

For many years Abbot George has researched the identity of Jesus Christ and his teachings with India and Sanatana Dharma, including Yoga. It is his conclusion that Jesus lived in India for most of his life, and was a yogi and Sanatana Dharma missionary to the West. After his resurrection he returned to India and lived the rest of his life in the Himalayas.

He has written extensively on these and other topics, many of which are posted at OCOY.org.

Light of the Spirit Monastery

Light of the Spirit Monastery is an esoteric Christian monastic community for those men who seek direct experience of the Spirit through meditation, sacramental worship, discipline and dedicated communal life, emphasizing the inner reality of "Christ in you the hope of glory," as taught by the illumined mystics of East and West.

The public outreach of the monastery is through its website, OCOY.org (Original Christianity and Original Yoga). There you will find many articles on Original Christianity and Original Yoga, including *Esoteric Christian Beliefs*. *Foundations of Yoga* and *How to Be a Yogi* are practical guides for anyone seriously interested in living the Yoga Life.

You will also discover many other articles on leading an effective spiritual life, including *The Yoga of the Sacraments* and *Spiritual Benefits of a Vegetarian Diet*, as well as the "Dharma for Awakening" series—in-depth commentaries on these spiritual classics: the Upanishads, the Bhagavad Gita, the Dhammapada, and the Tao Teh King.

You can listen to podcasts by Abbot George on meditation, the Yoga Life, and remarkable spiritual people he has met in India and elsewhere, at http://ocoy.org/podcasts/

READING FOR AWAKENING

Light of the Spirit Press presents books on spiritual wisdom and Original Christianity and Original Yoga. From our "Dharma for Awakening" series (practical commentaries on the world's scriptures) to books on how to meditate and live a successful spiritual life, you will find books that are informative, helpful, and even entertaining.

Light of the Spirit Press is the publishing house of Light of the Spirit Monastery (Atma Jyoti Ashram) in Cedar Crest, New Mexico, USA. Our books feature the writings of the founder and director of the monastery, Abbot George Burke (Swami Nirmalananda Giri) which are also found on the monastery's website, OCOY.org.

We invite you to explore our publications in the following pages.

Find out more about our publications at
lightofthespiritpress.com

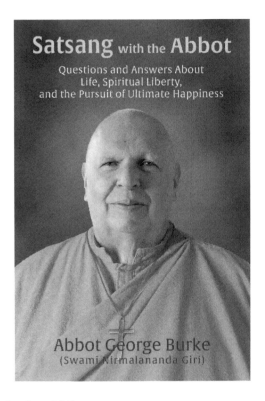

Satsang with the Abbot
Questions & Answers about Life, Spiritual Liberty, and the Pursuit of Ultimate Happiness

Grounded in the perspective of classic Indian thought, directly taught by such luminaries as Swami Sivananda of Rishikesh and Sri Anandamayi Ma, and blessed with the clarity and originality of thought that can only come from years of spiritual practice (sadhana), Abbot George Burke's answers to inquirers' questions are unique, fresh, and authoritative.

The questions in this book range from the most sublime to the most practical. "How can I attain samadhi? " "I am married with children. How can I lead a spiritual life? " "What is Self-realization? "

In Abbot George's replies to these questions the reader will discover common sense, helpful information, and a guiding light for their journey through and beyond the forest of cliches, contradictions, and confusion of yoga, Hinduism, Christianity, and metaphysical thought.

What Readers say:

"Abbot George speaks as one who knows his subject well, and answers in an manner that conveys an effortlessness and humor that puts one at ease, while, at the same time, a wisdom and sincerity which demands an attentive ear. "—*Russ Thomas*

ABBOT GEORGE BURKE (SWAMI NIRMALANANDA GIRI)

The Christ of India
The Story of Original Christianity

"Original Christianity" is the teaching of both Jesus of Nazareth and his Apostle Saint Thomas in India. Although it was new to the Mediterranean world, it was really the classical, traditional teachings of the ancient rishis of India that even today comprise Sanatana Dharma, the Eternal Dharma, that goes far beyond religion into realization.

In The Christ of India Abbot George Burke presents what those ancient teachings are, as well as the growing evidence that Jesus spent much of his "Lost Years" in India and Tibet. This is also the story of how the original teachings of Jesus and Saint Thomas thrived in India for centuries before the coming of the European colonialists.

What Readers say:

"Interpreting the teachings of Jesus from the perspective of Santana Dharma, The Christ of India is a knowledgeable yet engaging collection of authentic details and evident manuscripts about the Essene roots of Jesus and his 'Lost years'. ...delightful to read and a work of substance, vividly written and rich in historical analysis, this is an excellent work written by a masterful teacher and a storyteller." –*Enas Reviews*

SOHAM YOGA
The Yoga of the Self
Abbot George Burke
(Swami Nirmalananda Giri)

Soham Yoga
The Yoga of the Self

An in-depth guide to the practice of Soham sadhana.

Soham (which is pronounced like "Sohum") means: I Am That. It is the natural vibration of the Self, which occurs spontaneously with each incoming and outgoing breath. By becoming aware of it on the conscious level by mentally repeating it in time with the breath (*So* when inhaling and *Ham* when exhaling), a yogi experiences the identity between his individual Self and the Supreme Self.

The practice is very simple, and the results very profound. Truly wondrous is the fact that Soham Yoga can go on all the time, not just during meditation, if we apply ourselves to it. The whole life can become a continuous stream of liberating sadhana. "By the mantra 'Soham' separate the jivatma from the Paramatma and locate the jivatma in the heart" (Devi Bhagavatam 11.8.15). When we repeat Soham in time with the breath we are invoking our eternal being. This is why we need only listen to our inner mental intonations of Soham in time with the breath which itself is Soham.

What Readers say:

"This Soham meditation has been the most simple, effective kind of meditation I have practiced... This book is a complete spiritual path" –Arnold Van Wie.

The Unknown Lives of Jesus and Mary
Compiled from Ancient Records and Mystical Revelations

Compiled from Ancient Records and Mystical Revelations

"*There are also many other things which Jesus did, the which, if they should be written every one, I suppose that even the world itself could not contain the books that should be written.*" (Gospel of Saint John, final verse)

You can discover much of those "many other things which Jesus did" in this unique compilation of ancient records and mystical revelations, which includes historical records of the lives of Jesus Christ and his Mother Mary that have been accepted and used by the Church since apostolic times. This treasury of little-known stories of Jesus' infancy, his sojourn in the Orient as recorded in the famous Ladakh Manuscript, and his passion, crucifixion, and resurrection, will broaden the reader's understanding of what Christianity really was originally.

What Readers say:

"A tough one to put down once you start reading, insightful commentaries by the author add even more rich meaning."—*Dr. William Cunningham*

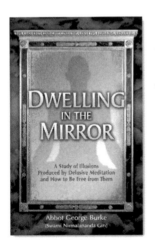

Dwelling in the Mirror
A Study of Illusions Produced by Delusive Meditation and How to Be Free from Them

"There are those who can have an experience and realize that it really cannot be real, but a vagary of their mind. Some may not understand that on their own, but can be shown by others the truth about it. For them and those that may one day be in danger of meditation-produced delusions I have written this brief study." –Abbot George Burke

In *Dwelling in the Mirror* you will learn:

- different types of meditation and the experiences they produce, and the problems and delusions which can arise from them.
- how to get rid of negative initiation energies and mantras.
- what are authentic, positive meditation practices and their effects and aspects.
- an ancient, universal method of meditation which is both proven and effective.

What Readers say:

"I totally loved this book! After running across many spiritual and self-help books filled with unrealistic promises, this little jewel had the impact of a triple Espresso."—*Sandra Carrington-Smith, author of Housekeeping for the Soul*

The Dhammapada for Awakening
A Commentary on Buddha's Practical Wisdom

The Dhammapada for Awakening brings a refreshing and timely perspective to ancient wisdom and shows seekers of inner peace practical ways to improve their inner lives today.

It explores the Buddha's answers to the urgent questions, such as "How can I find find lasting peace, happiness and fulfillment that seems so elusive?" and "What can I do to avoid many of the miseries big and small that afflict all of us?".

Drawing on the proven wisdom of different ancient traditions, and the contemporary masters of spiritual life, as well as his own studies and first-hand knowledge of the mystical traditions of East and West, Abbot George illumines the practical wisdom of Buddha in the Dhammapada, and more importantly, and make that makes that teaching relevant to present day spiritual seekers.

What Readers say:

"In this compelling book, Abbot George Burke brings his considerable knowledge and background in Christian teachings and the Vedic tradition of India to convey a practical understanding of the teachings of the Buddha. ...This is a book you'll want to take your time to read and keep as reference to reread. Highly recommended for earnest spiritual aspirants" *–Anna Hourihan, author, editor, and publisher at Vedanta Shores Press*

The Gospel of Thomas for Awakening
A Commentary on Jesus' Sayings as Recorded by the Apostle Thomas

"From the very beginning there were two Christianities." So begins this remarkable work. While the rest of the Apostles dispersed to various areas of the Mediterranean world, the apostle Thomas travelled to India, where growing evidence shows that Jesus spent his "Lost Years," and which had been the source of the wisdom which he had brought to the "West."

In *The Gospel of Thomas for Awakening*, Abbot George shines the "Light of the East" on the sometimes enigmatic sayings of Jesus recorded by his apostle Saint Thomas, revealing their unique and rich practical nature for modern day seekers for spiritual life.

Ideal for daily study or group discussion.

What Readers say:

"An extraordinary work of theological commentary, *The Gospel of Thomas for Awakening* is as informed and informative as it is inspired and inspiring".—*James A. Cox, Editor-in-Chief, Midwest Book Review*

The Tao Teh King for Awakening
A Practical Commentary on Lao Tzu's Classic Exposition of Taoism

With penetrating insight, Abbot George Burke illumines the the wisdom of Lao Tzu's classic writing, the Tao Teh King (Tao Te Ching), and the timeless practical value of China's most beloved Taoist scripture for spiritual seekers. With a unique perspective of a lifetime of study and practice of both Eastern and Western spirituality, Abbot George mines the treasures of the Tao Teh King and presents them in an easily intelligible fashion for those wishing to put these priceless teachings into practice.

Illumined with quotes from the Gospels, the Bhagavad Gita, Yogananda and other Indian saints and Indian scriptures.

What Readers say:

"Burke's evident expertise concerning both Western and Eastern spirituality, provides readers with a wide-ranging and intriguing study of the topic. For those who seek spiritual guidance and insight into Lao Tzu's wisdom, this work offers a clear pathway." – *Publisher's Weekly (BookLife Prize)*

The Bhagavad Gita for Awakening
A Practical Commentary for Leading a Successful Spiritual Life

With penetrating insight, Abbot George Burke illumines the Bhagavad Gita's practical value for spiritual seekers. With a unique perspective from a lifetime of study and practice of both Eastern and Western spirituality, Abbot George presents the treasures of the Gita in an easily intelligible fashion.

Drawing from the teachings of Sri Ramakrishna, Jesus, Paramhansa Yogananda, Ramana Maharshi, Swami Vivekananda, Swami Sivananda of Rishikesh, Papa Ramdas, and other spiritual masters and teachers, as well as his own experiences, Abbot Burke illustrates the teachings of the Gita with stories which make the teachings of Krishna in the Gita vibrant and living.

What Readers say:

"This is not a book for only "Hindus" or "Christians." Anyone desiring to better their lives mentally, emotionally, and spiritually would benefit greatly by reading this book."— *Sailaja Kuruvadi*

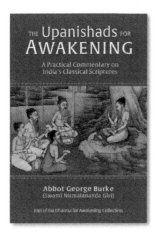

The Upanishads for Awakening
A Practical Commentary on India's Classical Scriptures

With penetrating insight, Abbot George Burke illumines the Upanishads' practical value for spiritual seekers, and the timelessness of India's most beloved scriptures. With a unique perspective of a lifetime of study and practice of both Eastern and Western spirituality, Abbot George mines the treasures of the Upanishads and presents them in an easily intelligible fashion for those wishing to put these priceless teachings into practice

The teachings of the Upanishads are the supreme expressions of the eternal wisdom, the eternal vision of the ancient rishis (sages) of India. The truths embodied in the Upanishads and their inspired digest-summary, the Bhagavad Gita, are invaluable for all who would ascend to higher consciousness.

What Readers say:
"It is always a delight to see how he seamlessly integrates the wisdom of the West into the East."
–Roopa Subramani

The Bhagavad Gita–The Song of God
A new translation of the most important spiritual classic which India has produced.

Often called the "Bible" of Hinduism, the Bhagavad Gita is found in households throughout India and has been translated into every major language of the world. Literally billions of copies have been handwritten and printed.

The clarity of this translation by Abbot George Burke makes for easy reading, while the rich content makes this the ideal "study" Gita. As the original Sanskrit language is so rich, often there are several accurate translations for the same word, which are noted in the text, giving the spiritual student the needed understanding of the fullness of the Gita.

For those unable to make a spiritual journey to India, a greater pilgrimage can be made by anyone anywhere in the world by simply reading The Holy Song of God, the Srimad Bhagavad Gita. It will be a holy pilgrimage of mind and spirit.

Robe of Light
An Esoteric Christian Cosmology

In *Robe of Light* Abbot George Burke explores the whys and wherefores of the mystery of creation. From the emanation of the worlds from the very Being of God, to the evolution of the souls to their ultimate destiny as perfected Sons of God, the ideal progression of creation is described. Since the rebellion of Lucifer and the fall of Adam and Eve from Paradise flawed the normal plan of evolution, a restoration was necessary. How this came about is the prime subject of this insightful study.

Moreover, what this means to aspirants for spiritual perfection is expounded, with a compelling knowledge of the scriptures and of the mystical traditions of East and West.

What Readers say:

"Having previously read several offerings from the pen of Abbot George Burke I was anticipating this work to be well written and an enjoyable read. However, Robe of Light actually exceeded my expectations. Abbot Burke explicates the subject perfectly, making a difficult and complex subject like Christian cosmology accessible to those of us who are not great theologians."—*Russ Thomas*

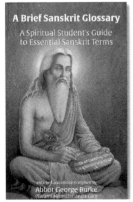

A Brief Sanskrit Glossary
A Spiritual Student's Guide to Essential Sanskrit Terms

This Sanskrit glossary contains full translations and explanations of many of the most commonly used spiritual Sanskrit terms, and will help students of the Bhagavad Gita, the Upanishads, the Yoga Sutras of Patanjali, and other Indian scriptures and philosophical works to expand their vocabularies to include the Sanskrit terms contained in them, and gain a fuller understanding in their studies.

What Readers say:

"If you are reading the writings of Swami Sivananda you will find a basketful of untranslated Sanskrit words which often have no explanation, as he assumes his readers have a background in Hindu philosophy. For writings like his, this book is invaluable, as it lists frequently used Sanskrit terms used in writings on yoga and Hindu philosophical thought.

"As the title says, this is a spiritual students' guidebook, listing not only commonly used spiritual terms, but also giving brief information about spiritual teachers and writers, both modern and ancient.

"Abbot George's collection is just long enough to give the meanings of useful terms without overwhelming the reader with an overabundance of extraneous words. This is a book that the spiritual student will use frequently."—*Simeon Davis*

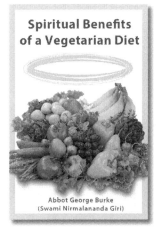

Spiritual Benefits of a Vegetarian Diet

The health benefits of a vegetarian diet are well known, as are the ethical aspects. But the spiritual advantages should be studied by anyone involved in meditation, yoga, or any type of spiritual practice.

Although diet is commonly considered a matter of physical health alone, since the Hermetic principle "as above, so below" is a fundamental truth of the cosmos, diet is a crucial aspect of emotional, intellectual, and spiritual development as well. For diet and consciousness are interrelated, and purity of diet is an effective aid to purity and clarity of consciousness.

The major thing to keep in mind when considering the subject of vegetarianism is its relevancy in relation to our explorations of consciousness. We need only ask: Does it facilitate my spiritual growth–the development and expansion of my consciousness? The answer is Yes.

A second essay, *Christian Vegetarianism*, continues with a consideration of the esoteric side of diet, the vegetarian roots of early Christianity, and an insightful exploration of vegetarianism in the Old and New Testaments.

Available as a free Kindle ebook download at Amazon.com.

Foundations of Yoga
Ten Important Principles Every Meditator Should Know

An in-depth examination of the important foundation principles of Patanjali's Yoga, Yama & Niyama.

Yama and Niyama are often called the Ten Commandments of Yoga, but they have nothing to do with the ideas of sin and virtue or good and evil as dictated by some cosmic potentate. Rather they are determined on a thoroughly practical, pragmatic basis: that which strengthens and facilitates our yoga practice should be observed and that which weakens or hinders it should be avoided.

It is not a matter of being good or bad, but of being wise or foolish. Each one of these Five Don'ts (Yama) and Five Do's (Niyama) is a supporting, liberating foundation of Yoga. An introduction to the important foundation principles of Patanjali's Yoga: Yama & Niyama

Available as a free Kindle ebook download at Amazon.com, as well as in paperback.

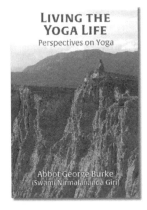

Living the Yoga Life
Perspectives on Yoga

"Dive deep; otherwise you cannot get the gems at the bottom of the ocean. You cannot pick up the gems if you only float on the surface." Sri Ramakrishna

Many people come to the joyous and liberating discovery of yoga and yoga philosophy, and then dive no deeper, resting on their first understanding of the atman, Brahman, the goal of yoga, and everything else the classic yoga philosophy teaches about "the way things are."

In *Living the Yoga Life* author Abbot George Burke shares the gems he has found from a lifetime of "diving deep." This collection of reflections and short essays addresses the key concepts of the yoga philosophy that are so easy to take for granted. Never content with the accepted cliches about yoga sadhana, the yoga life, the place of a guru, the nature of Brahman and our unity with It, Abbot George's insights on these and other facets of the yoga life will inspire, provoke, enlighten, and even entertain.

What Readers say:

"Abbot George eloquently brings the eastern practice of seeking God inwardly to western readers who have been taught to seek God outwardly."—*Bill Braddock*

May a Christian Believe in Reincarnation?

Discover the real and surprising history of reincarnation and Christianity.

A growing number of people are open to the subject of past lives, and the belief in rebirth–reincarnation, metempsychosis, or transmigration–is becoming commonplace. It often thought that belief in reincarnation and Christianity are incompatible. But is this really true? May a Christian believe in reincarnation? The answer may surprise you.

Reincarnation-also known as the transmigration of souls-is not just some exotic idea of non-Christian mysticism. Nor is it an exclusively Hindu-Buddhist teaching.

In orthodox Jewish and early Christian writings, as well as the Holy Scriptures, we find reincarnation as a fully developed belief, although today it is commonly ignored. But from the beginning it has been an integral part of Orthodox Judaism, and therefore as Orthodox Jews, Jesus and his Apostles would have believed in rebirth.

What Readers say:

"Those needing evidence that a belief in reincarnation is in accordance with teachings of the Christ need look no further: Plainly laid out and explained in an intelligent manner from one who has spent his life on a Christ-like path of renunciation and prayer/meditation."—*Christopher T. Cook*

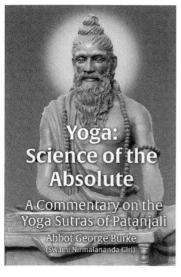

Yoga: Science of the Absolute
A Commentary on the Yoga Sutras of Patanjali

In *Yoga: Science of the Absolute*, Abbot George Burke draws on the age-long tradition regarding this essential text, including the commentaries of Vyasa and Shankara, the most highly regarded writers on Indian philosophy and practice, as well as I. K. Taimni and other authoritative commentators, and adds his own ideas based on half a century of study and practice.Serious students of yoga will find this an essential addition to their spiritual studies.

What Readers say:

"Abbot George has provided a commentary that is not only deeply informative, making brilliant connections across multiple traditions, but eminently practical. More importantly he describes how they can help one empower their own practice, their own sadhana."
—Michael Sabani

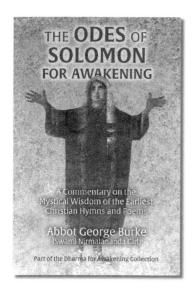

The Odes of Solomon for Awakening
A Commentary on the Mystical Wisdom of the Earliest Christian Hymns and Poems

With penetrating insight, Abbot George Burke illumines the practical value of the Odes of Solomon for spiritual seekers, and the timelessness of these ancient writings. With a unique perspective of a lifetime of study and practice of both Eastern and Western spirituality, Abbot George mines the treasures of the Odes and presents them in an easily intelligible fashion for those wishing to put these priceless teachings into practice.

What Readers say:

"Both Hierodeacon Simeon's lovely translation and Abbot George's deeply insightful commentary do great justice to this most ancient and exquisite work. It will rightfully hold an honored place in any seriously spiritual library." —Brother Julian-Ozana

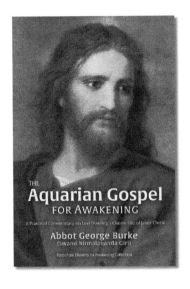

The Aquarian Gospel for Awakening, volumes 1&2

A Practical Commentary on Levi Dowling's Classic Life of Jesus Christ

In 1908 *The Aquarian Gospel of Jesus the Christ* by Levi H. Dowling appeared on the shelves of American bookstores. Immediately it evoked a response in those who intuited and sought for a deeper meaning of the person and teachings of Jesus of Nazareth. Abbot George illumines the practical value of the Aquarian Gospel for spiritual seekers, and the timelessness of this classic writing.

What Readers say:

"A perfect addition to any spiritual seeker's library, *The Aquarian Gospel for Awakening*...is a refreshingly different read about Christ's life. It is such an enjoyable book to read, I'm afraid I let my other tasks fall by the wayside - I couldn't put it down! I feel that it will enrich anyone's understanding of Jesus, no matter what your religious background is." —Mel Halloran

Light of Soham

The Life and Teachings of Sri Gajanana Maharaj of Nashik

At the beginning of the twentieth century, a young crippled boy in North India met a spiritual teacher in the Nath tradition of the great teachers Matsyendranath and Gorakhnath, who imparted to him the precious knowledge of yoga meditation. The boy began to apply himself to this meditation practice and became a very unusual saint indeed.

Gajanana Maharaj taught the ajapa-japa of the Soham mantra with the breath. In Light of Soham his teachings for success in Soham sadhana and spiritual life in general have been collected from the writings of himself and his disciples.

What Readers say:

"This book cuts straight to the problem of life - our separation from the Godhead - and without dwelling too much on this immediately cuts to the solution: Meditation." —Dylan Grant

Printed in Great Britain
by Amazon

85359230R00178